CW00822580

VENICE
&
THE VENETO

ALTA MACADAM
WITH ANNABEL BARBER

VENICE & THE VENETO
Updated chapter from *Blue Guide Northern Italy*

Published by Blue Guides Limited, a Somerset Books Company
Winchester House, Deane Gate Avenue, Taunton, Somerset TA1 2UH
www.blueguides.com
'Blue Guide' is a registered trademark.

ISBN 978-1-909079-78-5

The first Blue Guide, *London and its Environs*, was published in 1918 by two
Scottish brothers, James and Findlay Muirhead. The first edition of *Blue Guide
Northern Italy* was compiled by them and L.V. Bertarelli in 1924. Subsequent
editions were revised, compiled or written by the Muirhead brothers (1927, 1937);
Stuart Rossiter (1971); Alta Macadam (1978, 1984, 1991, 1998) and Paul Blanchard
(2001, 2005). This chapter was updated by Alta Macadam and Annabel Barber.

The author and publisher have made reasonable efforts to ensure the accuracy of
all the information in this book; however, they can accept no responsibility for any
loss, injury or inconvenience sustained by any traveller as a result of information
or advice contained in the guide.

Every effort has been made to trace the copyright owners of material reproduced
in this guide. We would be pleased to hear from any copyright owners we have been
unable to reach.

Statement of editorial independence: Blue Guides, their authors and editors, are
prohibited from accepting payment from any restaurant, hotel, gallery or other
establishment for its inclusion in this guide or on www.blueguides.com, or for a
more favourable mention than would otherwise have been made.

About the authors and contributor
ALTA MACADAM is the author of over 40 Blue Guides to Italy. She lives in the hills above Florence with her husband, the painter Francesco Colacicchi. She has worked for the Photo Library of Alinari and for Harvard University's Villa I Tatti. She is at present external consultant for New York University at the photo archive of Villa La Pietra in Florence, and as author of the Blue Guides to Florence, Rome, Tuscany, Venice, Central Italy, Umbria and Lazio (the last two e-chapters from *Central Italy*), she travels extensively every year to revise new editions of the books.

CHARLES FREEMAN is a freelance academic historian with widespread interests in Italy and the Mediterranean. His *Egypt, Greece and Rome, Civilizations of the Ancient Mediterranean* (Oxford University Press, 3rd ed. 2014) is widely used as an introductory textbook to the ancient world and is supported by his *Sites of Antiquity: 50 Sites that Explain the Classical World* (Blue Guides, 2009). His *The Horses of St Mark's* (Little Brown, 2004) is a study of the famous horses through their history in Constantinople and Venice. He is a Fellow of the Royal Society of Arts.

ANNABEL BARBER is the Editorial Director of the Blue Guides. She is contributing author of *Blue Guide Rome* and author of *Pilgrim's Rome* (available in print and digital), a short handbook to the monuments of early Christianity.

CONTENTS

THE GUIDE

PRACTICAL INFORMATION

MAPS & PLANS

Introduction & History

The Veneto region is particularly filled with interest for the visitor. Apart from Venice, it includes Verona, a particularly beautiful city with a celebrated Roman amphitheatre. The university town of Padua has important frescoes by Giotto; Vicenza was laid out by the great 16th-century architect Palladio. All over the Veneto are splendid country villas, some by Palladio, others by 17th- and 18th-century architects. Veneto is also home to perhaps the most beautiful of the Italian lakes: Lake Garda. The region was the birthplace of many of Italy's most celebrated artists, including Titian, Veronese and Tintoretto. Its wines—among them Amarone and Prosecco—are highly prized.

HISTORY OF THE VENETO

by Charles Freeman

In September 1786 the German poet Goethe entered northern Italy for the first time, over the Brenner Pass. The impact of the transition from northern Europe, down across an Alpine pass and into an ancient cradle of civilisation, was profound. At Verona he saw his first Roman building, the Arena, the great amphitheatre in Piazza Brà. At Vicenza he admired the works of Palladio. In Padua it was the 'astonishing' Mantegnas in the church of the Eremitani (tragically the victim of American bombs in World War Two) which enthralled him. Finally, in the late afternoon of the 28th September, Goethe had his first sight of Venice—a gondola coming out to meet him as his boat crossed the lagoon.

The modern traveller's entry to northern Italy is usually more abrupt, with the Alps some thousands of feet below; but the ranges have never been impassable. In fact the first human settlers probably came into Italy across them. The Romans used 17 of the 23 passes on a regular basis. When Jean-Louis David painted Napoleon at the top of the St Bernard Pass on his way to invade Italy in 1800, he engraved on the rocks the names of previous invaders: Hannibal (218 BC) and Charlemagne (AD 773). For centuries Italy, whether as the focus for invaders, the core of a great empire, the home of civic liberty or the cradle of artistic genius, has been etched into the European imagination as a culture profoundly different from those in the north. It needs a transition such as a passage through the Alps to make the point.

Those coming down into Italy from the Alps soon reached the peninsula's largest and most fertile plain, centred on the river Po, a river which, as the elder Pliny put it in the 1st century AD, 'deposits its soil and bestows bounteous fertility'. When the plain was settled and peaceful it provided, then as now, an underlying prosperity for the region; but the real fount of northern Italy's commercial and cultural wealth was the Mediterranean, to which it had full access through its ports and rivers. It was this same prosperity that made the area a lure for outsiders. The history of northern Italy alternates between periods of strong outside control (the Roman period, for instance) and virtual independence when, as in the Middle Ages, the larger cities struggled between themselves for land and trade routes. What follows is a simplification of a very complicated story.

CELTS AND ROMANS

The early history of Italy is being continually rewritten as new sites emerge and interpretations develop. If one starts, however, with the Bronze Age (2200–1000 BC), its culture seems to have been remarkably homogenous—but there is a break about 900 BC (with the coming of the Iron Age) when the indigenous peoples of northern Italy develop distinct cultures. The Veneti occupied the foothills of the Alps in the northeast, and early migrations led to settlement around the lakes. A much more determined migration of Celts, probably impelled by the breakdown of societies to the north and population increase, took place in the late 5th century. It was not peaceful. By the early 4th century Celtic warbands were raiding further south, reaching Rome in 390 BC.

Roman retaliation was inevitable. The exuberant but ill-disciplined Celtic warriors were no match for a Roman legion, and after Celtic tribes had helped the Carthaginian Hannibal in his invasion of Italy in 218, total subjection of northern Italy followed. Roman citizens, many of them former soldiers, were settled on the land in what were called *coloniae*. Originally the sites were chosen for strategic reasons, but many *coloniae* prospered in their own right. In contrast to the *coloniae* were the *municipia*. These were earlier urban settlements which were Romanised. Padua and Verona, for example, appear to have been founded by the Veneti. Many *municipia* flourished as a result of their position on roads or rivers. And with the Roman peace, the region prospered. Land was drained and vast quantities of grain were produced. The foothills provided excellent grazing for sheep. The landed elite enjoyed a lavish lifestyle, as the remains of villas around Lake Garda bear witness.

FROM THE FALL OF ROME TO THE HOLY ROMAN EMPIRE

The collapse of Roman civilisation was gradual. 476 traditionally marks the end of the western empire, but there was no abrupt transition. Many of the 'barbarians' had by now become Romanised, and in any case they were a small minority in a Roman population. When the Ostrogoth Theodoric became ruler of much of Italy in 493, it is estimated that his followers numbered 100,000 in a native population of four million. He ruled through Roman bureaucrats and was sympathetic enough to Roman culture to restore buildings in Rome.

The first abrupt break with the Roman past came with the invasion of northern Italy by the Lombards in 568. The Lombards were a mix of peoples from northern Europe, forged by their king Alboin into a military force who would cooperate when attacked by the Byzantine troops from the south or the Franks from the north. One reason for the Lombards' continuing success was a succession of charismatic kings who kept the allegiance of these dukes and through them sustained what remained of urban life. By the 8th century most Lombards had become Catholics, using Roman law alongside their own.

The Lombards met their match in 753 or 754, when Pepin the Short, King of the Franks, came over the Alps. Their kingdom collapsed and in 773, Pepin's successor, Charlemagne, received the iron crown of Lombardy in the old capital, Pavia. In 800 Charlemagne was crowned 'Roman Emperor' by Pope Leo III in Rome. The Holy Roman Empire, which passed from the Franks to German kings in the 10th century, was to survive until dissolved by Napoleon in 1806.

THE RISE OF THE CITY STATES

The problem for northern Italy was that the relative roles of pope and emperor within the empire were never clearly defined. The Church remained strong on the ground; the emperors claimed overall responsibility as successors of the Lombards. This, however, was also northern Italy's opportunity. Many cities, though greatly diminished from the days of the Roman empire, had remained relatively intact, while in a sheltered lagoon in the northern Adriatic tenacious settlements of refugees from the Lombard invasions were being forged into a trading community. These refugees, the Venetians, were nominally part of the Byzantine empire (their first patron saint, Theodore, was a soldier martyr from Asia Minor), but they were determined to achieve independent control of their destiny. Contemporary documents from the 8th century show trading links between Venice and Constantinople, Sicily, the whole of north Africa, Syria and France. Trading prosperity on the mainland was supplemented by the rise of a landowning class (made up, it appears, of both Frankish and Lombard aristocrats) on the plains. The rivers opened again to trade, and it was only now that cities such as Ferrara, well placed on the Po, became important.

Politically the most remarkable development was the rise of communal government. In the 11th century the weakening of imperial rule led to revolts by many northern cities, a sign of a vibrant local identity. There was also increasing irritation with the power of the Church, and bishops were expelled from a number of cities. Communal government can be seen as the political structure which filled a vacuum, with different social groups all interested in a share of power: local landowners anxious for a foothold in the local city, a rising merchant class, administrators whose knowledge of Roman law was instrumental in defining the checks and balances of communal government.

The most common form of communal government consisted of 'consuls' (an echo of Roman times), who took responsibility for internal order and foreign relations with an assembly of 'the people' who could check the misuse of power. The assemblies ratified major decisions such as the making of peace and war, the approval of alliances and the acceptance of new laws. It was the ability to create and sustain a legal structure of government which was especially important and which provided the impetus for cities to set up their own institutions for the study of the arts and law (notably Roman law). So were born the first universities, among them that of Padua, founded in 1222. They were organised on communal lines as if the teachers were the consuls and the students the citizens. Communal activities also spread to trade, and fraternities of citizens were formed for charitable purposes, such as the *scuole* of Venice which gave a continuing role to Venetian citizens after government was restricted to the nobility in 1297. In 1300 there were an estimated 142 guilds or trade associations in Venice, 48 in Verona and 38 in Padua.

The wealth of these cities was boosted by trade. The Italians were pioneers in every aspect of commerce from banking to the design of ships. They dominated the Mediterranean trade routes, their tentacles penetrating deep into the Islamic world. Islamic motifs are to be found in the architecture of Venice, and the city competed with its rival Genoa for trading concessions from the Byzantine emperors. The Venetians won a great coup when they manipulated the Fourth Crusade of 1204 to their advantage, ending up not in the Holy Land as intended but in Constantinople, which they sacked, on the grounds that the Greeks were heretics. Not only did they bring rich treasures back home (the famous Horses of St Mark's among them), but they also awarded themselves strategic trading posts throughout the East. The returns were fantastic. 'While the burghers and barons of the north were building their dark streets and grisly castles of oak and sandstone, the merchants of Venice were covering their palaces with porphyry and gold', wrote John Ruskin in *The Stones of Venice*. In Padua, the vast Palazzo della Ragione, built first in the early 1200s and then rebuilt a hundred years later, acted as law court and assembly hall, with shops for merchants on the ground floor. Its size was also a symbol of the city's wealth and status. The ambiguous attitude to wealth creation in a Christian society is beautifully illustrated in Padua. Giotto's frescoes in the Scrovegni Chapel were commissioned by a wealthy merchant who sought, by his piety, to distance himself from the usury of his father, who had been named by Dante amongst the denizens of Hell.

FROM *COMUNE* TO SEIGNIORY
Despite its successes, northern Italy always remained vulnerable to invasion from its nominal overlord, the Holy Roman Emperor. Frederick Barbarossa, elected in 1152, waged five campaigns over 30 years, although at last he was forced to accept the independence of the *comuni*. Barbarossa's grandson Frederick II launched further campaigns between 1225 and 1250, but again was unsuccessful. The invasions placed immense burdens on the *comuni*, with factions in the cities supporting either the emperors (the Ghibellines) or the papacy (the Guelphs). These factions were often a mask for local ambitions and the combination of marauding imperial armies and social tensions was devastating. 'O servile Italy, breeding ground of misery, ship without a pilot in a mighty tempest' wrote Dante, himself a Guelph. After his exile from Florence in 1302, Dante's wanderings around the courts and universities of northern Italy—he sheltered in Verona and taught at Padua—are symbolic of a troubled age. He yearned for the return of a strong emperor who would rule under the auspices of the papacy.

The *comuni* were idealised by later generations but, as Dante's experience suggests, their history was also filled with factional in-fighting and popular unrest. One pragmatic response was to elect, often from outside the city, a *podestà*, an official given wide powers for a fixed period of time. This proved the forerunner of the next development in northern Italy: the emergence of the seigniories, governments based on one man, with power then being passed on to the next generation of his family. As with communal government it is difficult to generalise: sometimes the lord enjoyed popular support, in other cases he emerged from aristocratic in-fighting, and the path to power was invariably tortuous. The Della Scala of Verona are an example of such a family. The Visconti of Milan are another. Matteo Visconti used his aristocratic position to achieve prominence in the city in the 1280s, which he then strengthened by being elected *capitano del popolo* in 1288. He further consolidated his position with marriage alliances with other seigniorial families, and placed members of his own family as lords of neighbouring cities. His son Galeazzo Visconti, originally subject to his father as lord of Piacenza, incorporated Cremona, Como, Bergamo, Piacenza and Brescia into Milanese territory. This dominance over Lombardy was extended to Bologna (1350), Genoa (1353), and ultimately into the Veneto.

The stories of individual seigniorial families are too varied to be followed here, but many cities of northern Italy have monuments of their rule. The lives of the *signori* were often precarious, with the result that their residences were as much fortresses as palaces. A good example is the Castelvecchio of the Della Scala in Verona (1350s), still with its tall battlements.

In their time the *signori* attracted both praise and blame. For those who retained the ideal of *libertas*, the ancient rallying cry of republican Rome, revived by the *comuni*, they were tyrants, 'a breed of cruel destruction', as one opponent of the lords of Milan put it. Others stressed that strong rule brought an end to factional squabbles and that the *signori* were often effective patrons. Not that seigniorial rule was universal. The most important example of a city which maintained its republicanism is Venice. Although political participation was restricted to the nobility, a variety of councils and a doge led to a balanced government which survived intact for centuries.

THE RISE OF FRANCE AND SPAIN

A new period of vulnerability for northern Italy began in 1494, with a sequence of invasions from French, Spanish and imperial troops. The cities were no match for these well organised states, although they tried to play one off against another. It was Venice who encouraged the French to attack Milan, their main rival on the mainland, in 1499, with the result that Lombardy fell under French control. However, Venice had its come-uppance when an alliance under the pope defeated its forces at Agnadello near Milan in 1509. The French in their turn were defeated at Pavia in 1525 by the new Holy Roman Emperor Charles V. Charles, whose territories already extended across Europe from Spain to Austria, now stamped his rule on northern Italy. Venice was allowed to survive as a republic (and she regained much of her mainland territory) but Milan became a capital of a province of the Holy Roman Empire.

The 16th century saw another challenge with the opening up of trade routes round the Cape to the Far East and across the Atlantic. Mediterranean trade fell into decline and wealth creation shifted to the more lively and untrammelled (by guilds) economies of England and Holland. The prosperous merchant families began to transform themselves into an aristocracy living on the land, and villas and palaces replaced the warehouses of earlier centuries. The cultural interests of these patricians were broad, as can be seen from their patronage of Palladio in Vicenza. The Palladian villa was designed to exploit the aesthetic appeal of the landscape without losing touch with the labour on the land, which was required to sustain the ideal.

The universities of northern Italy had long had an international clientèle. (Teaching was, of course, in Latin, still the universal language of scholarship.) The Palazzo del Bo, the 16th-century core of the university of Padua, is filled with the insignia of students from all over Europe. The area was now also attractive to collectors, prominent among them Thomas Howard, second Earl of Arundel, who in a seminal trip to Italy in 1613 was enthused by Italian art and architecture. Among his retinue was the architect Inigo Jones, who had already encountered Palladio's work in England through the latter's *I Quattro Libri dell' Architettura* (1570); Arundel's purchase of several chests full of Palladio's drawings proved the catalyst by which Britain became the first country outside Italy to adopt Palladianism. In the same period, Charles I bought up many of the treasures of the now bankrupt Gonzaga. Italy was being redrawn as a place to go for cultural improvement, the Grand Tour providing the 'gap year' experience for the European aristocracy.

THE 18TH CENTURY AND NAPOLEON

In the 18th century came the War of the Spanish Succession, fought between the Bourbon French and the Austrian and Spanish Habsburgs. Once again northern Italy became a playground for imperial ambitions. In 1707 the Austrians acquired Milan. This was also the Age of Enlightenment, and there was some response in Italy. Reforming rulers and intellectuals tried to confront the nobility and the Church, but as these two groups controlled 70 percent of the land in the north, sustained programmes of reform were difficult. Reform was further hampered by the mass of small semi-independent cities and duchies, each with its own legal systems and weights and measures. Venice survived as an independent republic, but her territories in the East had long succumbed to the Ottoman Empire and her façade of opulence was now sustained by outsiders buying their way into the nobility. (Ca' Rezzonico on the Grand Canal is an excellent example of a grand 18th-century palace completed by a wealthy Lombard family.) Abroad the city was no longer taken seriously. 'The English use their powder for their cannon, the French for their mortars. In Venice it is usually damp, and, if it is dry, they use it for fireworks', as one observer recorded. The antics of its aristocratic revellers in their villas on the mainland are brilliantly evoked by the comedies of Carlo Goldoni.

The outbreak of the French Revolution in 1789 was greeted in Italy with a mixture of fear and enthusiasm. The momentous significance of the event hit Italy in 1796, when one of the revolution's generals, Napoleon Bonaparte, arrived over the Alps. His campaigns saw the destruction of Austrian rule in Lombardy and, in 1797, the bullying of the Venetian Republic into an ignominious dissolution. Having conquered the Veneto, Napoleon then transferred control of the region to Austria. The rest of northern Italy was incorporated into the Kingdom of Italy, with

Napoleon as its monarch (he had himself crowned at Milan). Napoleonic rule was a powerful experience: the emperor broke down the intricate network of legal and administrative boundaries and replaced them with a centralised state. Some Italians responded to the siren song of reform and of new opportunities in government, but primarily the kingdom, like all Napoleon's fiefdoms, existed to be milked for taxes and men. By 1812 Italians were fighting Napoleon's battles all over Europe, and suffering heavy casualties. Few regretted the collapse of his empire in 1814.

UNIFICATION: THE KINGDOM OF ITALY
In the settlement which followed at the Congress of Vienna (1814–15), Austria retained control of the Veneto. The Austrians were not particularly brutal rulers, but the Italians had a growing sense of national consciousness, partly a reaction to Napoleonic rule, but also given inspiration through the impassioned writings of Giuseppe Mazzini (1805–72), the founder of the revolutionary movement 'Young Italy'. This was the period known as the Risorgimento, literally the 'resurgence', denoting an awakening of Italian nationalist feeling. The sophistication of Italian intellectuals can be seen from the meeting rooms of the Caffè Pedrocchi in Padua (opened in 1831), which were dedicated to the great civilisations of the past. Such people needed to be treated sensitively but the inept response of Metternich's Austria to the economic tensions of the 1840s ensured that Italy was at the forefront of the revolutions of 1848. The Austrians were thrown out of Milan and a Piedmontese army came to support the rebels. From then on, the mountain kingdom of Piedmont remained the focus of nationalist hopes. By now a constitutional monarchy, it enjoyed a relatively prosperous economy and had, in Camillo Cavour (1810–61), an able and pragmatic statesman. In 1859 Cavour engineered the support of Napoleon III in a war against Austria which led to the absorption of Lombardy and later central Italy into a new Kingdom of Italy under the Piedmontese monarch Vittorio Emanuele II. After the killing fields of Magenta and Solferino, Napoleon III began to question the wisdom of what he had set in motion. Bismarck had no such qualms. His Prussian armies conclusively defeated Austria in 1866, after which Venice itself was joined to the new Kingdom of Italy.

This historical introduction has covered the background to the major historical monuments a visitor is likely to encounter from the rich past of northern Italy. Themes of invasion (the appalling fighting in the Veneto of the First World War), centralised rule (the Fascist era), desires for independence (the Northern League of the 1980s and 1990s), and an underlying prosperity have persisted through the 20th century. The north has, like the rest of Italy, deep-rooted social and political problems which the visitor often passes by. However, the cities of the region are alive and immensely proud of their heritage. Restoration work is effective and expert. There are happy signs of a post-industrial society which will sustain ancient traditions. The 'Slow Food' movement in a region where good food and wine has always been linked to courteous hospitality offers much hope. It is even possible that Venice will not sink beneath the weight of all her tourists.

Venice

Venice is unique: a city where canals replace roads and everyone gets about on foot or by boat. Its entire urban framework has been preserved intact over the centuries, and its churches and palaces are among the most beautiful in the world. Because of this it is crowded with tourists all through the year except in the depths of winter (late Nov or Jan), which is the best time to visit. But no matter when you go, it is difficult to come away without the sensation of having been to a place which uplifts the spirit and produces a calm sense of well-being.

NB: Venice and its lagoon is covered in much greater detail in the separate *Blue Guide Venice* (available in print and digital formats).

HISTORY OF VENICE

The unique position of Venice has given her a history of proud independence. At first a Byzantine province, by the 11th century the power of the Doges had been circumscribed to ensure that their position never became that of an autocrat. In time, complicated voting systems were devised to keep corruption to a minimum, and only Marin Falier (in 1355) dared to make his dogeship into a tyranny—and was promptly beheaded as a result. Indeed the Venetian State, the *Serenissima*, was always recognised as a Republic.

Internal policy was to maintain independence from neighbouring city states on the Italian mainland and as well as from European powers and the Papacy, as far as possible. Every year, as soon as the weather grew warmer, the great galleons would set sail from the Arsenal, protecting the interests of her wealthy merchants, and her fleet ensured the duration of her maritime empire for centuries.

From the early 15th century there was a policy of expansion onto the *terraferma* as well and in just a few years all the major towns in the Veneto (Padua, Verona, Treviso) decided to throw in their lot with the *Serenissima* and were well rewarded as a result, enjoying some 300 years of peace and prosperity under Venetian protection. Still today carved lions of St Mark can be seen on columns and buildings thoughout the region—though many of them were defaced by Napoleon and survive in mutilated form.

Apart from the 'democratic' controls of the doges' powers, many strata of Venetian society lower down the scale were given fundamental roles to play in the running of the state as well as in the ceremonial spectacles—always important as statements of the magnificence and security of Venice. The *arsenalotti*, for example, who were employed in the great shipyard, were given specially advantageous working conditions (their number had reached some 16,000, an eighth of the total population of the city, by the 15th century). Other privileged citizens included the many brethren of the hundred or so *scuole*, or charitable confraternities (which excluded patricians from their ranks).

In 1797, Venice fell to Napoleon, who symbolically burned the *Bucintoro*, the doge's great state barge. After helping himself to a choice of plunder (including the Horses of St Mark's, which he shipped to Paris), he then handed Venice to Austria, a move that caused long resentment. Venice never settled down happily under Austrian rule, and in 1848, the great year of European revolution, she rose up under Daniele Manin, winning a brief 17 months of freedom. Austria returned, and was to rule Venice until she finally joined the new Kingdom of Italy in 1866. By this time a romantic concept of the city's past glory had developed in the minds of her many foreign visitors, and as the next century proceeded, preoccupation about her preservation began to grow. In the 20th century, problems of depopulation and conservation had to be faced—and still remain great challenges. But the city remains a truly extraordinary place, filled with reminders of a great history but also with an atmosphere kept alive by the Venetians themselves.

The city is divided into six *sestieri* or districts: San Marco, Castello, Dorsoduro, San Polo, Santa Croce and Cannaregio.

At present the greatest problem facing Venice is the notable increase in the number of days when the city suffers from *acqua alta* (a flood tide over 80cm above mean sea level). When the tide reaches 110cm about 12 percent of the city is affected by flooding; exceptional conditions can cause the level of the tide to reach 140 cm and in this case 59 percent of the city is under water for a number of hours. *Acqua alta* is caused not only by subsidence but also by the gradual rise in the mean sea level and climate change in general. (*For more on acqua alta, see p. 53.*)

The project known as Mo.S.E. (*modulo sperimentale elettromeccanico*) aims to regulate tides of over 110cm by the installation of moveable barriers at the three lagoon entrances, using a system similar to those already functioning in the Netherlands and Britain. Work has been underway since 2003, and the present predictions, subject to funding, assume the entire project will probably not be functional before 2016. The sluice gates, filled with water, are designed to lie on the seabed, and they will be raised (by replacing the water with compressed air) only when a particularly high tide is expected. The gates have been designed to withstand a tide of 3m (the disastrous 1966 flood reached a level of 1.94m), and so take into account the predicted increase in the level of the sea (to a maximum of 60cm).

THE GRAND CANAL

The best introduction to the city, if you are visiting Venice for the first time, is to take vaporetto no. 1, which carries its passengers sedately down the Grand Canal. This great waterway is Venice's main thoroughfare and it is bordered on both sides by a continuous line of palaces dating from all periods, their façades rising directly from the water. They are all provided with water-gates which serve as their main entrances (their land-entrances are usually hidden in the narrow *calli* behind). Those that are open to the public as museums are described in more detail elsewhere in the text.

The vaporetto stops at 16 landing-stages before it reaches San Marco, so its leisurely pace allows you to take in the splendid scene along the way. The water is always busy with motor traffic of all kinds, giving a clear picture of how the city works. The gondoliers, on their beautiful vessels which have decorated Venice's canals for centuries but which today serve only tourists, take precedence over all the other boats. Gondolas are also used as ferries (known as *traghetti*) between the two banks: rowed by two oarsmen they provide Venetians with a very convenient way of getting from one bank to the other at various points along the Grand Canal, and are often full to the brim with passengers who stand for the short trip.

Just after the vaporetto leaves the bus and car park at Piazzale Roma, it passes under the **Calatrava Bridge** (*map Venice Left 3*), designed by Santiago Calatrava in 2008 to provide a link between the terminus of the road from the mainland and the railway station. At the first bend, the Cannaregio Canal enters the Grand Canal and just beyond, on the right, is the **Fondaco dei Turchi** (*map Venice Left 2*), a palace built in the 12th–13th century in a style which is known at Veneto-Byzantine and which can still be seen in many of Venice's buildings influenced by the East. It takes its name from the Turkish merchants who used it as their warehouse from the early 17th century onwards. It was very over-restored in the 19th century and now houses Venice's Natural History Museum. The battlemented building next to it, with the lion of St Mark, was used as a granary in the days of the Republic.

Opposite rises the splendid Renaissance **Palazzo Vendramin Calergi**, built by Mauro Codussi in Istrian stone and marble, in the early 16th century. Here Wagner died in 1883 and today it is used as the winter home of Venice's Casinò. On the right, beyond the delightful Baroque church of San Stae, rises the huge **Ca' Pesaro** (*map Venice Left 4*), an elaborate Baroque palace by Baldassare Longhena, begun in 1658. It houses the Gallery of Modern Art. Further on, on the opposite bank, is the most beautiful of all the Gothic palaces along the Canal, the **Ca' d'Oro**. Its very well preserved delicate features were designed between 1420 and 1434. It is also open to the public as one of the most interesting museums in the city.

The vaporetto now enters the area of the Rialto markets, always busy on weekday mornings: fish are sold in the building with red awnings and in the *campo* are the fruit and vegetable stalls. The **Rialto Bridge** (Ponte di Rialto; *map Venice Left 4*), lined with two rows of shops, is at the topographical centre of the city. A bridge of boats here was replaced by a wooden bridge in the mid-13th century, renewed over the next two centuries, and in 1588 it was rebuilt in stone by Antonio da Ponte (it remained the only bridge across the Canal throughout the life of the Republic). Today it is Venice's most famous landmark.

At the bend known as the *Volta del Canal*, where the Rio Nuovo, a canal cut from the station in 1933 comes in, stands the beautifully proportioned Gothic **Ca' Foscari** (*map Venice Left 5*), a grand residence built in the mid-15th century for Francesco Foscari, when almost 80 years old and after 34 years as doge. It is now the seat of Venice University, which is always named after this palace. On the left, by Campo San Samuele, is the vast **Palazzo Grassi** (*map Venice Left 6*), begun in 1748 by Giorgio Massari for Angelo Grassi whose family was one of the richest in Venice by the end of the century. It was opened by its new owner, François Pinault, in 2006 to exhibit part of his huge collection of contemporary art. Opposite is **Ca' Rezzonico** (*map Venice Left 5*), a superb building begun around 1667 by Longhena, his most successful secular work. It houses the city's collection of 18th-century works of art.

The vaporetto now passes under the wooden **Accademia Bridge** and enters the final stretch of the Grand Canal. **Palazzo Venier dei Leoni** on the right, named after its frieze of colossal lions' heads at water level (only the ground floor was ever built) was the residence of Peggy Guggenheim and is now home to the Peggy Guggenheim Collection of Modern Art (*map Venice Left 8*). Opposite rises the huge **Palazzo Corner**, also called **Ca' Grande**, a dignified edifice in the full Renaissance style commissioned from Jacopo Sansovino in 1537 by the Corner family. On the right bank, across a *rio*, is the charming **Ca' Dario**, with numerous delightful chimney-pots. It was built in 1487 and faced with a profusion of varicoloured marbles and porphyry in roundels in all shapes and sizes. A marble pavement opens out before the magnificent church of **Santa Maria della Salute**, a masterpiece of Baroque architecture by Longhena. The **Punta della Dogana**, with a handsome long low 17th-century façade extends to the end of the promontory (now used for contemporary art exhibitions).

The boat now enters the open lagoon and crosses the Bacino di San Marco (with a view of the island of San Giorgio and its church by Palladio, to dock at two landing-stages (either San Marco or the less-crowded San Zaccaria) for Piazza San Marco, where most passengers disembark.

PIAZZA SAN MARCO

This is the largest open space in the city (*map Venice Right 5*), spread out before its most venerable monument, the Basilica of St Mark. It had more or less reached its present vast dimensions by the 12th century. On three sides it has a continuous line of porticoes beneath handsome symmetrical arcaded buildings designed in the 16th century as the residence of the Procurators of St Mark's, who looked after the basilica. The two most famous cafés in Venice (Florian and the Caffè Quadri), which face each other across the square, have elegant period interiors and tables outside grouped around their orchestra podiums. Beside the wonderful façade of St Mark's is the Doge's Palace. Throughout the Republic the waterfront here was the official entrance to the city. At the back of the Piazza, the decorative clock-tower (Torre dell'Orologio) provides an entrance to the Merceria, the main pedestrian

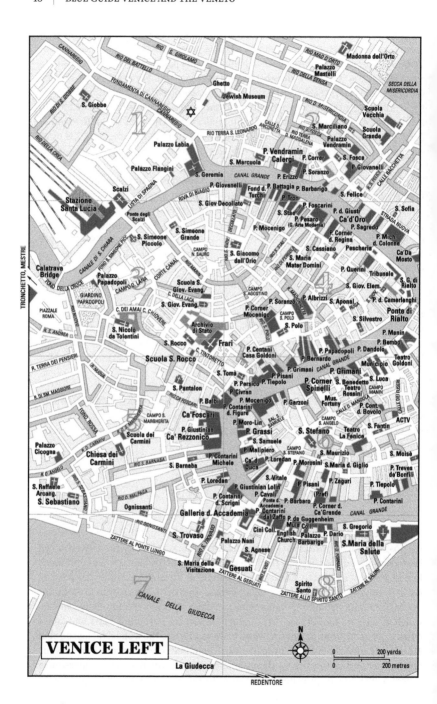

VENICE LEFT

La Giudecca

N

0   200 yards
0   200 metres

REDENTORE

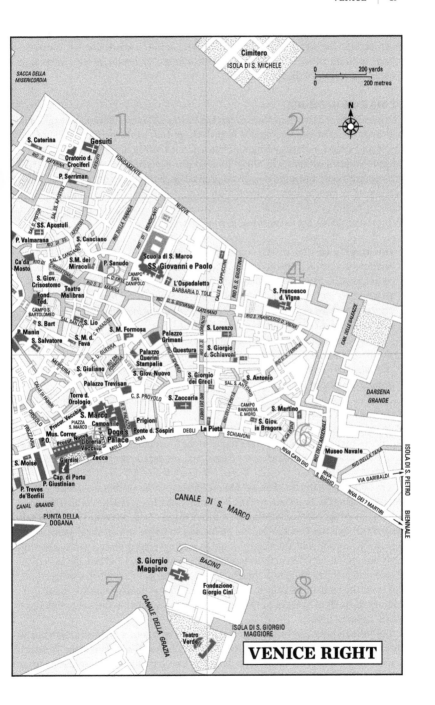

VENICE RIGHT

thoroughfare of the city, which leads directly to the Rialto. On days when there is an *acqua alta*, the piazza is one of the first places in the city to be flooded; the duck-boards used on these occasions are usually stacked in readiness (the water first reaches the atrium of the basilica).

ST MARK'S BASILICA

The basilica of St Mark (San Marco; *map Venice Right 5*) is one of the most venerable buildings in christendom, founded in the 9th century as the private chapel of the doges and used for state ceremonies throughout the life of the Republic (it only became Venice's cathedral in 1807). Its plan was derived from the great churches of Constantinople and it has numerous original Byzantine carvings as well as works carried out in Venice in the 12th and 13th centuries, inspired by Byzantine art. The mosaics, begun by craftsmen from Constantinople and continued in the same spirit by local mosaicists, are its most wonderful feature.

> **Opening times:** *The basilica is open to visitors daily 9.45–4.30 or 5; Sun and holidays 2–4.30 or 5. However, it is difficult to fully appreciate the beauty of the mosaics unless they are illuminated: they are only lit for one hour on weekdays, 11.30–12.30, and on Sun and holidays from 2–5. From Easter to the end of Oct you can book the visit for a small extra fee at www.venetoinside.com, although the interior is almost always unpleasantly crowded.*
>
> *Once inside you are restricted to a 'one-way' route in the nave, unless you pay the small entrance fee to see the gilded and enamelled high altarpiece known as the Pala d'Oro (open 10–4 or 6; Sun and holidays 3–6) and in this way you can also explore the east end of the church (the Treasury is open at the same times).*

Exterior of St Mark's

Five great arches with clusters of precious marble columns surround the five entrances to the narthex. Above are copies of the four splendid Horses (the originals are in the Museo di San Marco; *see below*) and the façade is crowned with Gothic tracery.

The archway on the extreme left **(A)** preserves its original mosaic lunette (1260–70) illustrating the Translation of the Body of St Mark to the Basilica, which includes a depiction of the basilica façade with the four Horses. Legend relates that **St Mark** passed through the Venetian lagoon on his way to Rome and an angel appeared to him in a vision and told him Venice would be his final resting place. In 828, when his body was stolen by two Venetian merchants from Alexandria and brought to Venice, the doge decided to build this church. Since then the saint's symbol, a winged lion, has been the emblem of Venice. When the church was damaged by fire in the 10th century the body of St Mark was lost, only to be miraculously 'rediscovered' by Doge Vitale Falier in 1094.

The Romanesque carving dating from the mid-13th century on the three arches of the central doorway **(B)** is particularly fine and includes illustrations of the Venetian trades, the months, the Virtues, and daily life. The very ancient doors, dating from the 6th century, are wonderful Byzantine works.

Low down on the corner of the façade towards the Doge's Palace is a famous statue group of four porphyry figures dressed in Roman garb. Known as the **Tetrarchs (C)**, after the four rulers of the Roman Empire, they come from Constantinople but were probably carved in Egypt in the 4th century.

The narthex of St Mark's

The narthex is thought to have been built around 1063–72, and the north side was added before 1253. It provides a fitting vestibule to the basilica, although it is today sadly cluttered with barriers and notices, and now only partly accessible, given the strictly imposed routes for entering and leaving the basilica. The superb mosaics of the six small domes and arches represent stories from the Old Testament, and are mainly original works of the 13th century. The door of San Clemente (**D**; right of the main entrance) was cast in the East in the second half of the 11th century. The Byzantine capitals of the columns flanking it are beautifully decorated with birds.

On the first arch the mosaics show the *Story of Noah and the Flood*. Here lies Doge Vitale Falier (d. 1096) who consecrated the basilica two years before his death, and who was responsible for much of its most beautiful decoration. The tomb, made up of Byzantine fragments, is the oldest surviving funerary monument in the city.

In front of the main door two tiers of niches contain the earliest mosaics in the basilica (c. 1063), doubly precious since they have never had to be restored. They represent the Madonna with eight Apostles and the four Evangelists beneath. The *St Mark in Ecstasy* in the semi-dome was added centuries later (in 1545, on a cartoon attributed to Lorenzo Lotto). We know that the great central door in Byzantine style (protected between two wooden doors) was commissioned in 1113.

Interior of St Mark's

The plan is a Greek cross, and the splendid mosaics on a gold ground which cover all the domes and barrel vaults of the ceiling and the sumptuous marbles which cover the walls below, as well as the many exquisite sculptural details (and the absence of paintings) produce an atmosphere entirely Byzantine in spirit. Beyond the rood screen and the two ancient pulpits (one with an oriental style dome) is the raised sanctuary. The vaulted aisles have numerous columns with exquisite foliated capitals. The venerable pavement in precious marbles has fascinating geometric designs as well as representations of birds and beasts.

The earliest **mosaics** were made by Greek masters who were succeeded in the 12th century by very skilled Venetian mosaicists working in the same style. The five great mosaic domes survive intact from this time: the earliest is probably the Dome of the Pentecost (**E**) at the west end, showing the descent of the Holy Spirit with the twelve Apostles seated in a circle. At the crossing is the Dome of the Ascension (**F**), with Christ seated on a rainbow with the symbols of the Evangelists and four figures representing the Rivers of Paradise. In the south transept (**G**) the dome has four early 13th-century figures of saints (Nicholas, Clement, Blaise and Leonard). In the Sanctuary (**H**) the dome illustrates the Religion of Christ as foretold by the prophets, with the bust of Christ Emmanuel holding a half-revealed scroll, surrounded by the Virgin between Isaiah and Daniel and eleven other Prophets. In the apse at the east

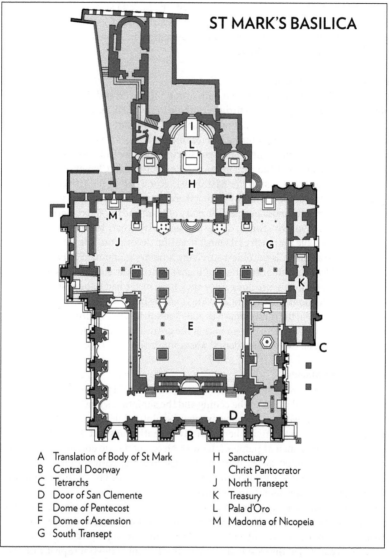

ST MARK'S BASILICA

A	Translation of Body of St Mark	H	Sanctuary
B	Central Doorway	I	Christ Pantocrator
C	Tetrarchs	J	North Transept
D	Door of San Clemente	K	Treasury
E	Dome of Pentecost	L	Pala d'Oro
F	Dome of Ascension	M	Madonna of Nicopeia
G	South Transept		

end is *Christ Pantocrator* **(I)**, the ruler of the universe, remade in 1506 (many of the mosaics elsewhere in the church were also replaced in later centuries). The four patron saints of Venice here: St Nicholas, St Peter, St Mark and St Hermagorus, are among the earliest mosaics in the basilica (probably completed before 1100). The dome in the north transept **(J)** is dedicated to the life of St John the Evangelist.

In the south transept is the entrance to the **Treasury (K)** (*for admission, see p. 20*) with one of the most important collections of Byzantine goldsmiths' work of the 12th century in existence, most of it looted from Constantinople in 1204, when Venice sacked it during the Fourth Crusade.

Also from this transept is the entrance to the Sanctuary and Pala d'Oro (*for admission, see p. 20*). The carved altars here (by Antonio Rizzo), and the statues on the rood screen (by Jacobello and Pier Paolo dalle Masegne) are by the leading Venetian sculptors of the 15th century. The works in bronze in the choir and apse were made in the mid-16th century by the great architect Jacopo Sansovino, who is buried in the Baptistery and carried out many restoration projects in the basilica. The baldacchino over the high altar (beneath which is the sarcophagus of St Mark) has four intricately carved alabaster columns, early Byzantine works. Behind the altar is the **Pala d'Oro (L)**, the most precious work of art in the basilica. It was commissioned by Doge Pietro Orseolo I in Constantinople in the 10th century, but subsequently enlarged and re-set by medieval goldsmiths. The enamels were made using the cloisonné technique, and it is considered one of the most exquisite examples of this art, typical of Byzantine craftsmanship.

Another very precious Byzantine work is on an altar in the north transept (*the chapel is reserved for services*): this is the greatly revered **Madonna of Nicopeia (M)**, an icon of the *Madonna and Child*. Known as the 'Victory-maker', since it would often be carried by the Byzantine emperor into battle at the head of his army, it was also stolen from Constantinople in 1204 and became the protectress of Venice. Probably dating from the 12th century, it is also surrounded by a fine enamelled frame encrusted with jewels.

MUSEO DI SAN MARCO

The museum is entered from the Narthex (entrance porch). Open 9.45–4.45. From the gallery you get a remarkable view of the interior of the basilica and come very close to some of the mosaics. There is also a superb view from the exterior loggia.

The mosaic of the *Last Judgement* above the gallery dates from the 16th century. Some of the earlier mosaics can be seen from the walkways. In the huge Sala dei Banchetti are ten tapestries of the Passion by Venetian masters (dating from 1420). The magnificent **Horses of St Mark's** are the only quadriga figures to have survived from Classical times. They came to Venice as loot from the Fourth Crusade in 1204 and in 1267 it was decided to install them on the façade of the basilica. Made in gilded copper, it seems that they are Roman works dating from around 195 AD, probably part of an imperial triumphal monument set up in Constantinople. From the loggia (where the horses are replaced by copies) there is a wonderful view of Piazza San Marco.

THE CAMPANILE

The basilica was given its brick bell-tower in the 9th century. It was completed in the 12th century and restored in succeeding centuries until 1902, when it crashed to the ground without warning. Fortunately it caused very little damage and there were no human casualties. It was reconstructed ten years later, an exact replica of the origial. There is a lift up to the bell-chamber (*open daily 9 or 9.30–dusk*). The wonderful view takes in the entire lagoon and stretches as far as the Alps on a clear day.

At the base of the campanile is the Loggetta, in red Verona marble, Jacopo Sansovino's first work to be completed in Venice (1537–46). Its form is derived from the Roman triumphal arch and its sculptures celebrate the glory of the Republic.

THE DOGE'S PALACE

This great palace (*map Venice Right 5; open 1 April–31 Oct 9–6; 1 Nov–31 March 9–5*) was the magnificent official residence of the doges and chief magistrates. It was begun around 1340 with a room big enough to contain the 1,212 members of the Great Council. Inaugurated in 1419, its two façades are superb examples of florid Gothic architecture. The portico on the ground level (the columns appear somewhat stumpy since the height of the pavement has risen over time) has magnificent carved capitals representing the virtues of wise government and the importance of justice. Each arcade of the portico supports two arches of the loggia decorated with quatrefoil roundels. This in turn is surmounted by a massive wall 12.5m high lightened by a delicate pattern of white Istrian stone and pink Verona marble. Marble ornamental crenellations crown the façade. At the three corners are high reliefs inspired by Old Testament subjects to underline the importance of the Christian faith. The highly decorative Porta della Carta next to the Basilica (now used as an exit from the palace) was added in 1438.

The quay extends in front of the Doge's Palace as far as the Ponte della Paglia, from which you can see the famous **Bridge of Sighs** (Ponte dei Sospiri), an elegant little flying bridge in Istrian stone added in 1600 to connect the law courts in the Doge's Palace to the prisons. It only received its popular name in the 19th century when the idea of the 'sighing' prisoners on their way to trial fired the imagination of the Romantics.

MUSEO DELL'OPERA AND COURTYARD

The entrance to the palace is through the Porta del Frumento at the centre of the waterfront façade. In the **Museo dell'Opera**, on the ground floor, there is a splendid display of the original capitals and columns (mostly dating from 1340–55) from the exterior portico, where they were replaced by fine copies in 1876–87. The largest and most beautiful depicts the *Creation of Adam*, with the planets and signs of the zodiac.

From the **courtyard** you can admire the magnificent east façade of the palace (after 1483), which has four storeys with a double row of porticoes and numerous windows. The carved decoration is extremely beautiful and is partly the work of the Lombardo family of sculptors. The façade itself is the work of Antonio Rizzo, who also provided the ceremonial **Scala dei Giganti**, the stairway which was used as the setting for the doge's coronation ceremony (which up to then had not been held in public). Built of Istrian limestone, it is famous for its exquisitely-carved reliefs. On the wide landing at the top, the doge was crowned (over a white skull cap) with the jewelled and peaked *cornu*, modelled on a Byzantine head-dress and always an important symbol of his position. The statues of Neptune and Mars (the *giganti* of the stairway's name) symbolise the maritime and terrestrial might of the Republic. They are late works (c. 1554) by Jacopo Sansovino, added in order to diminish the figure of the doge during his coronation.

INTERIOR OF THE DOGE'S PALACE

In the vast interior almost nothing remains from the 14th century since it was devastated by fire several times. However, when the palace was restored after the last fire in 1577, a decorative programme glorifying Venetian history was drawn up to cover the walls and ceilings of the main rooms used by the governing bodies of the Republic by the greatest Venetian painters of the 16th–17th centuries, and so the present sumptuous appearance of the interior dates from that time.

From the courtyard, the Scala dei Censori leads up to the inner loggia. From here the Scala d'Oro, built in 1558–9, to Sansovino's design and decorated with brilliantly gilded stuccoes by Alessandro Vittoria, continues up to the first floor (the *primo piano nobile*) and the **Doge's Apartments,** reconstructed after a fire in 1483. These rooms have gilded and stuccoed ceilings and fine chimneypieces by Tullio and Antonio Lombardo, and in one of them are displayed four charming paintings of the winged lion of St Mark, the famous symbol of Venice, including one by Vittore Carpaccio (1516) which shows the lion between the sea and the *terraferma* and has a very accurate view of the Doge's Palace and the Campanile and domes of St Mark's in the background, as well as a group of galleons setting sail from the Arsenale.

The Scala d'Oro continues up to the *secondo piano nobile*. The grand **state rooms** on this floor were decorated after 1577 with a series of paintings glorifying Venice and her history, commissioned from the leading artists of the day (including Titian, Veronese and Tintoretto) on a scheme carefully worked out to include the most important military and naval victories of the Republic, as well as allegories of wise government, and scenes of the most significant events in the reigns of the most highly regarded doges.

The **Sala delle Quattro Porte** was the magnificent waiting-room where ambassadors and heads of state would attend their turn to be received by officials of the Republic or by the doge himself. It was also the room through which the Venetian patricians would pass to and fro on their way to meetings of the most powerful organs of the Venetian State (the Collegio, Senate and Council of Ten) and so its grandeur and allegorical decorations exulting the power of the Republic took on special significance. It was designed by Palladio and has very fine stucco work. On the long wall is a painting commissioned from Titian, in 1555: it apparently escaped damage in the fire since it had not yet been completed and was still in the painter's studio. It represents *Antonio Grimani Kneeling before the Faith*, and was completed around 1600 by Titian's nephew Marco Vecellio, but the parts attributed to Titian's own hand are the figure of St Mark, the helmeted warrior, and the view of the waterfront.

In the **Sala del Collegio** the doge and the Collegio, or cabinet, deliberated and received ambassadors. The Collegio's 26 members included the doge himself, six councillors (one for each *sestiere* of the city) and the three judges of the criminal tribunals. The room is a treasure house of art, and its decorations, carried out from 1575–81, survive almost intact, including the original rostrum and benches. The carved wood ceiling is set with wonderful paintings by Veronese: the most remarkable is that in the centre at the farther end: *Justice and Peace Offering the Sword, the Scales and the Olive-branch to Triumphant Venice*. The painting over the entrance, showing *Doge Andrea Gritti before the Virgin*, is by Jacopo Tintoretto, while above the throne Veronese painted *Doge Sebastiano Venier Offering Thanks to Christ for the Victory of Lepanto*. Facing the fireplace are three more magnificent paintings by Jacopo Tintoretto: *Marriage of St Catherine, Doge Niccolò da Ponte Invoking the Virgin*, and *Doge Alvise Mocenigo Adoring Christ*.

The **Sala del Senato** was where the Senate, or legislative body of the Republic, sat. They were elected from among the patricians by the Great Council, and held office for just one year. At the centre of the political life of the Republic, they also nominated magistrates, ambassadors, bishops and the patriarch. They treated with foreign courts, and only they could take the grave decision to declare war. The room has another fine ceiling (1581), with *Venice Exalted among the Gods*, by Jacopo Tintoretto, in the central panel. Tintoretto also painted the *Descent from the Cross, with doges Pietro Lando and Marcantonio Trevisan in adoration*, over the throne. The prolific painter Palma Giovane, who was overshadowed by his contemporaries Veronese and Tintoretto, but who carried out some of his best works for the Doge's Palace, painted the three works on the left wall: *Venice Receiving the Homage of Subject Cities Presented by Doge Francesco Venier, Doge Pasquale Cicogna in Prayer*, and an *Allegory of the League of Cambrai*, as well as *Doges Lorenzo and Girolamo Priuli Praying to Christ* on the end wall. Tintoretto painted *Doge Pietro Loredan Praying to the Virgin*, also on the left wall.

The **Sala del Consiglio dei Dieci** was where the Council of Ten met. This court, which tried political crimes, became a notoriously severe organ of government. The ceiling contains more paintings by Veronese, notably an *Old Man in Eastern Costume with a Young Woman*.

In the Sala della Bussola can be seen a *Bocca di Leone* (or 'mouth of truth'), a box in which denunciations were posted from the outside. These could only be opened in the presence of all three magistrates and there were notoriously severe punishments for false denunciations (and they were disregarded if anonymous).

Back on the *prima piano nobile* is the vast **Sala del Maggior Consiglio**, the seat of the governing body of the Republic. It was first built on this scale in 1340, and was large enough to hold the entire assembly of Venetian patricians. Here laws were ratified and the highest officials of the Republic were elected. The 14th–15th-century frescoes by leading artists of the time and the magnificent ceiling were all destroyed in fire in 1577, but the following year the best known Venetian artists of the day were commissioned to begin the work of replacing them with painted panels—a task which was only completed in 1595. On the entrance wall is a huge painting of *Paradise* (1592), the most important work by Jacopo Tintoretto's son Domenico. The magnificent gilded ceiling frames 35 paintings, but the most important are the three central panels: nearest the throne is *Venice Surrounded by Gods and Crowned by Victory (Apotheosis of Venice)*, a masterpiece of light and colour by Veronese (painted just before he died in 1588); the central panel, *Venice Surrounded by Gods Gives an Olive-branch to Doge Niccolò da Ponte*, is by Jacopo Tintoretto; and at the far end is *Venice Welcoming the Conquered Nations around her Throne* by Palma Giovane. These three artists also worked on some of the large historical canvases around the walls, recording important events in the history of the Republic: on the wall towards the courtyard the 12th-century battles between Church and Empire, culminating in peace proclaimed by Venice in 1175, are commemorated. On the wall towards the Bacino are the events of the Fourth Crusade of 1204, including Domenico Tintoretto's *Capture and Sack of Constantinople*. On the wall opposite the throne, Veronese's *Triumph of Doge Contarini after the Battle of Chioggia*, commemorates the Venetian victory over the Genoese in 1379.

The **Prisons**, approached across the famous Bridge of Sighs, can also be visited. The *Itinerari Segreti*, literally 'secret tours', are guided tours (also in English) of the lesser-known parts of the palace (booking necessary: *T: 041 4273089 or www. visitmuve.com.*) and include the seven prison cells called the *Piombi* because they were high up beneath the leaden roof. Giacomo Casanova was detained in one of them in 1756 before his celebrated escape across the rooftops. His lifestyle had been condemned since he was accused of being a mason, a gambler and a cheat, of frequenting people from every walk of life, of practising alchemy and magic, of showing little respect for Christians, and of writing irreverent and satirical verse and reading it in public.

PIAZZETTA DI SAN MARCO

The Piazzetta (*map Venice Right 5*) is an extension of Piazza San Marco from St Mark's to the waterfront: this was where the ships from the open sea once docked carrying ambassadors and foreign dignitaries as well as the boats from the terraferma and all visitors would thus at once be confronted with Venice's most magnificent buildings.

Near the water's edge are two huge monolithic granite **columns** brought back to Venice from Constantinople by Doge Vitale Michiel II and erected here at the end of the 12th century. One bears a winged lion and the other is crowned with a copy of a statue of the first patron saint of Venice, the Greek soldier St Theodore, and his dragon.

The **façade of the Libreria Marciana**, opposite the Doge's Palace, is the masterpiece of Jacopo Sansovino. This great Tuscan architect and sculptor at first worked in Rome but in 1527 was called to Venice by Doge Andrea Gritti and put in charge of the fabric of St Mark's. Begun in 1537, the library is built of Istrian stone, its ornate grand design derived from Classical Roman architecture, with a Doric ground floor, and an Ionic *piano nobile* with an elaborate frieze beneath a balustrade crowned by obelisks and statues of gods and heroes.

By the public gardens known as the Giardini Reali, laid out c. 1814, is the rusticated Doric façade of the **Zecca**, which was Jacopo Sansovino's first commission in Venice, begun in 1536. It is on the site of the 13th-century mint from which the first golden ducat was issued in 1284, and at the height of the Republic the Venetian *zecchini* were used as currency throughout the world.

MUSEO CORRER, MUSEO ARCHEOLOGICO & LIBRERIA MARCIANA

Map Venice Right 5. Open 9–5 or 7. Entrance beneath the Ala Napoleonica at the far end of the Piazza. The ticket includes entrance to the two museums and two monumental rooms of the Libreria Marciana.

The museums are housed in the Procuratie Nuove which were used, from the days of Napoleon onwards, as a royal palace by the French and Austrian courts during their occupation of the city before Unification in 1866, and then, up until 1920, by the Italian royal family. You can also visit some of the 19th-century rooms in the Ala Napoleonica, the central wing built by Napoleon, where works by Antonio Canova, Italy's greatest Neoclassical sculptor, are displayed. There is a grand ballroom of 1822 and a suite of rooms furnished for Princess Elisabeth ('Sisi') of Bavaria, the young bride of Franz Joseph, who stayed here in the 1850s and '60s.

MUSEO CORRER
The rooms display paintings and objects illustrating the **history of Venice**, with particular reference to the doge and officials of the Republic, as well as the maritime exploits of the *Serenissima*. One of the most interesting exhibits is the wood engraving (and its six original blocks) of the city made in 1500 by Jacopo de' Barbari. De' Barbari invented the idea of the perspective view of a city, as seen from above: his work was to influence the long series of maps and views of cities which were produced right up until the 18th century. Very few representations of Venice had been made before this time, and this bird's-eye view is of fundamental importance to historians of Venice.

Upstairs, the **picture gallery** is arranged chronologically with paintings from the Gothic period up to the late 15th century. Among the masterpieces are Antonello da Messina's *Pietà* and Vittore Carpaccio's portrait of two Venetian ladies on a balcony.

MUSEO ARCHEOLOGICO AND LIBRERIA MARCIANA
The **Museo Archeologico** was founded in 1523 from a bequest of Classical sculpture to the Republic from Cardinal Domenico Grimani. It has some precious ancient Greek statues, and a very fine Roman bronze portrait head.

The **Libreria Marciana**, the Library of St Mark, was designed by Jacopo Sansovino in 1537. Petrarch gave his books to Venice in 1362 and the library was formally founded in 1468 with an important donation of Greek and Latin manuscripts by Cardinal Bessarion. Two rooms can be visited (access from the Museo Archeologico): the magnificent Great Hall, the former reading room, with its walls and ceiling decorated with paintings by Venetian Mannerist artists including Tintoretto and Veronese; and the Vestibule, from which can be seen the monumental staircase with a splendid stuccoed vault by Alessandro Vittoria, which descends to the original entrance. The central panel of the Vestibule ceiling has an *Allegory of Wisdom* by Titian. In 1587 Cardinal Domenico Grimani arranged a public gallery of some 200 pieces of statuary on the walls of this room, and this has been partially reconstructed, also with the use of casts. Here also is displayed a celebrated world map dating from around 1450, drawn by Fra' Mauro, a monk in the monastery on the island of San Michele, 40 years before the discovery of America. It is annotated with some 3,000 inscriptions which illustrate the geographical knowledge of the period, as well as descriptions by travellers including Marco Polo. It is one of the library's most precious possessions.

THE SESTIERE OF SAN MARCO

The small *sestiere* of San Marco is very much at the heart of Venice: it stretches from Piazza San Marco to the Rialto Bridge, cradled in the curve of the Grand Canal and bounded by the narrow *calle* known as the Merceria. It has nearly all Venice's most fashionable shops and art galleries and a great number of restaurants of all categories, as well as numerous hotels. It is the district which is always the most crowded with visitors.

ALONG THE MERCERIA TO THE RIALTO

The highly decorated **Torre dell'Orologio** (*map Venice Right 5*), on the north side of Piazza San Marco, was designed by Mauro Codussi to house a remarkable astronomical clock constructed in 1493–9. Above hangs a great bell cast at the same time, which is struck every hour by two giant mechanical figures in bronze. *The tower can be visited daily but only by appointment at the Museo Correr or Doge's Palace, or T: 848082000; www.torreorologio.visitmuve.it. Ticket includes admission to Museo Correr.*

Beneath the tower begins the busy Merceria, the shortest route from Piazza San Marco to the Rialto. At the first bend is the church of **San Giuliano** (San Zulian) rebuilt in 1553 by Jacopo Sansovino. The façade records the wealthy physician and scholar from Ravenna called Tommaso Rangone, who supplied the funds for its construction (and includes his portrait in bronze attributed to Alessandro Vittoria). The pleasing simple interior preserves its 16th-century decorations.

The church of **San Salvatore** (*map Venice Right 3*) has a good Renaissance interior and two splendid works by Titian: an *Annunciation* (third south altar) and *Transfiguration* (over the high altar). In the south transept is the tomb of Caterina Cornaro (or Corner). Close to the foot of the Rialto Bridge is the busy **Campo San Bartolomeo**, at the crossroads of the city. The statue of the playwright Goldoni, the dramatist of Venetian life, in a tricorn hat and flowing frock coat, was set up here in 1883.

FROM PIAZZA SAN MARCO TO THE ACCADEMIA BRIDGE

This busy route takes you past some of the city's grandest and most fashionable shops. It begins at the far end of Piazza San Marco, beneath the entrance to the Museo Correr and takes you past the famously over-elaborate façade of **San Moisè** (*map Venice Right 5*) with its sculpted camels. Once across the *rio*, you can take a detour to the north to see the grand Neoclassical entrance **La Fenice** (*map Venice Left 6*), famous in the history of operatic art and still one of the most important opera houses in Italy (*it can be visited daily 9.30–6 with an audio guide in English*). First built in 1786, a fire in 1996 caused by arson destroyed 80 percent of the building, but the immediate decision was taken to rebuild a replica, which opened in 2004. The première of Rossini's *Tancredi* took place here in 1813, and many of Verdi's operas had their opening nights at the Fenice: *Rigoletto* was received with great enthusiasm in 1851, but *La Traviata*, which was specially written for the Fenice, had a disastrous reception two years later.

The church of **Santa Maria del Giglio** ('Zobenigo' in Venetian dialect) has one of the best Baroque façades in Venice, built by Giuseppe Sardi in 1678–81 as a monument to the Barbaro family, who paid for the rebuilding of the church. Inside, the quaint Cappella Molin contains a *Madonna and Child* attributed to Rubens (the great Flemish painter is known to have stopped in Venice in 1600 on his way to the court of Vincenzo Gonzaga in Mantua, on the first of many trips to Italy). The *campo* opens onto the Grand Canal beside Palazzo Pisani, now the **Hotel Gritti**, one of Venice's best luxury-class hotels. John and Effie Ruskin stayed here in 1851, the year that *The Stones of Venice* was published.

The huge **Campo Santo Stefano** (*map Venice Left 6*) has some exceptionally large palaces including the 17th-century Palazzo Morosini, and (behind its garden railings) Palazzo Cavalli-Franchetti, both owned by the Istituto Veneto di Scienze, Lettere ed Arti, an academy of arts and sciences founded in 1838. Peep into the church of **San Vitale** (used for concerts) to see, over the high altar, a splendid painting of the titular saint mounted on a white horse, signed and dated 1514 by Carpaccio. At the other end of Campo Santo Stefano is the brick flank of the church of **Santo Stefano** (*open Mon–Sat 8–7; museum 10–5 with Chorus Pass*). Its lovely early Gothic interior, dating from the 14th–15th century, has three apses, and tall columns alternately of Greek and red Veronese marble beneath the wonderful tricuspid wooden roof in the form of a ship's keel. There is a little museum in the sacristy with four paintings by Tintoretto.

A bridge leads over to Campo Sant'Angelo from which it is a short way to the **Museo Fortuny** in the grand 15th-century Palazzo Pesaro degli Orfei, with a magnificent Gothic exterior (*open Tues–Sun 10–6*). From 1930 this was the home of the Spanish painter Mariano Fortuny (1871–1949), who designed the famous Fortuny fabrics here. His gorgeous silks and velvets were derived from ancient Venetian designs, and he set up a factory on the Giudecca (*map Venice Left 7*; near the Mulino Stucky), which is still in operation. His huge atelier on the first floor has a remarkable *fin de siècle* atmosphere, and it is filled with curios.

SESTIERE OF DORSODURO

This district, across the Grand Canal from San Marco, is principally a residential area, with a very peaceful atmosphere and some of the most picturesque canals in Venice. To the south it looks over the Giudecca Canal, and here the wide and sunny Zattere promenade is one of the most congenial spots in Venice. There are also important museums: the Gallerie dell'Accademia, Ca' Rezzonico and the Peggy Guggenheim collection of modern art. The great church of the Salute crowns Dorsoduro's easternmost tip where the Grand Canal enters the city from the lagoon.

GALLERIE DELL'ACCADEMIA

The Gallerie dell'Accademia (*map Venice Left 6–8, open 8.15–7.15, Mon 8.15–2*), at the foot of the Accademia Bridge, is one of the most important art galleries in Italy, with the best collection in existence of paintings from all periods of Venetian art from the 14th–18th centuries, and especially memorable for its Madonnas by the city's greatest 15th-century painter, Giovanni Bellini.

The collection, first opened in 1817, occupies the former church and Scuola Grande of the Carità (founded in 1260) as well as its old convent where major construction work has been in progress since 2005 to expand the gallery space. The earliest works exhibited in the 15th century chapter house of the Scuola, with its splendid gilded wooden ceiling, include polyptychs by **Paolo Veneziano**, born in the last years of the 13th century. He is considered the first truly Venetian painter: though his works show the influence of Byzantine art (it is thought that he may even have visited Constantinople), they also provide a prelude to the great Venetian school of painting.

Giovanni Bellini, son of the painter Jacopo Bellini, was born c. 1433 and was an innovator who throughout his long life (he lived to be over 80) produced wonderful works which epitomise the Venetian Renaissance (in 1482 he was made official painter of the Republic). His exquisite paintings of the Madonna and Child here show mother and child in an extraordinary variety of poses and moods, sometimes accompanied by saints. His large altarpiece from the church of San Giobbe illustrates the profound influence it had on his contemporaries, including Carpaccio and Cima da Conegliano, whose monumental altarpieces are also present in the gallery.

Giorgione's most famous painting is also here, the enigmatic *Tempesta*, the subject of which is still much discussed, and which includes a wonderful landscape. Born around 1476, Giorgione has always been one of the best known Venetian painters despite the fact that very little is known about his life and very few paintings can be attributed with certainty to his hand.

The gallery is famous, too, for its cycles of paintings made at the end of the 15th and beginning of the 16th century for two *scuole* of the city. Those which used to decorated the Scuola of San Giovanni Evangelista relating especially to miracles associated with a relic of the True Cross, are particularly remarkable for their depiction of Venice, including the old Rialto Bridge and the brightly-painted Gothic palace façades, and the richly clothed Venetians. They are the work of Lazzaro

Bastiani, Gentile Bellini, Giovanni Mansueti, Benedetto Diana and Carpaccio. For the Scuola di Sant'Orsola, Carpaccio painted single-handed the delightful cycle of nine paintings of scenes from the life of St Ursula.

Large canvases painted for the Scuola Grande di San Marco include scenes from the saint's life commissioned in 1492 first from Gentile and Giovanni Bellini and then after their death from Giovanni Mansueti (who had worked in Gentile's studio). When Mansueti died in about 1527, Paris Bordone and Palma Vecchio were chosen to complete the cycle. For the chapter hall of the same *scuola* **Jacopo Tintoretto** painted four masterpieces in the 1560s illustrating the transport of the Body of St Mark from Alexandria to Venice, and three dramatic miracles related to the saint.

Paolo Veronese's most famous work here is the huge painting of *Christ in the House of Levi* (1573), a splendid Venetian banquet scene framed in a Palladian loggia, with some 50 figures busy enjoying themselves, dressed in splendid, colourful costumes, and including servants, clowns and dogs. In the background are extravagant buildings against a twilight sky. It was the secular character of this painting that brought Veronese into conflict with the Inquisition, and the name had to be changed from 'The Last Supper' to 'Christ in the House of Levi' before it was allowed to be hung in the refectory of Santi Giovanni e Paolo.

Amongst the portraits present in the Gallery, perhaps the most memorable is **Lorenzo Lotto**'s *Gentleman in his Study*, painted around 1530. The sitter has a striking pallor, and the lizard, rose petals and book all have symbolic meaning (fleeting life, disappointed love).

A *Holy Family with Saints* by **Palma Vecchio** is one of his best works, left unfinished at his death in 1528. It is thought that Titian completed the head of St Catherine and the landscape in the background.

A moving *Pietà* is one of the last works by **Titian**, painted the year before his death in 1576, when Venice was devastated by a plague (which eventually killed the painter himself). The muted tones produce a strikingly dramatic and tragic effect, and the kneeling figure of the old man disguised as St Jerome is a self-portrait. In the former Sala dell'Albergo of the Scuola della Carità (with a very fine carved 15th-century ceiling) is Titian's wonderful *Presentation of the Virgin*, painted in 1534–39 for its present position. The details such as the man dressed in red above at the window, and the old woman seated at the foot of the steps beside her basket of eggs, are particularly beautiful, as well as the two splendid female figures in the centre of the picture scrutinising Mary. The large triptych by Antonio Vivarini and his brother-in-law Giovanni d'Alemagna was also painted (in 1446) for this room, one of the first works in Venice to be painted on canvas.

THE PEGGY GUGGENHEIM COLLECTION

Map Venice Left 8. Open daily except Tues 10–6. Entrance at no. 704 on Fondamenta Venier.

The collection provides one of the most representative displays of modern art (after 1910) in Europe. It is housed in the single-storey Palazzo Venier dei Leoni (left incomplete in the mid-18th century) on the Grand Canal, which was the residence of Peggy Guggenheim from 1949 until her death in 1979.

The permanent collection, which is frequently changed round, is very well labelled, also in English. The paintings include important Cubist works by Picasso, Braque and Duchamp. The Italian Futurists are represented by Giacomo Balla and Umberto Boccioni, and there are Metaphysical paintings by Giorgio de Chirico. Other famous painters whose works are here include Kandinsky, Mondrian, Arp, Max Ernst (Peggy's second husband), Chagall, Klee, Miró, Magritte and Dalí. Two mobiles and a silver bedhead (made on commission for Peggy) are by Alexander Calder. In 2012 the Hannelore B. and Randolph Schulhof Collection was left to the museum with paintings from the 1950s and 1960s by Jasper Johns, Andy Warhol, Afro, Lucio Fontana, Cy Twombly and Jean Dubuffet.

SANTA MARIA DELLA SALUTE AND THE PUNTA DELLA DOGANA

In one of the best sites in the city, at the entrance to the Grand Canal from the lagoon, this **church of the Salute** (*map Venice Left 8; open 9–12 & 3–5.30, 6.30 in summer. Sacristy open 3–5.30 and when possible also 10–12*) was the most magnificent last addition to the townscape in the 17th century (built some hundred years after Palladio had erected San Giorgio Maggiore and the Redentore, both just across the water from here). The masterpiece of Baldassare Longhena, it has a central octagonal plan raised above a monumental flight of steps. The huge Baroque volutes surmounted by statues support the drum of the great dome crowned by a lantern, and another smaller dome covers the east end. The water is reflected on its bright surface, built partly of Istrian stone and partly of *marmorino* (brick covered with marble dust. Dedicated to the Madonna 'of health', it was begun in 1631in thanksgiving for the deliverance of Venice from the terrible plague of the same year, which had left some 46,000 dead (30 percent of the city's population). The doge visited the Salute annually on 21st November in a procession across a pontoon of boats from San Marco: this Venetian festival is still celebrated every year on the same date.

In the interior, the sanctuary has an allegorical sculptural group by Juste le Court of the Virgin casting out the plague (represented by an ugly female figure). The Byzantine icon was seized from the cathedral of Herakleion in Crete by Francesco Morosini in 1669.

In the circular aisle are three altarpieces of the life of the Virgin by Luca Giordano. Beneath the *Pentecost* by Titian is a 15th-century Flemish tapestry of the same subject, with charming landscapes of exquisite workmanship. Here is the entrance to the sacristy, which has some good paintings: the *Wedding at Cana* is a splendid work by Jacopo Tintoretto, with very beautiful light effects, and *St Mark Enthroned between Sts Cosmas and Damian and Sts Roch and Sebastian* is an early work by Titian (who also painted the three very fine ceiling paintings).

The last building on the promontory is the **Punta della Dogana**, which from the 14th century onwards was the site of a customs' house for goods arriving in Venice by sea. Its attractive late 17th-century exterior was preserved when the Japanese architect Tadao Ando restored it as an exhibition space for the François Pinault Foundation (*open 10–6 except Tues; combined ticket available with Palazzo Grassi*).

THE ZATTERE

The Fondamenta delle Zattere, which skirts the Giudecca Canal, takes its name from the cargo boats (*zattere*, literally 'rafts'), which used to pull in here and unload into the warehouses along the quay. In full view of the island of the Giudecca with Palladio's church of the Redentore, this is a delightful peaceful place to walk. Bridges lead across some of the most picturesque canals in this *sestiere*.

The most important church on this waterfront, near the busy vaporetto stops, is the **Gesuati** (*map Venice Left 8; open Mon–Sat 10–5; Chorus Pass*), with a good Rococo interior. It has two very fine works dating from 1739 by Giambattista Tiepolo: the fresco of the *Institution of the Rosary*, and the *Virgin in Glory with three Saints*. The *Crucifixion*, with a beautifully composed group of mourning women at the foot of the Cross, is by Jacopo Tintoretto (c. 1570).

SAN TROVASO

The **Squero di San Trovaso**, outside the church of the same name (*map Venice Left 7*), is a picturesque little boatyard, which was already here in the 17th century but has been restored over time. It was in yards such as this that the great Venetian fleet of warships and merchant ships was built before the end of the 15th century; after that date boat-building was concentrated in the Arsenale. This *squero* now specialises in the construction and repair of gondolas.

The church of **San Trovaso** (*open 8.30–11 & 2.30–5.30; closed Sun*) is an old foundation, though the present Palladian-style exterior dates from 1584. In the interior the altarpieces in the chapels on the north side are all by Palma Giovane, including (third altar) *Birth of the Virgin*, a very well composed painting. In the chapel to the left of the sanctuary is the *Temptation of St Anthony* by Tintoretto (c. 1577), and (dating from the previous century) a charming decorative painting of St Chrysogonus on horseback, by Michele Giambono painted in a flowery archaic Gothic style. In the adjacent chapel is a *Last Supper* by Jacopo Tintoretto. In another chapel the altar bears a lovely, very low bas-relief in Greek marble of angels holding signs of the Passion or playing musical instruments, thought to date from around 1470.

SAN SEBASTIANO

San Sebastiano (*map Venice Left 5; open Mon–Sat 10–5; Chorus Pass*) was the parish church of the great Venetian painter **Veronese** and he decorated it in 1555–70 with a wonderful series of paintings. Paolo Caliari, the son of a stonemason, was known as Veronese since he was born in Verona, where he learnt his skills. When he moved to Venice in 1555 he first began work for this church and soon became celebrated and was commissioned to paint many other works for Venice's churches, as well as large canvases for the Doge's Palace. He is buried here.

The eye is drawn at once to the three central panels of the beautiful ceiling, with its elaborate wooden framework, with scenes from the Old Testament Book of Esther, the 'fair and beautiful' Jewish orphan who 'obtained favour in the sight of all them that looked upon her', so much so that the Persian King Ahasuerus, after banishing his wife Vashti, decided to make her his queen. Subsequently her cousin Mordechai saved the king from danger. The scene nearest the door depicts the grim expulsion of Vashti; the central scene the joyful crowning of the beautiful Esther (with a conspicuous white dog seated beneath the throne); and the far scene, the triumph of Mordechai, whom the grateful king ordered to be honoured with a procession through the streets of the city, dressed in royal apparel wearing the king's own crown, and mounted on a splendid grey charger next to a dark horse in attendance—both of them with their hooves raised as they seem to prance down to us out of the ceiling, while the crowds wave him on from the top of a huge marble palace. Most of the other paintings in the church and sacristy are also by Veronese.

THE CARMINI AND CAMPO SANTA MARGHERITA

The church of the **Carmini** (*map Venice Left 5; open 7.30–12 & 2.30–7*) has a spacious basilican interior with gilded wooden sculptural decoration in the nave. By the side door, *St Nicholas in Glory with St John the Baptist and St Lucy* is one of the best works of Lorenzo Lotto (1529), with a remarkable landscape beneath. The charming small painting of the *Holy Family* is by Paolo Veronese. A small bronze plaque (c. 1474) with an exquisite relief of the *Deposition* is the only work in Venice by the great Sienese artist Francesco di Giorgio Martini. There is also a beautiful painting of the *Nativity* by Cima da Conegliano (c. 1509) and a vault frescoed by Sebastiano Ricci. The side door of the church has a Romanesque porch decorated on one side with Byzantine Greek marble *paterae* dating from the 11th and 12th centuries.

The **Scuola Grande dei Carmini** (*open every day 10–5 or 6*) is in a building of 1668 with an elaborate double staircase and *salone* on the upper floor both attributed to Baldassare Longhena. Here the nine superb paintings in the ceiling are among the masterpieces of Giambattista Tiepolo (1739–49), with allegories of the Virtues around the central *Virgin in Glory* (the *Apparition of the Madonna del Carmelo to the Blessed Simon Stock*). They illustrate the legend of the English hermit Simon who became the sixth general of the Carmelite order in 1247. **Giambattista Tiepolo** (1696–1770) was the most important fresco painter in Venice in the 18th century. He received many commissions from the Venetian aristocracy and the Church, and carried out famous works also in Germany and Spain. His decorative Rococo style, with numerous charming details, was particularly well suited to ceilings and he had a great influence on European painting. Tiepolo's son, Gian Domenico worked with him, and later developed his own style to depict delightful scenes of Venetian social life, many of which can also be seen in Venice.

Campo Santa Margherita is one of the liveliest squares in the city, always full of local families and their children, who come here to pass the time of day or visit the little daily market. It has a miscellany of shops and simple cafés with tables outside.

CA' REZZONICO

This great palace (*map Venice Left 5; open 10–5 except Tues*) on the Grand Canal was begun by Baldassare Longhena around 1667, and then modified (and the upper storey added) by Giorgio Massari for the Rezzonico family, who bought it in 1751 (a few years before Carlo Rezzonico became Pope Clement XII). It fittingly contains the city's collection of 18th-century art, displayed in sumptuously decorated rooms.

On the first floor are the ballroom, the throne room and the library linked by other reception rooms, some with ceiling frescoes and paintings by **Giambattista Tiepolo**, as well as portraits by Bernardino Castelli and pastels by Rosalba Carriera. Ebony and boxwood vase-stands, statues of Moors, and armchairs are part of a famous set of furniture elaborately carved by Andrea Brustolon, the most important wood sculptor at work in the Veneto in the Baroque period.

The most important paintings in the collection are on the second floor, including works by Giovanni Battista Piazzetta and two early Venetian views by **Canaletto**. A group of rooms are filled with charming frescoes by Gian Domenico Tiepolo. The scenes depict amusing satyrs and fauns; carnival antics with Pulcinella and acrobats; everyday life with masqueraders and satyrs on court life, country idylls, a crowd at a fairground, and birds.

Genre scenes of typically Venetian life are represented with small paintings by Francesco Guardi and Pietro Longhi.

The attic on the third floor has a huge collection of paintings left to the city in the 20th century by Egidio Martini, displayed more or less chronologically in 13 rooms.

The mezzanine floor houses the choice little **Mestrovich Collection**. The corner room here retains its decorations from Browning's time, when he stayed here in 1889 as an old man and widower with his son Pen. Pen had purchased the entire palace a few years earlier thanks to the wealth of his wife, Fanny Coddington. The great poet died here in the same year.

SESTIERE OF SAN POLO

The *sestiere* of San Polo takes its name from the church of San Polo, which sits in one of the largest *campi* in Venice, far away from the crowds. Goldoni lived close by, and his charming little house can be visited. The *sestiere* also includes the lively area at the western foot of the Rialto Bridge, with its busy markets. There are numerous grocer's shops and bakeries in the *calli* close by. This area must have been just as crowded in the days of the Republic, when it was the commercial centre of the city, attracting merchants, bankers, brokers and traders of all kinds.

Close together at the western limit of the *sestiere* are the famous church of the Frari, filled with Venetian masterpieces of sculpture and painting, and the Scuola Grande di San Rocco, where the walls and ceilings are covered with superb works by Tintoretto.

THE RIALTO

The area known as the Rialto (*rivo alto*, high bank) is thought to have been one of the first places to be settled by the earliest inhabitants of the lagoon because it was one of the highest points and the best protected. Since the beginning of the Republic it has been the commercial and economic centre of Venice. The famous Rialto Bridge is described on p. 16. Venetians still come to shop at the excellent produce stalls open on weekday mornings at the foot of the bridge. It is known that there were markets here as early as 1097, but the medieval buildings were burnt down in 1514, so had to be reconstructed by Scarpagnino. These are the porticoed **Fabbriche Vecchie di Rialto** and they are adjoined by the long arcaded **Fabbriche Nuove di Rialto**, begun by Jacopo Sansovino in 1554, now used by the Assize court. Fish is sold in the neo-Gothic **Pescheria** (*map Venice Left 4*), built in 1907.

Scarpagnino's porticoes also extend around Campo San Giacomo where the church of **San Giacomo di Rialto** (*open 9.30–7*), preceded by a Gothic portico, dates from 1152 or earlier. The domed Greek-cross plan on a tiny scale, derived from Byzantine models, with its six ancient Greek marble columns and capitals, was faithfully preserved in the rebuilding of 1601.

San Giovanni Elemosinario (*open Mon–Sat 10–5; Chorus Pass; inconspicuous entrance on Ruga Vecchia San Giovanni*) was the first church to be built in the Rialto area (mentioned in documents as early as 1051) and it still has its campanile of 1398–1410. It was rebuilt after the Rialto fire of 1514 by Scarpagnino. In the interior, on a Greek-cross plan, the high altarpiece of *St John the Almsgiver* was painted for the church by Titian (c. 1545). In the chapel to the right of the sanctuary there is a lovely altarpiece of *Sts Catherine, Sebastian and Roch*, by Pordenone, who also carried out the frescoes on the dome of the church.

San Cassiano (*open 9–12 & 5.30–6.45*) is another ancient church a short distance away from the market area, perhaps dating from the 10th century. In the sanctuary are three remarkable paintings by Jacopo Tintoretto: *Crucifixion, Resurrection,* and *Descent into Limbo.*

CAMPO SAN POLO

This peaceful *campo* (*map Venice Left 4*) is one of the largest and most attractive squares in the city, used as a playground by local children. The church of **San Polo** (*open Mon–Sat 10–5; Chorus Pass*) has one of the best of the Tintoretto's many paintings of the *Last Supper*. The Oratory of the Crucifix has a wonderful series of small paintings by Gian Domenico Tiepolo (1749), illustrating the Stations of the Cross: Christ's Passion is portrayed in a sumptuous Venetian setting.

The **Casa Goldoni** (*open 10–3.30 or 4.30 except Wed; entrance in Calle dei Nomboli beyond the courtyard*), in the 15th-century Palazzo Centani, is where the playwright Carlo Goldoni (1707–93) was born. His brilliant comedies give a vivid idea of social life in 18th-century Venice, since they satirise the old Venetian aristocracy as well as describing the ordinary people of the city. The house has a picturesque Gothic courtyard with a charming staircase and a pretty well-head dating from the 15th century. In the interior you can visit just three rooms, at present evocatively furnished with stage sets and costumes for some of his plays. There is also an 18th-century puppet theatre and display of puppets.

SANTA MARIA GLORIOSA DEI FRARI

This church, commonly known as 'the Frari' (*map Venice Left 3; open Mon–Sat 9–5.30; Chorus Pass*), is dedicated to the Assumption of the Virgin. It is the church of the mendicant order of Friars Minor, or Franciscans, founded in the mid-13th century, and in size rivals that of the other mendicant order, the Dominican church of Santi Giovanni e Paolo. It contains numerous masterpieces of painting and sculpture. Its majestic campanile is the tallest in the city after St Mark's.

The huge brick Gothic interior was begun c. 1330 but not finished until after 1443. The 15th-century monks' choir, with its lovely carved screen by Bartolomeo Bon and Pietro Lombardo, has three tiers of stalls with fine intarsia. The apse is lit by stained glass windows and is filled with Titian's *Assumption* (1518), the largest altarpiece in Venice, celebrated among his early masterpieces. **Titian** (Tiziano Vecellio; 1488–1576) succeeded Giovanni Bellini as the most important painter in Venice, and was one of the greatest Italian painters of all time. He was painting at a time when Venice flourished and was at the height of her power. Although there are numerous paintings by Titian in Venice, he also worked for the most important Italian courts, as well as for the papacy, the Habsburg emperors, and Philip II of Spain.

There are two 15th-century Doge's tombs in the sanctuary: that of Doge Niccolò Tron by Antonio Rizzo is considered one of the finest Renaissance monuments in the city. The choir chapels have more tombs and paintings including two by Bartolomeo Vivarini, and a gilded polychrome statue of St John the Baptist signed and dated 1438 by Donatello, his first documented work in the Veneto, and the first that he made in wood.

The monuments in the south transept commemorate two admirals who served the Venetian state. The peaceful **sacristy** here preserves an exquisite triptych of the *Madonna and Child and four Saints*, painted for the chapel in 1488 by Giovanni Bellini, and some fine carvings. In the adjoining Chapter House, above the sarcophagus of Doge Francesco Dandolo, is a lunette signed and dated by the first great Venetian painter Paolo Veneziano, which includes a portrait of the doge and his wife Elizabeth.

In the south aisle is a 19th-century monument to Titian above the place he is traditionally believed to have been buried, and in the opposite aisle is his wonderful painting of the Madonna, commissioned by Bishop Jacopo Pesaro. The extraordinary tomb of Doge Giovanni Pesaro, who died in 1659, is a bizarre Baroque work, and one of the most elaborate funerary monuments in Venice, and is in striking contrast to the pyramidal mausoleum of Canova the great Neoclassical sculptor, which was erected by his pupils in 1827 to a design similar to others that Canova had himself executed for the tombs of his patrons.

THE SCUOLA GRANDE DI SAN ROCCO

The building (*map Venice Left 3-5; open 9.30–5.30*), made for this important confraternity of St Roch, founded in 1478, was begun in 1515 by Bartolomeo Bon and finished by Scarpagnino (1549), who added the elegant main façade, usually considered his masterpiece. San Rocco (St Roch) was born in Montpellier in 1295. He caught the plague when he came to Italy to help cure victims of this contagious disease, but he retired alone to a wood where he was miraculously saved by an angel. He was particularly venerated in Venice and in 1576 he was declared a patron saint of the city. Members of the confraternity offered their services especially during the frequent plagues which broke out in the city, the worst of which (after the Black Death of 1348) occurred in 1575–77 and 1630.

The interior of the Scuola is exceptionally well preserved in all its decorative details, and is famous above all for the 50 or so **paintings by Jacopo Tintoretto**, a brother of the confraternity, who here produced one of the most remarkable pictorial cycles in existence. He began work in 1564 and spent the next 23 years working on the paintings (largely without the help of collaborators). On the walls of the columned hall on the ground floor his paintings illustrate the life of the Virgin Mary. Scarpagnino's grand staircase leads up to the huge Chapter House, still dimly lit by the processional lanterns above the carved wooden benches which line the walls. Tintoretto's paintings here depict Old Testament subjects on the ceiling, and New Testament subjects on the walls. They were chosen in a careful iconographical scheme related to the teaching of St Roch and his efforts to relieve thirst, hunger and sickness. In the adjoining Sala dell' Albergo the vast *Crucifixion* is generally considered to be the painter's masterpiece (on the opposite wall are three Passion scenes, and on the ceiling is *St Roch in Glory*). Here also is displayed a fragment of a frieze from the ceiling of three apples, showing Tintoretto's remarkable painting technique.

TINTORETTO

Jacopo Robusti, born in Venice around 1519, was called **Tintoretto** because his family were *tintori* (dyers). Throughout his long life (he died at the age of about 75) he worked exclusively in Venice, producing a remarkable number of superb paintings in the *scuole* and churches, commissioned from him by the Venetian middle classes, as well as official works for the Doge's Palace. He was one of the most daring painters who ever lived, and his creative fervour was without parallel. His output was enormous, and evidently he had an extraordinary capacity for work. Tintoretto was deeply religious, and his highly dramatic scenes, often in humble settings and always infused with a spiritual content, were given added intensity by his wonderful use of light, producing intense contrasts between the illuminated areas and those in shadow. His style of painting was transmitted to his large *bottega* as well as to his son Domenico, who also produced a great many paintings for Venetian buildings.

The church of **San Rocco** (*map Venice Left 3; open 9.30–5.30*), rebuilt in the 18th century, has a number of paintings by Jacopo Tintoretto including (in the sanctuary) *St Roch Curing Victims of the Plague*. It is set in an isolation hospital, many of which operated on the islands of the lagoon during the dreaded outbreaks of pestilence.

The **Scuola Grande di San Giovanni Evangelista** (*map Venice Left 3*), also one of the most important confraternities in Venice, founded in 1261, is particularly interesting for the beautiful marble screen and portal by Pietro Lombardo (1481) in its courtyard. The interior, with a splendid double staircase by Mauro Codussi built in the following decade, is not usually open.

SESTIERE OF SANTA CROCE

The *sestiere* of Santa Croce takes its name from a huge monastery demolished in 1810. Both the elaborate Baroque church of San Stae and the magnificent Ca' Pesaro (open as Venice's Modern Art Gallery) present their grand façades to the Grand Canal. There are some interesting little-visited churches tucked away in particularly quiet areas.

The church of **San Stae** (*map Venice Left 4; open Mon–Sat 2–5; Chorus Pass*) has a very fine façade on the Grand Canal built in the 18th century. The numerous paintings inside date from the same century and are by some of the most important artists of the day including Giambattista Tiepolo, Sebastiano Ricci and Giovanni Battista Piazzetta. The **Museo di Palazzo Mocenigo** (*open April–Oct 10–5 except Mon; Nov–March 10–4 except Mon. Entrance at no. 1992 Salizzada di San Stae*) was the residence of the distinguished Mocenigo family (who provided the Republic with no fewer than seven doges), and it retains its late 17th-century furnishings. There are usually displays of 18th-century costumes (the palace houses a study centre devoted to costumes and fabrics from the 16th century up to the 1950s).

Ca' Pesaro (*map Venice Left 4*) houses the Galleria Internazionale d'Arte Moderna and the Museo Orientale (*open 10–5, 10–4 in winter*). This great Baroque palace, built in the 17th century for the Pesaro family by Baldassare Longhena, has a splendid façade on the Grand Canal. The collection of modern art, founded in 1897, is arranged mostly on the first floor, and includes 19th-century Venetian masters such as Ippolito Caffi, the Tuscan Macchiaioli, and some works exhibited at the Biennale art exhibitions, notably paintings by Gustav Klimt and Marc Chagall, and some of the most important protagonists of the Italian *novecento* movement.

The Oriental Museum is on the top floor (although for years there have been plans to move it to a more suitable space in another palace). It has a huge collection of paintings, sculpture, arms and armour, lacquer-work, bronzes, ivory, jade, musical instruments, decorative arts, fabrics and costumes (and is especially noted for its Japanese paintings of the Edo period, 1600–1868).

San Giacomo dell'Orio (*map Venice Left 4; open Mon–Sat 10–5; Chorus Pass*) has massive low Byzantine columns below a beautiful 14th-century wooden ship's keel roof. In the sanctuary hangs a Crucifix attributed to Paolo Veneziano (c. 1350), and on the east wall is a *Madonna and Four Saints* by Lorenzo Lotto (1546). On the left pier of the sanctury is a quaint little statuette of the *Virgin Annunciate* dating from the mid-13th century.

San Simeone Grande (or San Simeone Profeta; *map Venice Left 3; open 8–12 & 5–7*) sits in a pretty little *campo* which opens directly onto the Grand Canal. The low interior has a wide nave with antique columns and statues above the arcade. A remarkable effigy of St Simeon is the only signed and dated work by Marco Romano, a Sienese sculptor who also worked in Tuscany in the first two decades of the 14th century. Near the main door is a large painting of the *Last Supper* by Jacopo Tintoretto.

SESTIERE OF CANNAREGIO

This, the most northerly of the *sestieri*, takes its name from the *Canal Regio*, or Royal Canal (now the Canale di Cannaregio), once the main route into Venice from the mainland. Today this peaceful canal has a little row of shops and cafés, the lovely church of San Giobbe, and is also at the entrance to the old Ghetto. The bustling Rio Terrà San Leonardo, with its daily food market, and the broad Strada Nuova both have quite a different character, with lots of local shops. A few steps from the Strada Nuova is the Ca' d'Oro, perhaps the most beautiful of all the palaces on the Grand Canal. In the lovely remote area of northern Cannaregio is the church of the Madonna dell'Orto, Other unexpected delights in this *sestiere* include the little church of the Madonna dei Miracoli.

CA' D'ORO

This palace (*map Venice Left 4; open 8.15–7.15, Mon 8.15–2*) is famous for its extraordinarily elaborate 15th-century Gothic façade on the Grand Canal. The palace was carefully restored by Baron Giorgio Franchetti in 1894, and he presented it to the state in 1916, together with his very fine collection of sculpture and paintings.

On the first floor is Mantegna's *St Sebastian*, one of the artist's last works. Although he was Giovanni Bellini's brother-in-law he spent most of his life working for the court of Mantua and this is the only large painting by him in Venice. The other rooms have a splendid display of small Venetian sculptures dating from the end of the 15th and beginning of the 16th century including masterpieces by Tullio Lombardo and his father Pietro, Antonio Rizzo and Il Riccio. On the second floor are detached frescoes by Pordenone and (fragments) by Titian and Giorgione.

San Giovanni Crisostomo (*map Venice Right 3; open 7.30–7.30 pm*) is the last work of Mauro Codussi (1504), who built many palaces and churches in the city in a new Renaissance style. The lovely interior, on a Greek-cross plan, contains a superb high altarpice by Sebastiano del Piombo and a beautiful late painting by Giovanni Bellini of three saints.

Behind the church the Corte Seconda del Milion is surrounded by ancient houses which incorporate 12th–15th-century elements, and a beautiful Byzantine arch, richly carved with animals and birds. Marco Polo probably lived in this area, and the name of the courtyard recalls his nickname, earned because his contemporaries thought he always talked in 'millions' and exaggerated his description of his travels in the East: in fact probably the first account of Asia ever to reach the West, and which remained the most accurate for centuries. The great traveller set out in 1271 on a four-year overland journey, from Trebizond on the Black Sea through Persia, Tibet, and the Gobi Desert to Peking. He was then employed for 17 years at the court of the Mongol ruler, Kublai Khan, grandson of Genghis Khan, and was sent as envoy throughout the Empire from Siberia to southern India and Japan. He returned to Venice by sea along the coast of China and India.

Santa Maria dei Miracoli (*map Venice Right 3; open Mon–Sat 10–5; Chorus Pass*), one of the few churches in Venice where you can see all four external walls, is an exquisite Renaissance work by Pietro Lombardo (1481–9). It is sumptuously decorated with elegant polychrome marble inlay in geometric designs and delicately carved friezes both inside and out. The nave walls are entirely lined with patterned marble panels and the raised choir and domed apse are beautifully decorated by Pietro and his son Tullio Lombardo.

THE CANNAREGIO CANAL AND THE GHETTO

The Cannaregio Canal is the widest waterway in Venice after the Grand Canal, and has peaceful *fondamente* on both sides. In a secluded *campo* at the far end is the church of **San Giobbe** (*map Venice Left 1; open Mon–Sat 10–1*), built in the mid-15th century, with a very beautiful domed sanctuary. The Cappella Martini has a vault lined with majolica tiles and roundels in glazed terracotta attributed to the Florentine master Andrea della Robbia.

The **Ghetto** (*map Venice Left 1–2*), approached through a passageway off the Cannaregio Canal, gave its name to all the other areas in Europe where the Jews were segregated. It was called thus from an iron foundry which used to exist here (the Venetian word *geto*, indicates a place where metal was cast). Although Jews from the East, northern Europe, Spain and Portugal had been coming to Venice for short periods (in which they were sometimes tolerated and sometimes expelled), it was not until 1516 that the Great Council permitted Jews to live permanently in Venice, though they compelled them to inhabit only this area. It is estimated that as many as 5,000 Jews lived here during the 16th–17th centuries, and just four wells supplied them with water (the wells in the rest of the city were barred to them). They were permitted to operate as money-lenders so their offices here were busy during the day with Venetian clients. Not until 1797 were Jews allowed (by Napoleon) to leave the Ghetto and live in other parts of the city. During the Austrian occupation, the Jews were asked to return to the Ghetto, and it was only definitively opened in 1866. There are still a number of shops here which sell Jewish objects as well as good bakeries and grocery stores frequented especially by the Jewish community. The five main synagogues (or *scuole*), on the upper floors of houses, remain here, two of them still in use. Built for the first time in the 15th century, they are named after the various different communities who erected them, in their own distinctive styles of architecture, as meeting places and places of worship. The Jewish cemetery is on the Lido. The *campo* on the **island of Ghetto Nuovo** has bronze reliefs set up in 1985 in memory of the Venetian Jewish war victims, many of whom were deported to concentration camps in Germany. The **Jewish Museum** is here (*open 10–4.30 or 5.30, Fri 10–sunset; closed Sat and Jewish holidays; the ticket includes a guided tour of some of the synagogues*).

NORTHERN CANNAREGIO

The church of the **Madonna dell'Orto** (*map Venice Left 2; open Mon–Sat 10–5; Chorus Pass*) has a Gothic façade with good 15th-century sculptures. In the choir are two magnificent huge paintings by Jacopo Tintoretto, the *Last Judgement* and *Making of the Golden Calf*. Because of their size they were probably painted *in situ* around 1562–4 and the artist donated them as a gift to this, his parish church. On the wall of the south aisle is another famous work by him: the lovely *Presentation of the Virgin in the Temple*. In the chapel on the right of the choir a modest slab marks the great painter's resting-place. On the first south altar, still in its original frame, is *St John the Baptist and Four Saints*, a masterpiece by Cima da Conegliano painted around 1493.

Campo dei Mori has three quaint statues of Moors, popularly supposed to be the Levantine merchants of the Mastelli family, whose palace is close by. Further along the *fondamenta*, a plaque at no. 3399 marks the charming house where Jacopo Tintoretto lived from 1574 until his death in 1594. Incorporated into the façade, along with several other ancient sculptural fragments, is a quaint turbanned figure, similar to those in Campo dei Mori.

At the eastern limit of the *sestiere* is the highly elaborate Baroque church of the **Gesuiti** (*map Venice Right 1; open 10–12 & 3.30–5.30*), rebuilt for the Jesuits in 1714–29 by Domenico Rossi. It contains a splendid painting of the *Martyrdom of St Lawrence* by Titian (1548).

SESTIERE OF CASTELLO

Castello is the largest *sestiere* of the city and its name is thought to come from the 8th-century fortress on the island of San Pietro, which is also where—as legend tells us—St Mark found shelter during a storm and his association with Venice began. San Pietro di Castello was the cathedral of Venice until 1807. Castello was also the maritime heart of the Republic, with the shipyards of the Arsenale, from which her trading and naval fleets set sail. The area boasts some superb treasures: the magnificent church of Santi Giovanni e Paolo, that of San Zaccaria, and Carpaccio's delightful cycle of paintings in the little Scuola di San Giorgio degli Schiavoni. Beyond the Arsenale, away from the crush of tourists and souvenir stalls, Castello becomes an area where life goes on untrammelled by visitors, with washing strung out across the canals, and the delightful Via Garibaldi has local shops and market stalls.

RIVA DEGLI SCHIAVONI

This wide, busy quay, often overcrowded around its first few bridges, was called 'Schiavoni' from the inhabitants of *Schiavonia* (now Dalmatia), because the waterfront here was often used as a mooring for the trading vessels from Slavonic ports.

San Zaccaria (*map Venice Right 5; open 10–12 & 4–6, Sun and holidays only 4–6; approached off the Riva by Sottoportico San Zaccaria*) was founded in the 9th century, at the same period as the Basilica of St Mark, and by the same doge, Giustiniano Particiaco. The very beautiful façade was finished by Mauro Codussi. Inside is Giovanni Bellini's *Madonna Enthroned and Four Saints*, one of the artist's greatest works, signed and dated 1505, when he was perhaps 75 years old. It is the last of a series of altarpieces with similar subjects he painted for the churches of

Venice. Off the south aisle is the entrance (*very small fee*) to the peaceful Chapels of St Anthanasius and St Tarasius, both well worth visiting for their interesting contents, and to see the water-logged crypt.

With its façade on the Riva, **La Pietà** (*map Venice Right 6; open 10–12 & 3–5, Sat & Sun 10–5*) was the church of an orphanage and hospital (*ospedale*) founded in 1346, and famous for its musical orphans. Vivaldi, son of a barber and violinist, taught at the Pietà on and off for most of his life. The bright interior was sumptuously rebuilt in the present oval plan (particularly suitable for musical performances) by Giorgio Massari (1745–60), with galleries for choir and musicians and an oblong vestibule. The contemporary decorations remain intact, with a fine ceiling fresco of the *Triumph of Faith* by Giambattista Tiepolo (1755) and a high altarpiece by Giovanni Battista Piazzetta.

The church of **San Giovanni in Bragora** (*map Venice Right 6; open 9–11 & 3.30–5, Sun 9.30–12 approached off the Riva by Calle delle Dose*) has a *Baptism of Christ*, one of the most beautiful works in Venice by Cima da Conegliano, painted in 1494, and a number of works by his master Alvise Vivarini.

THE GREEK DISTRICT

Ponte dei Greci is named after the Greeks who settled in this area in the 15th century after the fall of Constantinople and the subsequent invasion of Greece by the Turks. Together with the Jewish community, this became the largest foreign settlement in the Renaissance city. The Greek College and the *scuola* were built in the 17th century by the great Venetian architect Baldassare Longhena. The **Museum of Icons** (*open 9–12.30 & 1.30–4.30, Sun and holidays 10–5*) has a well-labelled collection arranged chronologically from the 14th to the 17th century.

The **Scuola di San Giorgio degli Schiavoni** (*map Venice Right 4–6; open Tues– Sat 9.15–1 & 2.45–6, Sun and holidays 9.15–1 Mon 2.45–6*) was founded in 1451 by the Dalmatians who came to live in the city (many of whom were sailors). The walls of the evocative little room are entirely decorated with a delightful series of paintings by Vittore Carpaccio (carried out between 1502 and 1508), relating to the lives of the three Dalmatian patron saints, Jerome, Tryphon and George, and bursting with detail, incident and symbolism.

ON AND AROUND CAMPO SANTA MARIA FORMOSA

This is one of the liveliest *campi* near St Mark's. The church of **Santa Maria Formosa** (*map Venice Right 3; open Mon–Sat 10–5; Chorus Pass*) has a beautiful light interior designed by Mauro Codussi (1492). It contains a delightful triptych by Bartolomeo Vivarini and a celebrated altarpiece by Palma Vecchio.

The **Museo Querini-Stampalia** (*map Venice Right 3–5; open 10–6, closed Mon*) is on the *piano nobile* of the 16th-century Querini-Stampalia family palace, and contains their fine collection of paintings, including the *Presentation of Christ in the Temple*, attributed to Giovanni Bellini, genre scenes by Pietro Longhi, views of Venetian life by Gabriel Bella, and two intriguing portraits of the Querini by Palma Vecchio.

Palazzo Grimani (*map Venice Right 3; entrance in Ramo Grimani off Ruga Giuffa. Open 8.15–19.15, Mon 8.15–2*) was begun around 1530 and work continued up until the 1570s (the architect Jacopo Sansovino may have been involved). The courtyard and staircase are particularly fine, and many of the handsome rooms on the *piano nobile* have good frescoes and stuccoes. The famous Grimani collection of Classical sculpture is now in the Museo Archeologico, but here in the Tribuna, designed to display some of the masterpeices, is the Ganymede and eagle (a 2nd-century Roman copy of a Hellenistic original) hanging from the centre of the ceiling, just as it did in the Grimani's day. Four extraordinary panels painted by Hieronymus Bosch around 1503, and probably acquired in Antwerp in Bosch's lifetime by Cardinal Domenico Grimani, are also displayed in the palace.

SANTI GIOVANNI E PAOLO

In Campo Santi Giovanni e Paolo, on a high pedestal, silhouetted against the sky, rises the superb bronze equestrian statue of the *condottiere* Colleoni by Andrea Verrocchio: a Renaissance masterpiece. The church of **Santi Giovanni e Paolo** (*map Venice Right 3; open 9–6.30, Sun and holidays 12–6.30*) is the largest in Venice. Founded by the Dominicans in 1234, the present building was begun around 1333, and was not finished until 1385. It is the burial place of 25 doges, and from the 15th century onwards the funerals of all doges were held here.

The vast light interior has a beautiful luminous choir with a polygonal apse, lit by Gothic windows. Among the array of funerary monuments to doges and heroes of the Republic are some masterpieces of Renaissance sculpture by the Lombardo family, as well as earlier Gothic works. The monument on the west wall to Doge Pietro Mocenigo is undoubtedly the masterpiece of Pietro Lombardo who, together with his sons Tullio and Antonio carried out numerous sculptural commissions in Venice in the late 15th and early 16th centuries, when they were considered the most important sculptors at work in the city. The tomb of Andrea Vendramin in the sanctuary is another superb Renaissance work designed by Tullio Lombardo, with the help of his brother Antonio, and it is probably the most elaborate funerary monument in the city, complete with gilding. Similarly to the monument to Pietro Mocenigo, it takes the form of a Roman triumphal arch above the effigy of the doge, who died in 1478, surrounded by allegorical figures and warriors. On the opposite wall of the sanctuary is the Gothic tomb of Doge Michele Morosini, who died in 1382, with carving attributed to the dalle Masegne workshop.

In the south transept is a beautiful stained glass window made in Murano in 1473 and an interesting painting of St Antoninus dispensing charity to the poor by Lorenzo Lotto (1542). In the south aisle there is a theatrical Baroque tomb of two doges of the Valier family by Andrea Tirali (1708). At the west end of the aisle is the most beautiful painting in the church: the *Polyptych of St Vincent Ferrer*, a very early work by Giovanni Bellini.

The **Scuola Grande di San Marco** (*map Venice Right 3*), founded in 1261, was one of the six great philanthropic confraternities of the Republic. Members of these *scuole*, elected mostly from the middle classes, attended to each other's needs and administered public charity throughout the city, as well as offering medical assistance and visiting prisoners. They were often associations of people in a particular trade or of a certain nationality, and no priest or patrician could hold a position of responsibility in them. Many of them became rich through legacies and donations, and they were an important source of patronage as they commissioned numerous works of art for their headquarters. The *scuole* held a particularly prestigious place in Venetian life from the 14th–16th centuries (when it has been estimated that there were around 100 in the city), and they would take part in full regalia in all state ceremonies and celebrations.

When it had to be rebuilt after a fire in 1485, the sumptuous façade of this *scuola* was designed by Pietro Lombardo, assisted by Giovanni Buora (1489), but when half finished Lombardo's chief rival, Mauro Codussi, was called in to complete it (1495). The whole façade is an original work of great charm, where coloured marbles are used in a combination of styles, and on the lower part the four panels have unusual false perspectives (as if they were windows). The main portal leads straight into the columned ground-floor hall of the *scuola*, which has been remarkably well preserved (and is similar to those in the other main Venetian *scuole*), but now serves as the entrance to Venice's main hospital.

One of the most isolated churches in the city, some way east of Santi Giovanni e Paolo, is **San Francesco della Vigna** (*map Venice Right 4; open 8–12 & 3–7*), with a façade by Palladio. It contains a charming large painting of the *Madonna and Child* in the florid Gothic style by Antonio da Negroponte (1465), his only known work.

THE ARSENALE

The arsenale (*map Venice Right 6*, labelled Darsena Grande) occupies a vast area of the city, still protected by crenellated walls with towers. From 1104 onwards it served as the great shipyard for the Venetian Republic's fleet. Here the ships were overhauled and repaired, and from the end of the 15th century onwards shipbuilding was also concentrated here (it had formerly taken place in the numerous *squeri* which existed all over the city). Specialised workers made ropes and armaments and everything necessary to equip the warships and merchant galleys before they set sail. Known as *arsenalotti*, they held a privileged position in Venetian society, as well as enjoying advantageous working conditions. At the height of Venetian prosperity they numbered some 16,000 (out of a population of about 130,000). They had the honour of carrying the doge in triumph in the procession immediately following his election. Dante visited the Arsenale in 1306, and again in 1321 when he was sent as emissary to Venice from Ravenna, and described it in the *Inferno* (*Canto XXI*).

There are long-term plans to make the area accessible, but at present it is still partly occupied by the Italian navy, or used as maintenance docks. However during the Biennale shows the huge long *Corderie*, where the ropes were made, and the *Artiglierie*, where munitions were stored, provide magnificent exhibition spaces.

From the Riva on the basin of San Marco a *fondamenta* leads along the Arsenale canal to the wooden bridge beside the triumphal arch built in 1460 as the land entrance. The **four ancient Greek lions** guarding it are one of the most memorable sights of Venice, and their presence here are indicative of the extraordinary prestige of the Venetian Republic. The two largest, of colossal dimensions, were shipped from Piraeus by Admiral Francesco Morosini as spoils of war after his conquest of the Peloponnese (1687), and placed here a few yeas later after he had been elected doge. The one sitting upright on the left (which gave the name of *Porta Leone—Aslan Liman*—to Piraeus) is thought to be the fellow of one which stood on the road from Athens to Eleusis. The two smaller lions, one of them also brought to Venice by Morosini and the other added in 1716 in celebration of the reconquest of Corfu, may have come originally from the Lion Terrace at Delos.

The **Museo Storico Navale** or Maritime Museum (*map Venice Right 6; open 8.45–1 or 1.30 except Sun; the admission fee goes to an orphanage for sailors' children*) is housed in the former Granary of the Republic, at the beginning of the Arsenale canal. The exhibits are beautifully arranged on four floors, and very well labelled.

The **Biennale** is Venice's famous biennial international contemporary art show, and has been held almost continuously since 1895 from the summer to the autumn in odd years. Since 1980 the Biennale exhibition devoted to architecture has been held in even years. Besides the permanent venue in the Giardini on the waterfront, it is also now held in part of the Arsenale. There are always numerous free collateral events throughout the city in conjunction with both exhibitions.

The long, broad **Via Garibaldi** (*map Venice Right 6*), which leads away from the waterfront, is one of the most characteristic streets in this *sestiere*, with a miscellany of local shops and stalls, selling everything from clothes to food. It leads towards a solitary island where in a grass-grown campo stands the church of **San Pietro di Castello** (*open Mon–Sat 10–5; Chorus Pass*), the cathedral of Venice from the 11th century until 1807, when St Mark's assumed the role. The present church, with a bright interior, was built to a Palladian design of 1557. In the south aisle a venerable marble throne from Antioch is, incredibly enough, an Islamic work of the 13th century: the Arabic funerary stele is decorated with verses from the Koran. In the Cappella Lando the altar-front is made from a pluteus which may date from as early as the 9th century, and, in the pavement in front, there is a Roman mosaic with a vase of pomegranates probably made in the late 5th century. The striking half-figure of St Lorenzo Giustinian, made during his lifetime, is attributed to Antonio Rizzo.

The isolated campanile, in Istrian stone, by Mauro Codussi, dates from 1482–8, crowned with an octagon. This was the first bell-tower in the city to be faced with Istrian stone, and, at the eastern extremity of the city, it also served as a lighthouse.

THE ISLAND OF SAN GIORGIO MAGGIORE

There are frequent vaporetto services to the island (no. 2) from San Zaccaria or the Giudecca.

This small island (*map Venetian Lagoon*), standing at the entrance to the city, across the water from St Mark's and separated from the island of the Giudecca by a narrow channel, was given to the Benedictines in the 10th century and the convent became the most important in the lagoon. In 1951 the Giorgio Cini Foundation was established here.

The church of **San Giorgio Maggiore** (*open 9.30–dusk; Sun 9.30–10.40 & 12–dusk*) is one of Palladio's most famous churches, in a wonderful site and designed (in 1565) to have its greatest effect when seen from a distance across the water, and reflect the changing light of the lagoon. The white front, with its four giant columns, is modelled on a temple portico, and in the interior the numerous Classical columns are raised on pedestals, repeating the design of the façade. Numerous apertures provide natural light and in the absence of superfluous decoration and colour, the clean architectural lines are emphasized through the painted white stucco surfaces. On the walls of the chancel are two beautiful late works by Jacopo Tintoretto, thought to have been painted in the final year of his life (1594; the *Last Supper* and the *Shower of Manna*).

The campanile (*open as the church*) has a lift and provides one of the best views in the city.

The Giorgio Cini Foundation (*guided visits at weekends on the hour from 10–5; otherwise by appointment, segreteria@civitatrevenezie.it*) occupies the former monastery. The monumental buildings were restored by Vittorio Cini (1884–1977), patron of the arts, collector, philanthropist and politician, as a foundation set up as a memorial to his son, who was killed in an air crash in 1949. It is now a research institute and exhibitions are held here. The magnificent first cloister was designed by Palladio (1579). Off the second cloister is the handsome refectory, another splendid space designed by Palladio (1560). A superb facsimile photographic reproduction of Veronese's *Marriage at Cana* has been installed on the end wall, from which it was removed by Napoleon (it now hangs in the Louvre).

THE ISLAND OF THE GIUDECCA

The island of the Giudecca (*map Venetian Lagoon*) lies across the wide Giudecca Canal, facing the Zattere on Dorsoduro. It is home to many local families, and has an atmosphere all its own, with a few simple shops. There are wonderful views from the fondamenta along the Giudecca canal, always busy with boats, but the southern edge of the island is mostly inaccessible.

The Giudecca has three landing-stages: Palanca, Redentore and Zitelle. Vaporetto no. 2 stops at all of these (from San Zaccaria via the island of San Giorgio Maggiore), or from the railway station, Piazzale Roma, Sacca Fisola and San Basilio and the Zattere in the other direction. Vaporetto 4.2 also serves the Giudecca from San Zaccaria, and vaporetto 4.1 from the railway station, Piazzale Roma, Santa Marta and Sacca Fisola.

Two churches by Palladio face the Giudecca canal: Le Zitelle and the **Redentore** (*open Mon–Sat 10–5; Chorus Pass*), the most complete and perhaps the most successful of all his churches (begun in 1577). The wonderful interior is brightly lit by natural light, and its beautiful architecture has many elements derived from ancient Roman buildings. The charming little sacristy is worth a visit. Handbills are available.

THE ISLANDS OF THE LAGOON

The hauntingly beautiful Venetian Lagoon is separated from the open sea by the low, narrow sandbars of the Lido and Pellestrina, which are pierced by three channels: the Porto di Lido, the Porto di Malamocco, and the Porto di Chioggia. A shallow expanse of water, with an average depth of only about a metre, and an area of 544km square, it is the largest coastal lagoon in the Mediterranean, and the only one in the world which supports a large town in its centre.

There is an excellent service of public *vaporetti* to all the inhabited islands. No visit to Venice is complete without a trip to at least one of them, since this is the only way to understand the city's extraordinary setting. The most evocative island is that of Torcello, which was one of the first places of all to be settled: its cathedral is one of the most memorable sights in all Italy.

SAN MICHELE AND MURANO

The circular vaporetto services nos. 4.1 and 4.2 serve the island every 20mins from the Fondamente Nuove. On Murano boats call at the landing-stages of Colonna, Faro, Navagero, Museo, Da Mula and Venier. Boats leave Murano roughly every half hour from the Faro landing-stage, for Mazzorbo and Burano (from where you take the ferry for Torcello).

Before docking at Murano the boats call at the walled island of **San Michele** (*map Venice Right 2*) with its elegant and well-sited church which was Mauro Codussi's earliest Renaissance work in Venice, and the first church façade in Venice to be built in Istrian stone (1469–78). Beside the former monastery is Venice's cemetery. Diaghilev is buried here.

Murano (*Map Venetian Lagoon*), which has numerous canals, is much visited for its glass shops and factories, all of whom welcome visitors and in many of which the art of glass-blowing can be watched: since 1292 the Venetian glass industry has been concentrated here, and Murano glass has always been famous for its elaborate designs and delicate colour and lightness, and for the production of crystal ware and filigree glass. The Museo Vetrario (*open 10–4 or 5, except Wed*) contains an excellent display of glass, from the oldest Roman period to the 19th century. One of the most famous masters in the 15th century was Angelo Barovier, and the firm of the same name is still at work on the island.

The Veneto-Byzantine basilica of **Santi Maria e Donato** (*open all day 8–7*) is the most beautiful building on the island. Its magnificent apse faces a canal, once the entrance to Murano from the lagoon. It is splendidly decorated in an unusual and intricate design. The church was founded in the 7th century and rebuilt around 1141, the date incorporated in the splendid pavement in mosaic *opus sectile* and *opus tessellatum*, of the lovely interior. Beneath the early 15th-century ship's-keel roof, the columns of the nave with ancient capitals support stilted arches, and the wonderful apse mosaic of the Virgin, shown on a gold ground with her hands raised in prayer, dates from the 12th-century.

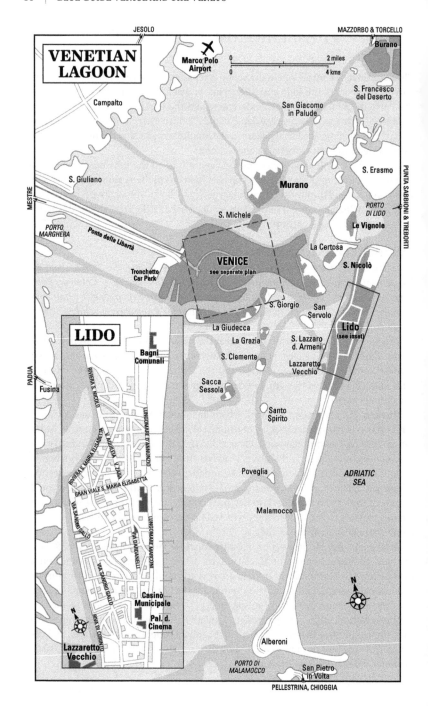

BURANO

Map Venetian Lagoon. Vaporetto no. 12 from the Fondamente Nuove (close to the Gesuiti) c. every 30mins via Murano (Faro) and Mazzorbo. Journey time c. 40mins.
Burano almost resembles a toy village with its tiny little houses brightly painted in a great variety of colours, and miniature canals and *calli*. It has a cheerful atmosphere and almost all the shops sell lace. There is just one wide main street, named after Baldassare Galuppi (1706–85), known as *il Buranello*, the organist and composer of operatic and sacred music, who was born here. **San Martino** (*open 7.30–12 & 3–6*) contains a splendid painting of the *Crucifixion* by Giambattista Tiepolo, commissioned by a pharmacist in 1722, and three charming small paintings by Giovanni Mansueti. The **Museo del Merletto** (*open 10–5 or 6, except Mon*) has a fine collection of lace (beautifully displayed chronologically from the 16th to the 20th century), and from Tues–Fri ladies from Burano still meet here to practise their art. The island was for centuries the centre of Venetian lace-making (first produced in Venice in the late 15th century).

TORCELLO

Vaporetto no. 9 from Burano (map Venetian Lagoon) in 5mins every half-hour. There are a number of restaurants but no shops.
Torcello, inhabited before Venice itself, is the most beautiful and evocative place in the Venetian lagoon. Though now only a remote small group of houses (and no cars), it still preserves some lovely relics of its days of splendour. The people of Altinum took temporary shelter on the island from Lombard invaders on the mainland in the 5th and 6th centuries, until their settlement there was finally abandoned and Bishop Paul moved the bishopric of Altinum to Torcello in 639, bringing with him the relics of St Heliodorus, Altinum's first bishop (still preserved in the cathedral).

At one time the island is said to have had 20,000 inhabitants and was a thriving centre of wool manufacturing, but it had started to decline by the 15th century. The rivalry of Venice compounded by malaria—due to the marshes formed by the silting up of the river Sile—brought about its downfall. In the 17th century the population had already dwindled to a few hundred; it now has only a handful.

From the landing-stage a brick path follows the peaceful canal to the island's group of monuments. There is a combined ticket for all of them, but they all have slightly different opening times. The **cathedral** (*open March–Oct 10.30–5.30; winter 10–4.30*) is a superb Veneto-Byzantine basilica which is one of the most beautiful churches in all Venice, famous for its mosaics. Founded in the 7th century, it was altered in 864 and rebuilt in 1008. The memorable interior is one of the highest achievements of Christian architecture. In the central apse, depicted on a bright gold ground, the mosaic figure of the Virgin is one of the most striking ever produced in Byzantine art. The large mosaic of the *Last Judgement* which covers the west wall dates from the late 11th century, and in the south apse are more ancient mosaics including a delightful vault decoration of four angels with the mystic Lamb. The iconostasis consists of four large marble *plutei* (11th century), elaborately carved with late Byzantine designs, and there are lovely 7th century marble panels in the apse. The pagan sarcophagus below the high altar contains the relics of St

Heliodorus. On the left, set into the wall, is the foundation stone of the church, which has somehow survived intact from 639. The superb pavement of the entire church has a mosaic design in black, red and white marble.

The tall, square, detached **campanile** (11th–12th century) is a striking landmark in the lagoon, and has a wonderful peal of bells which ring out across the water. When open, a brick ramp and a few steps ascend to the bell-chamber from which there is a wonderful view of the entire lagoon with its islands and mudflats, and, on a clear day, of the Alps in the far distance.

The church of **Santa Fosca**, with its octagonal portico, was built to house the body of St Fosca, brought to the island before 1011 and its design on a Byzantine Greek-cross plan survives from that time (although it has been drastically restored). The little **Museo Provinciale di Torcello** (*open 10.30–5; winter 10–4.30; closed Mon*) contains archaeological material and objects from the demolished churches on the island (which at one time numbered at least ten), as well as the Pala d'Oro in gilded silver from the cathedral.

THE LIDO

Map Venetian Lagoon. Vaporetto no. 1 (every 10mins) from San Zaccaria in c. 15mins via Arsenale, and Biennale (Giardini and Sant'Elena) to the Lido (Santa Maria Elisabetta). No. 5.1 (every 20mins) from the Ferrovia and Piazzale Roma via the Zattere and San Zaccaria (no. 5.2 makes the return trip). In summer there are usually more services including no. 8 from the Zattere and the Giudecca.

On the Lido ACTV buses (vaporetto tickets valid) A, B, and C depart from the vaporetto landing stage at Piazzale Santa Maria Elisabetta for San Nicolò, and (in the other direction) for Alberoni via Malamocco.

The Lido is a narrow island (about 12km long) between the lagoon and the open Adriatic sea. It is a pleasant spacious residential district, with fine trees and numerous gardens. But the atmosphere on the Lido is very different from that in the city of Venice itself, as it does not have many canals, and cars and buses are the means of transport. The first bathing establishments were opened here in 1857 and by the beginning of the 20th century it had become the most fashionable seaside resort in Italy. The beach on the Adriatic sea-front has some old-established luxury-class hotels each with their own *bagni* (provided with beach-huts, deck-chairs and cafés), and admission to some other *bagni* frequented by Venetian residents can be purchased for the day.

The two most famous hotels dating from the first decade of the 20th century are the **Grand Hotel des Bains** (*currently closed*; it provided the setting for Thomas Mann's *Death in Venice* in 1913) and the **Excelsior** (an elaborate building in Moorish style). The Palazzo del Casinò and the Palazzo del Cinema were both built in 1936–8 by Eugenio Miozzi in pure streamlined Fascist style.

In a remote spot near the northern tip of the island stands the Lido's most important church, **San Nicolò al Lido** (*usually open 9–12 & 4–7. Reached by bus C from the vaporetto landing-stage at Piazzale Santa Maria Elisabetta*), founded with its monastery in 1044. Its strategic position near the main entrance to the lagoon meant that it was often used by the doge as the official place to receive visitors.

VENICE PRACTICAL TIPS

INFORMATION AND VISITOR CARDS

The official Venice tourist office (*turismovenezia.it*) has offices at the Venice Pavilion, Giardini Reali and nearby, just off Piazza San Marco, close to the entrance to the Museo Correr. Smaller branches at the railway station, Piazzale Roma car park, and the airport.

The **Venice Card** valid for 7 days allows free entrance to the ten civic museums of Venice (including the Doge's Palace, where you can thus avoid the queue), the Palazzo Querini Stampalia, and the Jewish Museum in the Ghetto, as well as the 16 churches opened by Chorus, and reductions on some other museum entrances. There is also a combined ticket for the Museums in Piazza San Marco (the Doge's Palace and Museo Correr) and another ticket which allows you free entrance to all the civic museums of Venice.

The association called **Chorus** provides access to the following 16 churches with a single admission ticket (or, much cheaper, combined ticket for them all): Santa Maria del Giglio, Santo Stefano, Santa Maria Formosa, Santa Maria dei Miracoli, San Giovanni Elemosinario, the Frari, San Polo, San Giacomo dell'Orio, San Stae, Sant'Alvise, the Madonna dell'Orto, San Pietro di Castello, the Redentore, Gesuati, San Sebastiano, and San Giobbe. These are usually open Mon–Sat 10–5 except for the Frari which has longer opening hours (details are given in the main text).

ACQUA ALTA

Acqua alta, a high tide which floods parts of the city when above 110cm, usually occurs many times throughout the year (especially between Sept and April), but the frequency of these tides varies greatly from year to year. They are caused by the position of the moon as well as adverse atmospheric conditions including strong sirocco winds. The city is forewarned by digital acoustic signals: a prolonged sound at the same pitch announces a high tide of 110cm; two sounds on an increasing scale signify that the tide will be over 120cm; three sounds on an increasing scale that it will be over 130cm, and four sounds on an increasing scale announce an exceptionally high tide of 140cm, when nearly 60 percent of the city will be flooded (but this thankfully occurs very rarely). The flood tide usually lasts 2 or 3 hours, and passarelle or duck-boards are laid out in Piazza San Marco, by the landing-stages and in some of the calli. This raised thoroughfare throughout the city totals about 4km and can usually provide a dry route from Piazzale Roma and the railway station to Piazza San Marco. However, it is not possible to get about the city on these occasions without wellington boots. A map showing the calli which do not normally get flooded, and those where the duckboards are set up, is available on *actv.it*. For information there is an automatic call centre (*T: 041 2411996*) or see *comune.venezia.it/maree*, which also provides a weather forecast and warnings of *acqua alta* (and you can also ask to be forewarned by an SMS on your mobile phone).

ARRIVING IN VENICE

By air: Venice airport is 9km north of the city (*www.veniceairport.it T: 041 260 6111*). The best way of reaching Venice by water from the airport is by the yellow Alilaguna motorboat service (*www.alilaguna.it*) which runs frequently (every 15–30mins depending on the time of day and the route chosen). Water taxis are moored closer to the arrivals hall. There is also a frequent shuttle bus service run by ATVO (blue coaches; *www.atvo. it*) which takes just 20mins to reach Piazzale Roma where there are 24-hour vaporetto services to all destinations. There is also an ACTV bus to Piazzale Roma, which has services about every 15mins (*see www.actv.it or www. hellovenezia.it*). Treviso airport has a regular bus service to Venice (Mestre and Tronchetto). Tickets from the arrivals hall.

By rail: The railway station—Venezia Santa Lucia—is right on the Grand Canal, and water-taxis, *vaporetti* and *motoscafi* all operate from the quay outside. Some trains terminate at Venezia Mestre on the mainland, connected by frequent train services to Santa Lucia in 5mins. The Santa Lucia left luggage office is open 24hrs a day.

By car: Cars are not permitted in Venice; you have to leave your vehicle at one of the garages or open-air car parks (*see www.asmvenezia.it*). Parking space is very limited (the garages are used also by Venetian residents). At the most crowded times of year automatic signs on the motorway approaches indicate the space available. All car parks have *vaporetti* services into the centre of Venice. Piazzale Roma is the closest but always has limited space, whereas Tronchetto is a much larger park with rail shuttle service ('people mover') to Piazzale Roma, as well as a *vaporetto* service. There are other car parks on the mainland at the edge of the lagoon, as well as at Mestre and Marghera, which are both connected by frequent bus and train services to Venice.

GETTING AROUND

ACTV runs an excellent service of water-buses (*vaporetti* and *motoscafi*), also throughout the night. See *actv.it*, and *hellovenezia.it*. There are recorded schedules on T: 041 2424. Single tickets are expensive; it is usually best to buy an IMOB card, which gives unlimited travel on all lines valid for certain periods (from 12hrs up to 7 days; various tariffs available): choose the one which coincides with the length of your stay. These have to be presented at the reader machines on the landing-stages before each journey.

Water-taxis (motor-boats) charge by distance, and are much more expensive.

Gondolas are now used exclusively by tourists (they can be hired for 40-min periods and the tariffs are fixed) except for the excellent gondola ferries across the Grand Canal, which are a quick way of getting from one side to the other and provide the opportunity to board a gondola for those who cannot afford to hire one.

WHERE TO STAY

€€€€ Cipriani. In a secluded part of the city, on the island of the Giudecca (private motor-boat service), this hotel has been favoured by the rich and famous for many years. *Giudecca 10, T: 041 520 7744, hotelcipriani.com.*

€€€€ Danieli. One of the most famous hotels in Venice, frequented since the 19th century by the city's most illustrious visitors, it occupies a neo-Gothic palace and its extension built in 1948, a few steps from the Doge's Palace. Now owned by the Starwood hotel group. *4196 Castello (Riva degli Schiavoni), T: 041 522 6480, starwoodhotels.com/luxury.*

€€€€ Gritti Palace. ■ A famous old-established hotel in a 16th-century palace at the beginning of the Grand Canal, furnished with great taste in Venetian style. Less grand than the Danieli, although also owned by the Starwood group, it has a particularly friendly atmosphere. *2467 San Marco (Campo S. Maria del Giglio), T: 041 794 611, hotelgrittivenice.com.*

€€ La Calcina. In a delightful position on the Zattere overlooking the Giudecca canal. Ruskin stayed here in 1877. *780 Dorsoduro (Zattere), T: 041 520 6466, lacalcina.com.*

€€ La Residenza. ■ A small family-run hotel in a lovely old Gothic palace in the peaceful campo beside the church of San Giovanni in Bragora. *3608 Castello (Campo Bandiera e Moro), T: 041 528 5315, veneciaresidenza.com.*

€€ Locanda San Barnaba. ■ A nice little family-run hotel with a pretty garden courtyard in a 16th-century palace, a few steps from the Ca' Rezzonico vaporetto stop on the Grand Canal. *2785 Dorsoduro (Calle del Traghetto), T: 041 241 1233, locanda-sanbarnaba.com.*

€€ Locanda ai Santi Apostoli. ■ A charming little hotel on the third floor of Palazzo Bianchi-Michiel dal Brusà on the Grand Canal. *4391 Cannaregio (Strada Nuova), T: 041 099 6916, locandasantiapostoli.com.*

€€ San Sebastiano. Recently opened this is an attractive little hotel in a secluded position almost in front of the church of San Sebastiano, with a beautiful walled garden. *2542 Fondamenta San Sebastiano, Dorsoduro, T: 041 5231233, hotelsansebastiano.com.*

€€ Seguso. A *pensione* in an historic little house on the Zattere overlooking the wide Giudecca canal. Run by the same family for many years, it retains a delightful old-world atmosphere. *779 Dorsoduro (Zattere), T: 041 528 6858, pensioneseguso.it.*

€€ Tiziano. ■ A charming hotel in a small palace in a very peaceful position far away from the crowds, at the extreme western end of Dorsoduro. *1873 Dorsoduro (Calle Riello), T: 041 275 0071, hoteltizianovenezia.com.*

€ Casa Cardinal Piazza. A convent in a palazzo, in a very peaceful area with a large garden. *3539a Cannaregio (Fondamenta G. Contarini), T: 041 721 388, info@casacardinalpiazza.org.*

€ Casa Querini. ■ A simple friendly hotel in a central but extremely quiet position. *4388 Castello (Campo San Giovanni Nuovo), T: 041 241 1294, locandaquerini.com.*

€ Centro Culturale Don Orione

Artigianelli. A 'religious guest house' just off the Zattere. *909a Dorsoduro (Campo Sant'Agnese), T: 041 522 4077, donorione-venezia.it.*

€ **Istituto Canossiano.** This convent is on one of the prettiest and most peaceful canals in the Dorsoduro district. *1323 Dorsoduro (Fondamenta degli Eremite), T: 041 240 9711, romite1323.com.*

€ **Locanda al Leon.** ■ In a family house in a very central location. *4270 Castello (Calle Albanesi), T: 041 277 0393, hotelalleon.com.*

WHERE TO EAT

NB: The map references given here show the relative location of the restaurant. They cannot always point to the exact street, owing to the complexities of Venetian topography.

DORSODURO

€€€ **Pane e Vino.** In a delightful position away from the crowds, behind the church of the Angelo Raffaele. Reasonably priced and nicely run, with a warm interior and tables out in the campo. Closed Wed. *Campo Angelo Raffaele, T: 041 523 7456. map Venice Left 5.*

CANNAREGIO

€€ **Alla Vedova (Ca' d'Oro).** ■ This has been an excellent place to eat for a reasonable price for many years, and has a delightful atmosphere. Closed Thur and Sun lunch. *3912 Calle del Pistor, directly across the Strada Nuova from the Calle di Ca' d'Oro, T: 041 528 5324. map Venice Left 4–2.*

€€ **Antica Mola.** A very simple *trattoria* frequented mostly by Venetians, with tables outside on the canal front. Closed Wed. *2800 Fondamenta degli Ormesini, T: 041 717 492, just by the Ghetto Nuovo bridge. map Venice Left 2.*

CASTELLO

€€€ **Corte Sconta.** Very inconspicuous in a narrow calle, this is famous amongst Venetians for its good fish. Closed Sun and Mon. *3886 Calle del Pestrin, T: 041 522 7024. map Venice Right 6.*

€€€ **Da Remigio.** ■ Run by a delightful family, with excellent fish, caught locally. Closed Mon evening and Tues. *3416 Salizzada dei Greci, T: 041 523 0089. map Venice Right 6.*

€€€ **L'Osteria di Santa Marina.** A traditional Venetian *trattoria* with good food. Comfortable interior. Closed Sun and Mon lunch. *5911 Campo Santa Marina, T: 041 528 5239. map Venice Right 3.*

SAN MARCO

€€€€ **Harry's Bar.** The most renowned restaurant and cocktail bar in Venice, opened by the Cipriani in the 1920s. Even though it is on the Grand Canal it has no view and is rather too small, but this does not deter the famous and wealthy from coming here to enjoy the intimate atmosphere (and, one suspects, especially each others' company). The prices are perhaps what one would expect from such a celebrated establishment, and the food is not necessarily its strongest point, *Calle Vallaresso, San Marco, T: 041 528 5777. map Venice Right 5.*

SAN POLO

€€€€ **Da Fiore.** ■ Tucked away in a quiet corner east of Campo Sant'Agostino, with one tiny table perched on a balcony over the water. Excellent fish. Closed Sun and Mon. *2202 Calle del Scaleter, T: 041 721308. map Venice Left 4.*

€€€ **Alla Madonna.** Off Riva del Vin, very near the Rialto. According to some this famous old trattoria still serves the best fish in the city, and it has a faithful local and foreign clientèle. *594 Calle della Madonna, T: 041 522 3824. Closed Wed. map Venice Left 4.*

€€€ **Antiche Carampane.** ◼ High quality small restaurant in a quiet part of town, just north of Palazzo Albrizzi. Good meat and fish, excellent wines and home-made desserts. Closed Sun and Mon. *1911 Rio Terrà Rampani, T: 041 524 0165. map Venice Left 4.*

CHEAP EATING PLACES AND BACARI

Osterie, or *bacari* as they are known, are cheap eating places which sell wine by the glass and good simple food (usually crowded and often less comfortable than normal *trattorie*). Many of these are open only at lunch time and closed at weekends.

Da Mario. *Fondamenta della Malvasia (Rio Malatin), near Santa Maria del Giglio, San Marco, Open 12–2.30 & 7.30–9.30. map Venice Left 6.*

Do Mori. ◼ *Off Ruga Vecchia S. Giovanni Elemosinario, between 429 Sottoportego dei Do Mori and the parallel Ramo Prima Gallazza, with an entrance on each, San Polo, T: 041 522 5401. Open 8.30am–7.45pm except Sun. map Venice Left 4.*

Osteria ai Canottieri. *690 Fondamenta San Giobbe, Cannaregio, T: 041 717 999. Closed Sun and Mon. map Venice Left 1.*

Gislon, *Calle della Bissa, near Campo San Bartolomeo, 5424 San Marco, T: 041 522 3569*, Venice's most famous *rosticceria. map Venice Right 3.*

Schiavi (or Vini al Bottegon). ◼ *Rio San Trovaso, Dorsoduro, T: 041 523 0034. Closed Sun afternoon.* One of the most typical of all the Venetian *bacari. map Venice Left 7.*

FESTIVALS AND EVENTS

The Venetian **Carnival** was famous throughout the Republic, and since 1980 the week or ten days in February before Lent has been celebrated by ever-increasing numbers, and it has become the most crowded (and expensive) time of year. The city is invaded by merry-makers in fancy dress and masks, and numerous theatrical and musical events take place, both indoors and out. On some days during Carnival week the city more than doubles its population. The festivities end on Shrove Tuesday, when a huge ball is usually held in Piazza San Marco. *carnevale.venezia.it.*

The **Vogalonga** (literally 'long row') takes place on a Sun in May. It is open to anyone prepared to row from the mouth of the Giudecca Canal around the east end of Venice (Sant'Elena) up through the lagoon and back to Venice via the Cannaregio canal and the Grand Canal to the Punta della Dogana; a course of 32km. *vogalonga.net.*

On the **Festa del Redentore** (on the Sat before the 3rd Sun in July) a bridge of boats is constructed across the Giudecca canal; its vigil is celebrated with aquatic concerts and splendid fireworks.

The **Festa della Salute** (21st Nov) is also celebrated by a bridge of boats across the Grand Canal at the Punta della Dogana.

The **Regata Storica** (first Sun in Sept) starts with a historic procession on the Grand Canal followed by races.

The **Festa della Sensa** takes place on the Sunday after Ascension Day (usually in May), celebrated by the Mayor and Patriarch and other Venetian authorities who are taken by boat from the Bacino di San Marco out to San Nicolò al Lido.

The Venetian Lagoon

CHIOGGIA

Chioggia (*map Veneto East C3*), one of the main fishing ports on the Adriatic, lies at the southern extremity of the Venetian lagoon, connected to the mainland by a bridge. It is not part of Venice but it can be reached by bus and ferry from the Lido. The whole journey takes c. 90mins and is highly recommended particularly because it shows how the lagoon is protected from the open sea by the thin islands of the Lido and Pellestrina. Chioggia is the most important town after Venice in the lagoon. Its unusual urban structure—dating from the late 14th century—survives, with numerous narrow straight *calli* very close together on either side of the Corso del Popolo and Canale Vena. The Chioggia saltworks, first developed in the 12th century, were the most important in the lagoon and survived until the 20th century.

ACTV bus no. 11 operates c. every half hour from the Lido (terminus at the beginning of the Gran Viale Santa Maria Elisabetta, just across from the landing-stage of the vaporetti from San Marco). At Alberoni the bus drives straight on to the connecting ferry, which crosses to the island of Pellestrina. The bus terminates at the landing-stage of ACTV vaporetto no. 1, which continues to Chioggia.

The *vaporetti* from the Lido dock on the quay in at the beginning of Corso del Popolo, the lovely wide main street of Chioggia, which at certain times of day is crowded for the *passeggiata*. It passes a number of churches and the Town Hall, before reaching the Duomo, reconstructed by Longhena in 1624, with its incredibly tall campanile (1347). Nearby is the well-arranged **Museo Diocesano** (*open Thurs 10–1; Fri, Sun and holidays 5–8; in June–Aug Thur 10-1, Sat and Sun 8.30–10.30pm*), which has a remarkable group of Byzantine reliquaries in the form of ex-votos and a lovely polyptych of the *Madonna with four Saints* by Paolo Veneziano. The **Museo Civico della Laguna Sud** (*open Tues–Sat 9–1; Thur–Sat also 3–6; Sun and holidays only 3–6*), documents Chioggia's maritime history. The church of **San Domenico** contains a painting of *St Paul* by Carpaccio.

THE NORTHERN LAGOON

On the lagoon northeast of Venice, **Altino** (*map Veneto East C2*) was already settled by the 7th century BC. It became the Roman *Altinum*, and it was at the junction of several Roman roads where the Dese, Sile and Piave rivers enter the lagoon. The beauty of its country villas was admired by the Latin poet Martial and part of the Roman city has been excavated. It can be visited from the small Museo Archeologico Nazionale (*open daily 8.30–7.30pm*), which contains the finds, including mosaic pavements, stelae, Roman portrait busts (1st–2nd centuries AD), glass, amphorae and architectural fragments. A Roman road, thought to be part of the Via Claudia, has been exposed. The town was destroyed by Attila and the Lombards and, after floods and malaria, it was finally abandoned in the mid-7th century. The people took refuge on Torcello and are thus directly involved with the early history of Venice (many Roman stones from Altino were reused in the buildings of Venice, Torcello and Murano).

Across the lagoon towards the Adriatic is **Punta Sabbioni** (served by *vaporetti* from Venice) on the northernmost entrance to the Venetian Lagoon (the Porto di Lido). The tongue of land here extends from **Cavallino Treporti** to the **Lido di Jesolo**, a popular seaside resort, between the old and new mouths of the Piave. It has numerous hotels and campsites. The old village of **Jesolo**, formerly Cavazuccherina, perpetuates the name of an early medieval centre known also as *Equilium* (since horse were bred on the marshes here), the rival of Heraclea in the affairs of the lagoon.

Eraclea (*map Veneto North C4*), a modern village on east bank of the Piave, has taken the name of the ancient Heraclea (named after Emperor Heraclius), the episcopal and administrative centre of the Venetian lagoon in the 7th–8th centuries after the sack of Oderzo by the Lombards. The site of the ancient city, near Cittànova, has been identified by aerial photography. It was formerly surrounded by a lagoon, and it recalls Venice in plan, with a central canal and many smaller canals. From 750 onwards the inhabitants migrated to the safer islands of Malamocco and Rialto, and a leader from Heraclea is thought to have become the first Doge of Venice. Heraclea rapidly declined as its lagoon silted up and Venice grew in importance.

Caorle (*map Veneto North C4*) is an ancient fishing village and now a popular seaside resort near the mouth of the Livenza. Founded by refugees from Concordia (in Friuli-Venezia Giulia), it was a bishop's see for twelve centuries and has a cathedral of 1048 with a magnificent *Pala d'Oro* in the sanctuary, on the wall behind the high altar. Made of six panels of gilded silver, it is thought to date from the 8th century. The very fine cylindrical campanile was built in the 11th century, and in 2011 a spiral staircase was installed so that you can climb up it as far as the sixth floor. To the north is a beautiful lagoon with fishing huts and interesting wildlife

The Riviera del Brenta

The Venetians built the canal known as the Naviglio di Brenta or Brenta Vecchia to facilitate navigation between their city and Padua, diverting the river itself to the north to reduce the amount of silt pouring into the lagoon. The magnificent villas for which the area is famous first appeared in the 16th century when, in the face of Turkish expansion in the eastern Mediterranean, Venetian patricians shifted their investments from foreign trade to real estate. Portia's villa of Belmont in Shakespeare's *Merchant of Venice* was just one such. The great farms that grew up here were intended both to generate income and to provide a pleasant escape from the heat and humidity of the lagoon in summer. The principal façades of the residences faced the water, like the palaces on the Grand Canal—and not by chance, for the same festive lifestyle that graced the latter in winter continued in summer in the villas of the riviera. With the approach of the 18th century, the idyllic pleasures of country life merged with a taste for the exotic, and the architecture of the noble manors became more luxurious and extravagant, with spectacular parks, gardens, aviaries, greenhouses and even private zoos stocked with exotic animals. Meanwhile patricians of limited means (of whom there were quite a few), adventurers (even more) and the *nouveaux riches* rented lodgings in the towns, in order not to miss the great social events of the Venetian summer.

Those who, for one reason or another, chose not to make the trip up the canal in the family gondola took the *burchiello*, a large riverboat rowed by crews of oarsmen or pulled by horses—a 'marvellous and comfortable craft', as Goldoni recalls, 'in which one glides along the Brenta sheltered from winter's cold and summer's ardour'. Today, between March and Oct, a motorised *burchiello* lazily winds its way from Padua to Venice or vice versa, for a handsome fee, stopping to visit a couple of the 50-odd extant villas. The trip can also be made by bicycle (there are marked cycling routes) or by bus. For details, see p. 63.

Today, many of the villas are still privately owned and some are regularly open to the public (usually between April and Oct). Others, such as Villa Nani Mocenigo between Dolo and Mira and Villa Valmarana between Mira and Oriago, have found a new role as venues for weddings, gala events and conferences.

The villas that are open to the public, either regularly or by appointment, are described below in the order in which they appear if you depart from Venice.

LA MALCONTENTA
On a bend shaded by willows, on the first stretch of the canal (just before the small

town of Oriago), stands the **Villa Foscari**, also known as La Malcontenta (*map Veneto East C2; still privately owned by the Foscari family; open May–Oct Tues and Sat 9–12, lamalcontenta.com*), justly one of the most famous of all the Ville Venete. It was constructed around 1555–60 for the brothers Nicola and Alvise Foscari by Andrea Palladio, and is one of his most successful surburban villas, and the nearest he built to Venice but the only one he sited on the Brenta Canal. It was extremely influential in European country house architecture. The exterior is very slightly rusticated; the side towards the river is characterised by a noble six-columned Ionic porch, which projects outward and is raised on a tall basement with lateral ramps. It has a thermal window, and four characteristic Venetian chimneys. The interesting interior plan provided for two identical apartments for the brothers on the *piano nobile*, on either side of the central Greek-cross *salone* frescoed by Battista Franco and Giovanni Battista Zelotti. In one of the rooms is the frescoed figure of a woman, whom legend claims to be Elisabetta Foscari (the 'malcontent' of the name), exiled here for betraying her husband.

MIRA

It was here at Mira (*map Veneto East B2*) that Lord Byron wrote the fourth canto of *Childe Harold*, while staying at Villa Foscarini dei Carmini (on Via Nazionale overlooking the canal). On the outskirts to the east are the villas **Pisani Contarini** (or dei Leoni) on Riviera Trentin (*open for events*) and **Valier**, or 'La Chitarra', on Riviera Matteotti (*open for guided tours, see www.miratur.it/villa.valier.html*). A little further, on Via Nazionale, between Mira and Oriago, is **Villa Seriman-Widmann-Rezzonico-Foscari** (*open by appointment; T: 041 560 0690*), built in 1719 but remodelled in the French Rococo manner after the middle of the 18th century. The most famous of the villas of Mira, it has a two-storey façade with a curved tympanum, and frescoed rooms.

DOLO

Dolo (*map Veneto East B2*) was the principal town of the Riviera in the 18th century, and still preserves its mill, a *squero* (or boatyard) and one of the old locks. Like most of the places along the Brenta, once individual towns in their own right, is has now succumbed to urban sprawl. To the east of the centre, on Via Brenta Bassa, is the **Villa Ferretti Angeli**, designed in 1596–1608 by Palladio's pupil Vincenzo Scamozzi. Its Ionic pilastered façade is particularly elegant. The park is open to the public. Slightly further east, on the corner of Via Badoera, is the 18th-century **Villa Badoer Fattoretto**, which houses the Museo del Villano, which contains a collection of farm instruments and innumerable curiosities which document farming life near the Brenta.

STRA

The 18th-century **Villa Pisani** or Villa Nazionale at Stra (*map Veneto East B2; open summer Tues–Sun 9–7; winter 9–4; villapisani.beniculturali.it*) is the largest villa on the Riviera, named after its original owner, the Venetian doge Alvise Pisani. The interior is decorated by 18th-century Venetian artists, including Tiepolo, who frescoed the *Triumph of the Pisani Family* on the ceiling of the ballroom (1762). This grand residence was purchased by Napoleon in 1807, and in 1934 it was the scene of the first meeting between Mussolini and Hitler. In the vast park is the labyrinth (*open April–Sept*) described by Gabriele d'Annunzio in *Fire*. On the opposite bank of the canal rises the long front of the **Villa Lazara Pisani**, 'La Barbariga', with a Baroque central structure and symmetrical 18th-century wings.

FUSINA

Fusina (*map Veneto East C2*) is where the Brenta Canal enters the Venetian lagoon: if you are coming down the Brenta from Padua, it is here that you glimpse Venice, just 4km away. This was the place where boats were boarded for Venice, before the railway line was built in the 19th century. The trip took about one and a half hours and provided a splendid approach across the lagoon to the city. It was described by numerous travellers, including Charles Dickens in 1846:

'I was awakened after some time (as I thought) by the stopping of the coach. It was now quite night, and we were at the water side. There lay here, a black boat, with a little house or cabin in it of the same mournful colour. When I had taken my seat in this, the boat was paddled, by two men, towards a great light, lying in the distance on the sea...It soon began to burn brighter; and from being one light became a cluster of tapers, twinkling and shining out of the water, as the boat approached towards them by a dreamy kind of track, marked out upon the sea by posts and piles...Before I knew by what, or how, I found that we were gliding up a street—a phantom street; the houses rising on both sides, from the water, and the black boat gliding on beneath their windows. Lights were shining from some of these casements, plumbing the depth of the black stream with their reflected rays; but all was profoundly silent. So we advanced into this ghostly city, continuing to hold our course through narrow streets and lanes, all filled and flowing with water.'

Boats still leave Fusina for Venice; but the journey takes only half as long today as it did in Dickens' time.

RIVIERA DEL BRENTA PRACTICAL TIPS

GETTING AROUND

By boat: For boat trips on the Brenta Canal: 'Burchiello' boats operated by I Battelli del Brenta (*T: 049 8760233, battellidelbrenta.it*) depart from the Portello wharf in Padua (*beyond map Padua 4*) or from La Pietà landing stage in Venice (**map Venice Right 6**); Delta Tour (*T: 049 8700232, www. deltatour.it*) leave from Stra. The return journeys are not included, so you have to return by public transport. The fare is not cheap, but it includes a meal and guided visits to one or two villas. It is also possible to do partial tours, for example just from Venice to La Malcontenta. See the websites for details.

By bus: ACTV service no. 53 runs between Padua bus station and Piazzale Roma in Venice (*map Venice Left 3*). It stops at Stra, Dolo, Mira, Oriago and Malcontenta. For timetables, see *actv.it*. Go to the 'On the Mainland' section and choose 'Linee extraurbane'.

By bicycle: For cycling routes in the Veneto, see *bicycle.bonavoglia.eu/ itinerari/brenta_riviera.phtml*.

WHERE TO EAT

MIRA (*map Veneto East B2*)
€€ Trattoria Nalin. This has been the best-known place to eat on the Brenta Canal for many years. Run by the same family since 1914, it serves excellent fish from Chioggia, simply grilled on an open wood fire. Good selection of wines. Closed Mon. *Via Argine Sinistro Novissimo 29, T: 041 420083, trattorianalin.it.*

€ Trattoria alla Vida. A simple place with a little garden open in summer. Good fish. Closed Mon evening and Sat lunch. *Via Don Giovanni Minzoni 31, T: 041 422143, trattoriaallavida.it.*

Padua

Padua (*map Veneto East B2*; in Italian *Pádova*) is one of the most ancient cities in Italy with a famous university (the second oldest in the country) and a large student population. It is a busy, lively place, visited for its numerous important works of art, most famous of which is the Scrovegni Chapel with wonderful frescoes by Giotto. The town is also memorable for its busy markets in three adjoining piazze around the huge, early 14th-century Palazzo della Ragione, the ground floor of which is also occupied by good food shops. Many other shops nearby preserve their attractive old-fashioned premises. The town is supplied with numerous cafés, the most famous of which is the Caffè Pedrocchi, in an elaborate 19th-century building which dominates a central part of the town. Padua is the place where St Anthony carried out many miracles and his burial chapel in the town's most celebrated church, named after him but always simply called 'Il Santo'. It is visited every year by several million pilgrims, who come to touch his tomb and seek his comfort. Donatello was just one of the famous Renaissance artists who were commissioned by the city's enlightened patricians to carry out works of art to embellish the city, which was a leading centre of Humanism in the 15th century. Many pretty arcaded streets survive in the centre, but other districts had to be rebuilt after severe damage in the last War. Like all larger towns in the north of Italy, it has unappealing and less overtly friendly outskirts.

HISTORY OF PADUA

The Roman historian Livy, born near Patavium (Padua) in 59 BC, claimed that the cities of the Po valley were founded by Antenor, Aeneas' fellow refugee from Troy. In reality the site was probably already occupied before the 8th or 7th century BC by palaeo-Venetic tribes. Known to have been an important settlement of the Euganei and Veneti, it received full Roman franchise in 89 BC. The town prospered under Byzantine and Lombard rule, and declared itself an independent republic as early as 1164. The foundation of the university in 1222 attracted many distinguished teachers to Padua, including Dante and Petrarch, as well as numerous students from England, and the city came to be known as *La Dotta* ('The Learned'). In 1237–54 Ezzelino da Romano was tyrant of Padua, then after the suzerainty of the Carraresi (1318–1405) the city was conquered by the Venetians, and remained a faithful ally of Venice until the end of the Venetian Republic. Along with Venice, it was ceded to Austria in 1797 and its celebrated coffee house, Caffè Pedrocchi, was an important meeting-place for patriots during the Risorgimento. It became a command post for troop movements during WWI and the armistice that followed Austria's defeat at the battle of Vittorio Veneto was signed at Villa Giusti on the southeastern outskirts. Allied bombs did much damage in the final stages of WW2. Today it is a fairly prosperous town with many light industries.

ART IN PADUA

Giotto's frescoes in the Cappella degli Scrovegni gave rise to a flourishing local school of 'Giottesque' painters (including Guariento and Giusto de' Menabuoi). The Veronese Altichiero (c. 1330–95), who was active in Padua in the 1380s, was one of the most creative interpreters of Giotto's achievements before Masaccio, filling the gap between these two great names. Though he lacks the robust individuality of Giotto, and though he is less daring with colour, he is nevertheless the most important northern Italian mural painter of the late 14th century. His love of pageant and of decorative elements marks him out as an artist in the Gothic tradition. The Renaissance came to Padua with the arrival of Donatello in 1443, to work on his equestrian statue of Gattamelata and the high altar of the Santo. The painter Mantegna produced a superb fresco cycle in the church of the Eremitani between 1454 and 1457 (almost totally destroyed in the Second World War). In the late 15th century Bartolomeo Bellano (1434–96) and Andrea Briosco (Il Riccio, 1470–1532) created some of the finest small bronze sculpture of the Renaissance. Riccio's almost exact contemporary, Giovanni Maria Falconetto (1468–1534), was a painter but also an important architect: the two pretty little buildings he designed in Padua (where he died) for the erudite Venetian Alvise Cornaro, as ideal retreats where he could meet the great literary figures of his day, are his masterpiece.

Where to see works by the following artists in Padua:

Altichiero: Santo; Oratorio di San Giorgio

Bellano: Santo; San Francesco

Donatello: Santo; Gattamelata statue; Santa Maria dei Servi

Falconetto: Santo; Loggia Cornaro; Palazzo del Capitanio; Monte di Pietà; Porta Savonarola; Porta San Giovanni

Giotto: Scrovegni Chapel; Musei Civici

Giusto de' Menabuoi: Musei Civici; Eremitani church; Santo; Baptistery; Museo Diocesano

Guariento: Musei Civici; Eremitani church; Accademia di Scienze, Lettere ed Arti

Mantegna: Musei Civici; Eremitani church; Museo Antoniano

Il Riccio: Musei Civici; Santo; San Francesco; Santa Giustina.

SCROVEGNI CHAPEL

Map Padua 4. Open 9–7 every day. You are asked to book your visit in advance (T: 049 2010020, www.cappelladegliscrovegni.it) but you can also do so on the day if places are still available. A maximum of 25 visitors are allowed in the chapel at one time. Combined tickets with the Musei Civici Eremitani (where you buy or pick up your

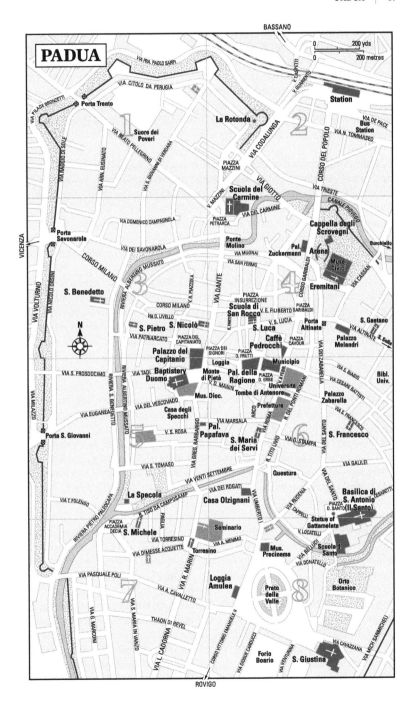

PADUA

BASSANO

0   200 yds
0   200 metres

VIA FRA. PAOLO SARPI

VIA CITOLO DA PERUGIA

VIA PILADE BRONZETTI

Porta Trento

La Rotonda

Station

VIA DE PACE
Bus
Station
VIA N. TOMMASEO

VIA CODALUNGA

CORSO DEL POPOLO

VIA GUERATO

V. CLASPETTI

VIA BEATO PELLEGRINO

Suore dei
Poveri

VIA ARR. BUSINATO

VIA S. GIOVANNI DI VERDARA

VIA RAGGIO DI SOLE

VICENZA

VIA DOMENICO CAMPAGNOLA

PIAZZA
MAZZINI

V. MAZZINI

VIA GIOTTO

Scuola del
Carmine

VIA DEL CARMINE

VIA TRIESTE

CANALE POVEGO

Porta
Savonarola

VIA DEI SAVONAROLA

PIAZZA
PETRARCA

Ponte
Molino

VIA MUGNAI

Pal.
Zuckermann

Cappella degli
Scrovegni

Arena

Burchiello

CORSO MILANO

RIVIERA ALBERTINO MUSSATO

VIA SAN FERMO

CORSO GARIBALDI

Musei
Civici

VIA CASSAN

VIA VOLTURNO

VIA NICOLO ORSINI

S. Benedetto

CORSO MILANO

VIA D. LIVELLO

PIAZZA
INSURREZIONE

Scuola di
San Rocco

V. R. PIAZZOLA

VIA DANTE

B. PARTIONI

V. E. FILIBERTO GARIBALDI

Eremitani

S. Gaetano

VIA ALTINATE

S. Sofia

S. Pietro

S. Nicolò

VIA PATRIARCATO

PIAZZA DEL
CAPITANIATO

S. Luca

V. S. LUCIA

Porta
Altinate

Palazzo
Melandri

N

Palazzo del
Capitanio

PIAZZA
D. FRUTTI

Caffè
Pedrocchi

PIAZZA
CAVOUR

VIA DEL ZABARELLA

VIA S. BIAGIO

RIVIERA S. BENEDETTO

VIA TADI

Baptistery

Duomo

Monte
di Pietà

VIA D. MANIN

PIAZZA
D. SIGNORI

Pal. della
Ragione

Municipio

PIAZZA
D. ERBE

V. A. FEBR.

Università

VIA CESARE BATTISTI

Bibl.
Univ.

VIA S. PROSDOCIMO

VIA EUGANEA

VIA DEL VESCOVADO

Mus. Dioc.

Casa degli
Specchi

Tomba di Antenore

VIA MARSALA

ARCO

VIA ROMA

R. DEI PONTI ROMANI

Prefettura

Palazzo
Zabarella

VIA S. FRANCESCO

Porta S. Giovanni

VIA GREG. BARBARIGO

V. S. ROSA

Pal.
Papafava

S. Maria
dei Servi

R. TITO LIVIO

VIA G. STAMPA

VIA DEL SANTO

S. Francesco

VIA GALILEI

VIA S. TOMASO

VIA VENTI SETTEMBRE

Questura

VIA MILAZZO

VIA T. FOLENGO

La Specola

R. TISO DA CAMPOSAMP.

PAGLIA

VIA DEI ROGATI

Casa Olzignani

VIA UMBERTO I

VIA RUDENA

VIA CAPPELLI

Basilica di
S. Antonio
(Il Santo)

PIAZZA
D. SANTO

VESAROTTI

RIVIERA PIETRO PALEOCAPA

PIAZZA
ACCADEMIA
DECIA

S. Michele

VIA TORRESINO

VIA A. MEMMO

Seminario

Statue of
Gattamelata

V. LOCATELLI

Scuola d
Santo

VIA PASQUALE POLI

VIA DIMESSE ACQUETTE

Torresino

Mus.
Precinema

VIA BELLUDI

VIA DONATELLO

VIA G. MARONI

VIA S. MARIA IN VANZO

VIA R. MARIN

VIA A. CAVALLETTO

Loggia
Amulea

Prato
della
Valle

Orto
Botanico

THAON DI REVEL

VIA L. CADORNA

CORSO VITTORIO EMANUELE II

VIA BIGUE CARDUCCI

Forio
Boario

S. Giustina

VIA VENTURINA

VIA CAVAZZANA

VIA A. MICH SANMICHELI

ROVIGO

ticket) and Palazzo Zuckermann are available Tues–Sun. Mondays are usually the least crowded days (but that is when the Musei Civici and Palazzo Zuckermann are closed), and in winter you can often book two time slots together so you can stay in the chapel for 40 instead of 20mins.

The chapel is approached through a little garden. While you are in the waiting room (approx 20mins), you are shown an excellent film (with English subtitles) about the chapel. The waiting time helps to stabilise the microclimate inside the chapel: once this is done, you are then admitted to the chapel itself for about 20mins.

This is the most famous monument in the city since the simple little barrel-vaulted chapel is entirely decorated with wonderful and well-preserved frescoes by the greatest early Italian master, Giotto. The chapel was built by Enrico Scrovegni in 1303, next to his palace (now demolished), in expiation for his father's usury. Dante, who may have been in Padua at the time Giotto was at work on these frescoes, singles out Scrovegni's father in his *Inferno (XVII. 64–75)* as one of three noblemen famous in his time for their usury (although none of them is named by the poet, they are easily identifiable by the description of their coats of arms).

Giotto may also have designed the chapel itself when he was commissioned to carry out the frescoes since its scale fits so precisely the painted decoration. The cycle was painted at the height of his power in just two years and is the only one by him to survive intact. The scenes depict the history of Christian redemption through the lives of Christ and the Virgin and reflect the painter's deeply religious spirit. Giotto's influence on all subsequent Italian painting can here be understood to the full: his painting has a new monumentality and sense of volume which had never been achieved in medieval art. The Biblical narrative is for the first time given an intensely human significance: as Bernard Berenson expressed it, Giotto's figures have remarkable 'tactile values'. The superb colouring (with strong blues) is exceptionally well preserved.

The frescoes are arranged in three bands, and were painted in chronological order. The cycle begins on the top band of the south wall nearest to the sanctuary with the story of the Virgin's parents, Joachim and Anne, and the Virgin's birth up to her betrothal and return home, as recorded in the Apocrypha. The numbering and description refers to the plan:

1. Joachim is expelled from the Temple after his offering has been rejected by the priests since, after 20 years of marriage to his wife Anne, God has not blessed them with children;
2. Joachim in sorrow takes refuge in a sheepfold among shepherds (where he is greeted by the friendly sheepdog), leaving Anne alone not knowing what has become of him;
3. An angel announces to Anne that she is to give birth to a daughter, and that she will find her lost husband at the Golden Gate of Jerusalem (as her handmaiden sits spinning in the porch);
4. Joachim kneeling in deep reverence makes a sacrifice of a burnt offering;
5. An angel appears to Joachim (still in the same sheepfold) in a vision and tells him of the imminent birth of the Virgin;

6. The meeting of Anna and Joachim at the Golden Gate.
7. The Birth of the Virgin;
8. The Presentation of the Virgin;
9. The high-priest Simeon orders all unmarried men of the lineage of David to present their rods at the altar, and declares that the man whose rod comes into bud (through the influence of the Holy Spirit) will marry the Virgin;
10. The Watching of the Rods, as all kneel in prayer;
11. Betrothal of the Virgin to Joseph (he is shown holding his rod in bud which also bears the Holy Spirit, while the others break their rods in despair);
12. The Virgin returns home with her seven companions to her father's house in Galilee, accompanied by joyous musicians.
13. God the Father, surrounded by elegant figures of angels, dispatches the angel Gabriel;

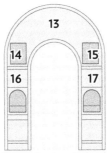

SCROVEGNI CHAPEL

East wall: triumphal arch

40
West wall

14. The angel Gabriel;
15. The Virgin Annunciate;
16. The Pact of Judas, with the black devil, is paired with the opposite scene:
17. The Visitation, in which Mary embraces the bent figure of her older cousin Elizabeth (mother of John the Baptist), one of the most moving scenes in the chapel.

The two lowest panels have a pair of unique scenes, particularly memorable: two empty rooms with vaults and Gothic windows (and the sky outside depicted at different times of day) are lit by two iron lanterns, symbolising the light which guides man to Virtue and the light which saves him from Vice.

The 22 other scenes depict much more familiar stories, relating to episodes in the life of Christ from the Nativity to the Ascension in a continuous narrative.

18. The Nativity;
19. The Adoration of the Magi;
20. Presentation in the Temple;
21. Flight into Egypt
22. The Massacre of the Innocents.
23. The young Christ disputing with the Elders in the Temple;
24. The Baptism of Christ;
25. The Marriage at Cana;
26. The Raising of Lazarus;
27. Entry into Jerusalem;
28. Expulsion of the money-changers from the Temple.
29. The Last Supper;
30. The Washing of the Feet;
31. The Kiss of Judas;
32. Christ before Caiaphas;
33. The Mocking of Christ: flagellation and crowning with thorns.
34. The Way to Calvary;
35. The Crucifixion (note the extraordinary skill with which the red tunic of Christ held up by the soldiers has been depicted);
36. The Deposition;
37. The Resurrection, with the Angels

at the empty tomb and the soldiers asleep (and the Noli me Tangere on the left);
38. The Ascension, showing Christ on a cloud surrounded by a choir of angels above the apostles;
39. Pentecost and the descent of the Holy Spirit.
40. Last Judgement. The west wall is entirely occupied by a depiction of this scene, full of fascinating figure studies, although it is the most damaged part of the cycle since the wall was the most exposed to the elements, after the portico and Scrovegni palace outside were demolished in the early 19th century and the intonaco was removed from the chapel façade. Above the door, in front of the Blessed, Scrovegni kneels before the Cross and presents the Chapel itself to the Virgin; on the right the numerous contorted figures of the Damned in Hell are shown much smaller and dominated by the huge monstrous Devil.

Around the socle on the two long walls are very beautiful monochrome allegorical figures of the Virtues and the Seven Deadly Sins or Vices, among the most original and striking part of the entire cycle. The seven Virtues are all turned towards the fresco of Paradise on the west wall, and the seven Vices on the opposite wall look in the direction of Hell. The panels in between, in imitation of marble, were painted with a technique used by the ancient Romans known as *stucco lustro*, similar to encaustic painting which involved the use of wax.

Nearest to the Last Judgement wall, the winged figure of **Hope (a)** is counterbalanced by **Despair (b)**, killing herself with a cord as the tiny Devil drags her towards the abyss on the west wall. **Charity (c)** has a triple flame on her head and holds a vase of flowers, while horned **Envy (d)**, enveloped in flames, is bitten on the forehead by a serpent issuing from her own mouth. The majestic figure of **Faith (e)** is crowned with a diadem and holds a Cross, while **Unbelief (f)** is represented by a helmeted warrior holding an idol. The serene figure of **Justice (g)** holds weighing scales, perfectly balanced, while **Injustice (h)** is shown as a judge armed with a sword and double hook sitting isolated in his fortress protected by trees, painted with extraordinary skill. **Temperance (i)** is a draped figure prevented from using arms, and **Anger (j)** is an ugly woman tearing at her dress. **Fortitude (k)** is also a female figure, fully protected by armour with the head of a lion on her head. **Inconstancy (l)** is represented by a girl vainly trying to balance herself on a wheel as it turns, while her veil flies away. **Prudence (m)** has two heads, one elderly and one youthful holding a mirror, while opposite **Folly (n)** is a pot-bellied grotesque figure wearing a headdress of feathers and defiantly shaking a mace.

The barrel vault is painted blue with stars, and has a bright medallion of Christ and the Virgin (and at the sides eight medallions of prophets).

On the altar are three very beautiful statues of the Virgin observed by two angels (or deacons) commissioned by Enrico Scrovegni at the same time as the frescoes from the greatest sculptor of the time, Giovanni Pisano. Enrico is buried in the tomb on the wall behind which bears his effigy. The frescoes here are by followers of Giotto.

Outside in the little garden can be seen the ruined walls of a **Roman amphitheatre** (1st century AD), an 'arena': the Cappella degli Scrovegni used to be known as the Arena Chapel.

MUSEI CIVICI EREMITANI

Map Padua 4. Open 9–7 except Mon. Tickets for the Scrovegni Chapel should be bought or picked up here. Combined tickets are available, also for Palazzo Zuckermann.

This huge museum is housed in the convent of the church of the Eremitani, rebuilt and modernised at the end of the 20th century by Franco Albini. It consists of an archaeological collection founded in 1825, a Pinacoteca with some masterpieces of painting, the extensive Emo Capodilista collection left to the city in 1864, as well as some sculpture and small bronzes.

THE ARCHAEOLOGICAL COLLECTION ON THE GROUND FLOOR

Exhibits include 14 stelae from pre-Roman Padua; Roman material found in Padua —funerary monuments, glass and monochrome mosaic pavements. The aedicular tomb of the Volumni family, dating from the Augustan period and found in 1879, has been reconstructed. The two fine black basalt statues of the ancient Egyptian goddess Sekhmet were given to the city by Giovanni Battista Belzoni (1778–1823), who was born in Padua. He was the first European to enter the tomb of Ramesses II at Abu Simbel, and supplied the British Museum with many of its largest Egyptian statues. A series of small rooms exhibit Etruscan pottery, antique gems, and vases.

A modern flight of stairs leads up past two lions and two griffins made in Padua in the 13th century.

THE EMO CAPODILISTA COLLECTION ON THE UPPER FLOOR
The small painting of a young Senator in the first room is an exquisite work by Giovanni Bellini. Also here are *St Augustine* and *St Gregory the Great* by Michele Giambono. In addition, the collection has works by Marco Basaiti, two tiny works by Giorgione (*Leda and the Swan* and a pastoral scene) and two panels from a *cassone* (marriage chest) with mythological scenes, attributed to Titian. There are also two paintings by Jan van Scorel (*Portrait of a Man*), who was in Venice in 1520, and Quentin Metsys (*St John the Evangelist*), from the previous generation of Netherlandish artists. Steps lead up to the cloister walk with a very good collection of small bronzes and plaquettes, particularly representative of northern Italian masters (Il Riccio, Moderno, l'Antico, Alessandro Vittoria, Tiziano Aspetti).

THE PINACOTECA ON THE UPPER FLOOR
The room at the end of the cloister walk displays two superb paintings by Giotto from the Scrovegni Chapel: the *Crucifix* and the *Redeemer* (from the top of the west wall). Also here are frescoes by Pietro da Rimini dating from the early 14th century, detached from a chapel on the ground floor of this monastery. Works by Guariento include a painting of the *Redeemer* and beautiful angels displayed in a reconstructed chapel. There are also works by Giusto de' Menabuoi, Jacobello del Fiore (*Crucifixion*), Cennino Cennini, and a lovely 14th-century tapestry made in France or Flanders. The exquisite painting of the *Madonna* by Mantegna (1491) has been on permanent loan to the museum since 2007.

Sculpture includes Madonna reliefs by the workshop of Donatello and Antonio Rossellino and two fragmentary heads, one by Tullio and one by Pietro Lombardo.

Displayed near a beautiful painting of the *Argonauts* by Lorenzo Costa, is a *Madonna and Child* by Lazzaro Bastiani and a *Portrait of a Man* by Alvise Vivarini.

In the upper walk of the cloister are terracotta heads from a Deposition group by Guido Mazzoni, Madonnas by Andrea Previtali and terracotta busts by Il Riccio.

Some of the most interesting paintings in the numerous subsequent rooms of the gallery are a *Crucifixion* and *Washing of the Feet* by Tintoretto, and two martyrdom scenes by Veronese. Works by painters from the Veneto school include the Bassano family, and there are later works from the 18th century.

THE CHURCH OF THE EREMITANI
Map Padua 4. Closed 12.15–4.
Beside the Musei Civici Eremitani stands this Augustian church built in 1276–1306,

with a façade of 1360. It was almost completely destroyed by bombing in 1944 but has been extremely well reconstructed: the splendid wooden ship's keel roof was entirely rebuilt.

The second chapel to the right of the sanctuary is the **Cappella Ovetari**, which contains all that remains of a famous fresco cycle by Mantegna, the destruction of which was the greatest individual disaster to Italian art in the Second World War. The great painter began work here in 1454 when he was only 23 and he took three years to complete the frescoes. He was clearly influenced by Donatello, who had begun work on his sculptures for the Santo just ten years earlier. The *Martyrdom of St Christopher* on the right wall was detached and removed to safety before the War and so survives in a much better state than that on the other wall of the *Martyrdom of St James*, which was partially recomposed from shattered fragments. Behind the altar can be seen the wonderful *Assumption*.

In the **sanctuary**, on the left wall, are frescoes by Guariento (1361–5) of scenes from the life of St Philip and St Augustine, and allegories of the planets and the ages of man. The Crucifix was painted in 1367 by Nicoletto Semitecolo. In the Cappella Sanguinacci, to the left of the sanctuary, the 14th-century votive frescoes include some by Giusto de' Menabuoi. Outside the sacristy door, photographs record the devastating appearance of the ruined church in 1944. The largest monument on the north wall is that of the law professor Marco Benavides (1489–1582) by Bartolomeo Ammannati, which shows how closely the artist was influenced by Michelangelo. The two polychrome altarpieces on this wall, of roughly the same date, are decorated with sculptures and a fresco by Giovanni Minello and his school. Near the west door are two similar hanging funerary monuments by Andriolo de Sanctis of Ubertino and Jacopo II da Carrara, who both died in the mid-14th century: Jacopo's epigraph was supplied by Petrarch. There are more Giottesque fresco fragments on the south wall by Giusto de' Menabuoi and Guariento.

PALAZZO ZUCKERMANN (MUSEI CIVICI)
Map Padua 4. Open 10–7 except Mon.
Across the road from the Musei Civici Eremitani, Palazzo Zuckermann is a monumental building of 1912/14 by Filippo Arosio. Its spacious Neoclassical interior, with parquet floors, houses the Museo Bottacin and the collection of decorative arts of the Musei Civici.

The **decorative arts collection**, on two floors, is chronological. On the ground floor is an interesting and well-displayed collection of ceramics, architectural fragments, sculpture, furniture, lace and glass dating from the 14th–16th centuries. Upstairs the display continues with furniture, majolica, costumes (including 18th-century men's apparel), Church silver, a wood relief of the *Fall of the Giants* by Andrea Brustolon, Rococo *objets d'art*, porcelain, musical instruments, silver and inlaid cabinets. There is a also a very fine collection of jewellery left to the city in 1882 by Leone Trieste. The prints and drawings collection is open to scholars. A drawing room of Palazzo Guadio in Padua, with furniture designed by Giuseppe Borsato, has been recreated.

A charming back staircase leads up to the **Museo Bottacin**, founded by Nicola

Bottacin, who left his important numismatic collection to Padua in 1870. There are coins from ancient Greece to the modern era. Another room is filled with statues, including *Flora* by Vincenzo Vela. A terracotta bust of Doge Paolo Renier is the work of Canova. The paintings and furniture all decorated Bottacin's residence in Trieste.

IL SANTO (BASILICA OF ST ANTHONY)

Map Padua 6. Open all day 6.30am–6.45pm

The most famous church in Padua and one of the great pilgrim shrines of Italy, this magnificent basilica was begun in 1232 as a temple for the tomb of St Anthony of Padua, who was canonised in the same year, just a year after his death. He had been born in Lisbon in 1195, but on a missionary journey to Africa he was forced in a storm to land in Italy and settled in Padua in the 1220s, where he preached with great fervour against heresy (a manuscript of sermons annotated in his own hand is preserved in the Biblioteca Antoniano in the monastery here). He was the closest companion of St Francis, and became one of the first Franciscan saints (and was made a Doctor of the Church in 1946). In 1257 he was declared a patron saint of Padua after it was believed that through his divine intervention the city had been saved from the tyranny of Ezzelino da Romano. Famous as a miracle-worker, he remains one of the best-loved saints in the country and millions of pilgrims visit his church every year.

From the north side of the piazza the massive **exterior** is a wonderful sight, somehow reminiscent of a fairy-tale palace, with its six spherical Byzantine-type domes and towers of different heights. Two of the slim bell-towers have the appearance of minarets, while another is much higher and highly decorated. One of the domes has a spire crowned with a golden angel blowing a trumpet. At the east end is the Gothic apse and the separate domed Chapel of the Relics, and the idiosyncratic façade combines several different styles. The exterior flank makes its greatest impact when approached either from Via del Santo or Via Cappelli, both narrow old streets lined with low houses over porticoes.

THE EQUESTRIAN STATUE OF GATTAMELATA

On an exceptionally high base, and silhouetted against the sky, is this famous statue, a masterpiece by Donatello dating from 1447–53, the first great bronze equestrian monument cast in Italy since the Roman era and the first to be exhibited in a civic piazza. Gattamelata (Erasmo da Nardo) was a celebrated Venetian *condottiere* and protector of the Venetian Republic. He died in 1443 and had a state funeral in Venice, but he was buried here in the Santo according to his wishes: it is thought to have been his widow who commissioned this work from the greatest sculptor of her time. The rider himself dominates the work, sitting—or almost standing—astride his charger (an extraordinary model in painted plaster for the head is preserved in the University museum here, but sadly is not usually on show). The horse was clearly influenced by Classical prototypes, including the ancient Horses of St Mark's and the bronze 4th-century BC horse's head owned by the Medici, which the young Donatello would certainly have seen in Florence (it is now in the Museo Archeologico there). The canon ball under the horse's front left hoof cleverly resolved the sculptor's problem of ensuring the equilibrium of the horse and rider. The monument was at once recognised as a masterpiece, and Alfonso V of Aragon, King of Naples, decided that he, too, wanted to be immortalised by Donatello, and asked the Florentine merchant Bartolomeo Serragli to try to arrange this. But Donatello only ever carried out the head of the horse (a remarkable work of art, carefully preserved in Naples in the Museo Archeologico: in fact Vasari noted that it was so well made that many people took it for a Classical work).

The stone reliefs on the base are good copies of the very damaged originals which the artist sculpted a few years earlier (they are now kept in the vestibule of the Biblioteca Antoniana). Unfortunately today the horse and rider are beset with pigeons and seem to be in need of restoration and protection. While at work on this monument, Donatello lived in the little house opposite the façade of the church (marked by a plaque).

INTERIOR OF THE SANTO
In the dark interior of the Santo, the chapel to which all visitors are first drawn, also because it is always brightly lit, is that in the left transept which is the **Cappella di Sant'Antonio (A)** with the greatly revered tomb of St Anthony. The green marble sarcophagus is touched every day by hundreds of devout worshippers, many of whom leave ex-votos, wax candles, or messages for the saint. From the 13th century onwards, indulgences were granted by the pope to pilgrims who visited the tomb.

When it was decided to reconstruct the chapel in the late 15th/early 16th century, the classical design is presumed to have been drawn up by Tullio Lombardo, with exquisite sculptural details. It seems that his pupil Giovanni Minello directed the work, and his son Antonio was also involved. It is one of the most beautiful works of the Italian Renaissance, perfectly preserved. It has blind arcades on all four sides, and more very delicate carving with busts in roundels and a carved architrave. The monumental entrance screen, supported on four lovely marble pillars and two exquisitely carved pilasters, was added by Giovanni Maria Falconetto in 1532. It also has beautiful marble details and delicate carving, and high up in niches are five statues of the patron saints of Padua, including St Justina on the left by Antonio Minello, and others made earlier by Buora and Minello. Falconetto also supplied the rich stucco vault inspired by the Domus Aurea in Rome, with the help of Tiziano Minio, Silvio Cosini and Danese Cattaneo.

What most claims the attention, however, are the nine large sculptured panels at eye level around the walls: they were presumably designed as a set by Tullio Lombardo, but were in the end carved by different hands (and over several decades, from 1500 to 1577). Each panel has life-size figures in both high and low relief, commemorating miracles of St Anthony in front of an architectural perspective in different marble. They are framed by blind arcades. The panels by the Lombardo brothers incorporate wonderful classically-inspired figures. The scenes are as follows:

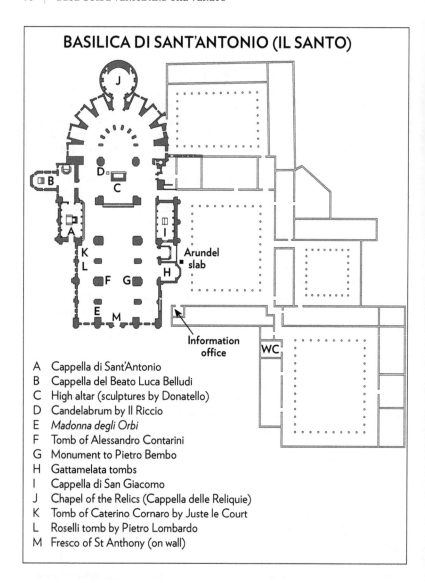

BASILICA DI SANT'ANTONIO (IL SANTO)

A Cappella di Sant'Antonio
B Cappella del Beato Luca Belludi
C High altar (sculptures by Donatello)
D Candelabrum by Il Riccio
E *Madonna degli Orbi*
F Tomb of Alessandro Contarini
G Monument to Pietro Bembo
H Gattamelata tombs
I Cappella di San Giacomo
J Chapel of the Relics (Cappella delle Reliquie)
K Tomb of Caterino Cornaro by Juste le Court
L Roselli tomb by Pietro Lombardo
M Fresco of St Anthony (on wall)

1. *St Anthony Kneeling to Receive the Franciscan Habit,* by Antonio Minello (1517).
2. *The Jealous Husband Prevented from Killing his Beautiful Wife Suspected of Adultery,* by Giovanni Rubino (1524) and completed after his death by Silvio Cosini in 1536.
3. *The Young Boy Brought back to Life,* a dramatic scene by Danese Cattaneo and Girolamo Campagna (1571–7). The boy's parents, shown kneeling in the background, had been accused of murdering him because his body had

been found in their garden. But the boy is about to reveal the name of his assassin, shown on the extreme right, wringing his hands in despair. In the background is Padua's Palazzo della Ragione.

4. *The Virgin Carilla Brought back to Life*. Having drowned, she is shown coming back to life in a dramatic scene while her mother, a striking-looking old lady, looks on. It is signed by Jacopo Sansovino (1540–50), 'Florentine sculptor and architect', and is in a style quite different from the other panels by the sculptors from the Veneto. The Basilica del Santo is shown in the background.

5. *Parrasio Brought back to Life*, by Antonio Minello (1528), finished by Jacopo Sansovino in 1532. Parrasio was St Anthony's nephew and had been drowned.

6. *The Heart of the Dead Miser Found in his Strong Box instead of in his Body* (representing a clear statement against usury), by Tullio Lombardo, dated by him 1525.

7. *The Irascible Youth's Severed Leg Restored to Him* (after confessing to the saint, he had amputated it in repentance, and here the saint is shown in person as he reattaches it), also by Tullio Lombardo. This is one of the most classical of the reliefs, with the figure of the woman, probably the boy's mother, tearing her hair, and the splendid nude body of the boy.

8. *The Glass Dropped by the Unbeliever Adelardino Remains Unbroken*, begun by Giovanni Maria Mosca and finished after 1529 by Paolo Stella. This was a miracle performed posthumously by St Anthony so he is not present: but Adelardino (in armour) has just dropped the glass and his companions are crowding round to see if it is still intact.

9. *The Newborn Babe Identifying his True Mother, Accused of Adultery by her Husband*, by Antonio Lombardo. This classical relief, the first to be completed, clearly influenced work on all the others.

The altar in front of the saint's tomb has eleven bronze statues by Tiziano Aspetti added at the end of the 16th century.

A door leads into a dark chapel off which is the **Cappella del Beato Luca Belludi (B)**, St Anthony's companion, who is buried here. It is decorated with early frescoes dating from 1382 by Giusto de' Menabuoi relating the story of this little-known Franciscan's life. It includes a scene of Padua itself enclosed in its walls.

THE SANCTUARY

Donatello produced the wonderful bronze statues and reliefs for the **high altar (C)** in 1446–49 but it has suffered many vicissitudes and its present reconstruction dates from 1895 (art historians still discuss just how Donatello intended to arrange the sculptures and the appearance of the original altar's architectural framework). Today the sanctuary is dark and the works are very difficult to see clearly unless you ask one of the uniformed custodians to unlock the gates at a time when Mass is not being held (the best time is often in the middle of the day).

Above twelve charming reliefs of angel musicians (only four of which are by Donatello's own hand) on either side of Christ as the Man of Sorrows, are four remarkable gilded bronze reliefs set in to the altar (two on the front and two on the back) which constitute some of Donatello's greatest works, the superb details in low relief highlighted in gold and silver leaf. They depict four of St Anthony's miracles: three of them later illustrated in marble in the Chapel of St Anthony (the Miser's Heart, the Irascible Boy, and the New-born Babe; *see above*), but the fourth, that of the mule which belonged to a non-believer kneeling before the Host, is the only depiction of this particularly charming miracle in the Santo and symbolises the Saint's crusade against heresy.

At the ends are the symbols of the Evangelists. The altar is crowned with seven superb bronze statues: in the centre is the Madonna rising from her throne, a disturbing figure in an unusual pose, holding the Christ Child in front of her; she is flanked by the four patron saints of Padua (Prosdocimus, considered Padua's first bishop; Justina and Daniel, two Paduans who were martyred for their faith; and Anthony) together with St Francis and the other great Franciscan, St Louis of Toulouse. It is clear that they were all designed to be seen from below. The bronze Crucifix above, another masterpiece by Donatello, is his first documented work here but was not made for the altar; it was probably intended for a more conspicuous position in the nave. On the back of the altar is a large stone relief of the *Entombment*, perhaps by an assistant of Donatello.

On the left of the altar is another bronze masterpiece: a **paschal candelabrum (D)** on a marble pedestal, the most important work of Il Riccio (1515), who also carried out two of the twelve exquisite small bronze reliefs with Old Testament scenes on the wall of the choir here. The others had been made some 20 years earlier by Riccio's master, Bartolomeo Bellano, who may have worked in Donatello's workshop.

THE NAVE

The basilica has been used over the centuries as the burial place of Padua's most eminent citizens. On the first north pillar there is a large greatly revered painting of the *Madonna degli Orbi* **(E)**, in gilded robes, by Stefano da Ferrara (early 15th century), which faces the tomb by Il Riccio of Antonio Trombetta (d. 1518), his erudition indicated by the piles of books on either side of his bronze bust. Against the second north pillar is the **tomb of Alessandro Contarini** (F), a Venetian general who died in 1553, by Sanmicheli with a bust by Danese Cattaneo and statues by Vittoria. The design of the **monument to Cardinal Pietro Bembo**, who died just a few years earlier, opposite **(G)**, is quite different: its simple classical lines have been attributed to Palladio. The bust is by Sansovino's gifted pupil Danese Cattaneo. This famous erudite Venetian humanist, who was a great scholar of Greek philosophy, spent the middle years of his life in Rome as secretary to Pope Leo X (where he befriended Raphael). From 1521 he came to live in Padua where he remained until 1539 when he was called back to Rome having finally achieved the status of cardinal. He died in Rome in 1547 and is buried there in Santa Maria sopra Minerva.

The first south chapel (reserved for prayer) has, on the left wall, the **tomb of Gattamelata (H)**, decorated with his coat of arms, and (right wall) that of his son. They were erected in 1458 by order of Gattamelata's widow.

In the south transept, opposite the Cappella di Sant'Antonio, is the wonderful **Cappella di San Giacomo** (or San Felice) **(I)**, designed in 1372–77 by Andriolo and Giovanni de Santi, with red pillars forming a portico at the entrance. At the same time it was entirely frescoed by Altichiero with stories from the life of St James of Compostela and a huge scene of the Crucifixion.

At the east end of the church there is an ambulatory with radiating chapels: the one in the centre, the **Cappella delle Reliquie (J)** (Chapel of the Relics) houses the rich treasury with more than a hundred reliquaries.

In the north aisle is the Baroque **tomb of General Caterino Cornaro**, by Juste le Court (1674) **(K)**, next to a beautiful **monument by Pietro Lombardo (L)** commemorating Antonio Roselli, who died in 1466. Above the main portal is a **fresco of St Anthony** preaching from a walnut tree by Pietro Annigoni (1985) **(M)**.

THE MONASTERY OF THE SANTO

Adjoining the basilica is the huge Franciscan monastery with no fewer than four handsome Gothic cloisters. The **Museo Antoniano** (*well signposted; open every day, 9–1 & 2–6*) is arranged on two levels in one large modernised room. On the lower level are four late 14th-century statues by Rainaldino di Pietro di Francia (the fifth, dating from 1503, is by Giovanni Minello). Also here are vestments, tapestries and inlaid wood panels from the sacristy. The paintings include works attributed to Giambattista Tiepolo and Giovanni Battista Piazzetta. On the upper level is the *navicella*, an elaborate incense burner in the form of a ship made around 1500 in Nuremberg. A reconstructed altar from the basilica has numerous bronze statuettes: the ones below date from the late 16th century and are by Girolamo Campagna, while those above by Bernardo Falcone date from a century later. From here a lunette painted by Mantegna (originally over the door of the Santo) is well seen.

In the **first cloister**, with a huge magnolia tree (close to the information office), is a modest slab which marks the burial-place of the entrails of Thomas Howard (1586–1646), Earl of Surrey and Arundel, English statesman and connoisseur. Inigo Jones had accompanied the Earl and Countess of Arundel on their Grand Tour in 1612–15, and the Earl is remembered for his interest in Classical sculpture: his collection known as the 'Arundel Marbles' was left by his grandson to the Ashmolean Museum in Oxford. The Biblioteca Antoniana (*open to scholars*) contains many MSS and incunabula.

THE SCUOLA DEL SANTO AND THE ORATORIO DI SAN GIORGIO

Map Padua 8. Open 9–12.30 & 2.30–5 (inclusive ticket).

In Piazza del Santo outside the basilica are the two little brick façades of the Scuola del Santo and the Oratorio di San Giorgio. The Oratorio, which dates from 1377–84, is entirely frescoed by Altichiero di Zevio, who was born in Verona but was active in Padua in the 1380s and was one of the most creative interpreters of Giotto's art. The large colourful scenes illustrate the life of Christ (on the entrance wall), with a Coronation of the Virgin above the Crucifixion (on the opposite wall). The side walls have scenes from the lives of the saints: St George is shown with the Dragon but also in much less well-known episodes of his life such as when he made a pagan temple collapse, and his death by decapitation. Harrowing scenes of martyrdom follow St Catherine and St Lucy's confessions of their Christian faith.

The **Scuola**, built in 1427–31 (with an upper story of 1504) is approached by a pretty flight of stairs installed in the early 18th century. The paintings of the miracles of St Anthony were carried out in 1511 by Venetian artists including Bartolomeo and Benedetto Montagna and Domenico Campagnola. The young Titian painted three of the scenes, and his elder brother Francesco Vecellio also worked here.

Set back from the piazza here, behind a very elaborate lamp post, can be seen the unusual façade of a building built in 1870–80 by Camillo Boito, now used for exhibitions. Its dome copies those of the Santo, although it is much flatter.

LOGGIA E ODEO CORNARO
Entrance at no. 37 of the arcaded Via Cesarotti (map Padua 6), which leads out of the north side of Piazza del Santo. Visits every half hour Tues–Fri 10–1, Sat and Sun also 3 or 4–6 or 7.

The classical-style **Loggia** was built in 1524 by Giovanni Maria Falconetto, his first work, for Alvise Cornaro, a cultivated Venetian who came to live in Padua and surrounded himself here with artists and intellectuals (Falconetto himself was Cornaro's guest for over 20 years). The Loggia was designed as a stage for theatrical representations (many of them with the participation of Angelo Beolco, called Ruzante) and the vault is decorated with stuccoes and mythological scenes. The delightful little **Odeo**, on the right of the lawn, is a remarkable centrally planned building, built a few years later as the seat of a literary society which Cornaro had founded. Derived from Classical models, it was also designed by Falconetto. It is interesting to note that Palladio was a frequent guest of Cornaro in 1538–40. The façade, by Tiziano Minio, has two stucco reliefs of allegories of Time (representing Apollo as the Sun and Diana as the Moon, copied from antique Roman reliefs). The tiny entrance admits to a charming central room with its umbrella vault covered with lovely grotesques on a white ground, inspired by similar decorations in the Vatican. The little side rooms have landscapes by Lambert Sustris and stuccoes by Tiziano Minio, including one room entirely decorated with white stuccoes of a triumphal procession. Here Cornaro and his erudite friends would meet to converse and listen to music.

PRATO DELLA VALLE, SANTA GIUSTINA & THE ORTO BOTANICO

From Piazza del Santo, Via Beato Luca Belludi leads past an interesting Art Nouveau house (no. 3) to the **Prato della Valle** (*map Padua 8*), the largest 'piazza' in Italy, surrounded by a miscellany of arcaded buildings. This huge area was used from Roman times for public spectacles and fairs (a large market is still held here on Saturdays) but by the 18th century it had become an unhealthy, marsh and so the land was reclaimed and laid out by Domenico Cerato in 1775 under the inspiration of Andrea Memmo, a distinguished Venetian who took up public office in Padua in the same year. He gave his name to the central Isola Memmia, which is approached by four bridges decorated with fountains, and encircled by a canal bordered by 18th-century statues of famous citizens (including Memmo himself), as well as professors and students of the University.

On the west side of the Prato is the **Loggia Amulea**, built in 1861 in the Venetian style with two Gothic loggias in brick and marble, with statues of Giotto and Dante by Vincenzo Vela. On the south side of the square is the monumental entrance to the former Foro Boario, now used as a car park and stadium. On the north side of the Prato, Palazzo degli Angeli houses the **Museo del Precinema** (*map Padua 8; open 10–4 except Tues*), which illustrates the history of the magic lantern shows which predated the cinema. It also has a collection of stereographs.

THE BASILICA OF SANTA GIUSTINA
Map Padua 8. Open 8–12 & 3–5 (8pm in summer)
This Benedictine church was designed by Il Riccio in 1502 but modified by its builder Andrea Moroni, with eight cupolas, four of which are invisible in the interior. It was built to protect the relics of two of Padua's patron saints, St Prosdocimus and St Justina.

The huge interior was provided with many works of art in the 17th century, including, in the **south aisle,** altarpieces by Pietro Liberi (second chapel), Johann Carl Loth (third chapel), and Luca Giordano (fourth chapel).

In the south transept is the so-called Arca di San Matteo, which has reliefs carved in Greek marble by Giovanni Francesco de Surdis in 1562. Behind it a door leads into a chapel with a cupola frescoed in the mid-18th century by Giacomo Ceruti above a well. In the niches are four terracotta statues by Francesco Segala (1565). Beneath the pavement can be seen a fragment of the original mosaic floor of the palaeochristian basilica. The altar beyond has a painting by Pietro Damini showing the finding of the well. A corridor, with two more terracotta statues by Segala and an unusual iron sarcophagus, leads down to the **Cappella di San Prosdocimo**, an oratory which retains its domed cruciform architecture dating from as early as 520 but which was decorated in 1565 when the effigy of the saint was carved. The only architectural element which survives from the 6th century is the very rare iconostasis with delicate columns and an inscription. Above the effigy, the roundel with a relief of the saint also dates from this time. On the wall outside the oratory are exhibited two plutei decorated with birds, and a tympanum from the door of the ancient building: the inscription on the latter records the date that the oratory was built. The interior used to be covered with very fine mosaics (destroyed in an earthquake of 1117), and a fragment of the pavement can be seen through an adjacent glass door.

In the **sanctuary** of the main church, the very fine choir stalls were carved in the 16th century and the high altarpiece of the *Martyrdom of St Justina* was painted by Veronese in 1575 (but these are all difficult to see from afar).

In the **north transept** is the marble sarcophagus supposed to be that of St Luke the Evangelist (forming a partner to that of St Matthew in the south transept). It was decorated with alabaster reliefs in 1313. In the **north aisle** are altarpieces by Luca Giordano (fourth altar) and Sebastiano Ricci (second altar).

ORTO BOTANICO
Map Padua 8. Open April–Oct daily 9–7: winter 9–3 except holidays; labelled also for the visually impaired.

This is the oldest botanic garden in Europe, founded in 1545. It is beautifully tended and all the plants are well labelled. It retains its original form and structure with a charming circular walled garden, entered through four symmetrical gates. The geometrical beds are protected by low iron fences, and there are a number of ponds and fountains. The various sections include medicinal and aquatic plants, rare species from northern Italy, flora from the Euganean Hills, and poisonous plants. Also here are a tamarisk tree, a ginkgo tree of 1750, a mimosa tree and an ancient magnolia dating from the mid-18th century. But the oldest plant of all is a palm tree dating from 1585 and known as 'Goethe's palm' (since he described it when he visited the garden in 1786). It survives here, now some 11 metres tall, in a little greenhouse. Outside the walled garden are interesting 19th-century hothouses, where succulents and carnivorous plants are kept, opposite which is a row of the plants first introduced into Italy in this garden, including the lilac, first cultivated in 1565, the sunflower in 1568, and the potato in 1590. There is also a greenhouse for orchids. Trees in the arboretum include swamp cypresses, magnolias, Chinese palm trees, cedars, pines, a plane tree dating from 1680, and ilexes.

CAFFÈ PEDROCCHI

The centre of city life, which gravitates around the university, is Via VIII Febbraio (*map Padua 6*), where there is a female bronze statue by Emilio Greco (1973).

Map Padua 4. Open 9.30–12.30 & 3.30–6 except Mon. The upper floor and museum are entered from the Doric loggia on the right in the piazzetta.

This historic café is one of the most celebrated in Italy and its spacious interior is still much frequented by Paduans and visitors. It is named after its founder, Antonio Pedrocchi, and was built on this triangular site in 1831–7 by Giuseppe Jappelli in an eclectic style: there are two protruding neoclassical Doric loggias on either side of a façade with an upper portico with Corinthian columns, and a Gothic-revival wing in a totally different style. It is the Venetian architect's most famous work. The lions (irresistible to children) are copies of those at the foot of the Campidoglio in Rome. In 1891 Pedrocchi's adopted son left the building to the city of Padua on condition that it would remain a café. Inside, the large main room on the ground floor is decorated in white and yellow, and the two smaller drawing rooms in red and green. All are prettily furnished in period style. It became famous soon after it was opened as a meeting place for intellectuals and used to be kept open 24 hours a day.

UPPER FLOOR AND MUSEO DEL RISORGIMENTO E DELL'ETÀ CONTEMPORANEA

The upper floor was added in 1842. A grand staircase, with a stuccoed apse decorated with the dancing Muses, leads up to a series of living rooms and meeting rooms decorated in styles that evoke the great civilisations of the past and which retain their original early 19th-century decorations and creaking wooden floors. Large windows give access to attractive terraces. Beyond the Etruscan Room is the octagonal Greek Room. The charming circular Roman Room has four views of Rome by Ippolito Caffi. There is also a Herculaneum Room and an elaborate ballroom (Rossini Room) with a stage for the orchestra. Off it is the delightfully decorated little Moorish Room, with a *trompe l'oeil* painting of an Arab and good wood carvings. The Egyptian Room was inspired by Jappelli's friend Giovanni Battista Belzoni, actor, engineer and famous Egyptologist, and it is decorated with mock porphyry and painted stucco statues. There is also a Gothic Room (with paintings on glass) and a Renaissance Room.

The **museum**, which documents the history of the Risorgimento and also the later history of Italy up to the end of the Second World War, occupies the rest of the upper floor. This is particularly appropriate since it was here that a revolt against the Austrians was planned in 1848. It is very well displayed and extremely interesting, with posters, uniforms, arms and mementoes (handlists in English are provided). The first room is dedicated to the period from the fall of the Venetian Republic in 1797 up to 1847. The next rooms document the insurrection against Austrian rule in 1848 and 1849, and the period of the Risorgimento from 1850 to 1866. Another room has material relating to the period of Italian Unity. The last three rooms have an excellent display illustrating the First World War, and then the period of Fascism up until the Second World War, and the aftermath of the War. There is also an illustrated record of how, in 1948, the Italian Constitution was drawn up, which established the present Republican government of Italy.

THE UNIVERSITY

Map Padua 6. Open Mon–Sat for guided tours, also in English, of around 30mins, at various times of the day which alter according to the season. See unipd.it/visite-guidate-palazzo-bo or T: 049 827 3047.

The University of Padua, founded around 1222, is the second oldest university in Italy (after Bologna). It was nicknamed 'Il Bo' (*bue*, or ox) from the sign of an inn, the most famous in the city, which used to stand on this site. Renowned as a medical school, it flourished in the 15th and 16th centuries, when it was the only university in the Venetian Republic.

The older façade dates from 1757 and the tower from 1572; the adjoining building to the right (with the entrance) was reconstructed in 1938–9. The dignified courtyard (1552) is by Andrea Moroni. In the old courtyard, at the foot of the stairs, is a statue of Elena Cornaro Piscopia (1646–84), who was the first woman to take a doctor's degree, in philosophy. It is by a little-known sculptor from Bassano del Grappa called Bernardo Tabacco, who was Elena's contemporary. From the upper loggia the Aula Magna is reached, covered with the coats of arms of rectors and 19th-century frescoes. Off it, in a room decorated with forty portrait frescoes of famous foreign students, Galileo's wooden *cattedra* is preserved. This great teaching desk is supposed to have been made as a sign of affection by his pupils so that they could see him better: the great scientist taught physics at the University from 1592–1610, a period he looked back on as the best of his life.

On the other side of the courtyard a door leads into a small museum related to the medical school of Anatomy, off which is the oldest anatomical theatre in Europe (1594). It was built by the surgeon Fabricius, master of William Harvey (who discovered blood circulation), who took his degree here in 1602. Founder of the Royal College of Surgeons Thomas Linacre (1492) and the future physician to Queen Elizabeth I John Caius (1539) also qualified here as doctors, and the anatomist Vesalius (1540) and Fallopius (1561, who lends his name to the fallopian tube) were among the famous medical professors (Fallopius died in 1562 and is buried in the Magnolia Cloister of the Santo). The theatre can unfortunately only be visited from below (where the dissecting table used to be); the wooden galleries above could accommodate (standing) some 250 students. It was in use up until 1874.

Opposite the University is the entrance to the Municipio (Town Hall), with a façade dating from 1930. Beyond the courtyard are buildings (and a tower) which were part of the 13th-century Palazzo del Podestà, and the 16th-century Palazzo Moroni.

PALAZZO DELLA RAGIONE & THE MARKET PLACES

PALAZZO DELLA RAGIONE

Map Padua 6. Open 9–6 or 7 except Mon. Excavations beneath the building carried out in 1992 including Roman and medieval remains can be visited by appointment (contact www.arcadia-web.it). An impressive flight of steps leads up to one of the entrances, but this is used only when exhibitions are in progress: the usual entrance is from the outside staircase off Piazza delle Erbe.

The immense Palazzo della Ragione, the former Palais de Justice, stands at the commercial and administrative heart of the old city, its double porticoes overlooking both market places in Piazza delle Erbe and Piazza della Frutta. It is one of the most extraordinary buildings in Italy, built by Fra' Giovanni degli Eremitani in 1306–8, although the huge roof had to be reconstructed in 1756 after storm damage. The food shops beneath the vaulted lower arcades on both sides of the building are an extension of the busy fruit and vegetable markets held outside on weekday mornings in the two piazze: Paduans still come here to do their shopping. The shop fronts, with their marble shelves and old signs, have been well preserved, and are mostly occupied by butchers and grocery shops.

The interior of the Palazzo della Ragione is if anything even more impressive: it is certainly one of the largest interior spaces in all Italy, nearly 80m long and 26m high, and quite takes your breath away. Its splendid proportions can only be fully appreciated when exhibitions are not in progress. It contains just three objects: a block of stone which once served as a stool of repentance for debtors (a reminder that this hall was built as a hall of Justice), a freely suspended pendulum which reproduces Jean Foucault's experiment in 1851 by which he proved that the earth rotates, and a giant wooden horse, which calls to mind the Trojan horse but is in fact a copy of Donatello's *Gattamelata* (*see p. 74*), made for a fête in 1466.

In 1313 Giotto and his assistants were called in to decorate the walls. Those frescoes where destroyed in a fire in 1420 and it fell to the far less well-known painters Nicolò Miretto and Stefano da Ferrara to repaint them: it is not known how closely they followed the original scheme. However, they are very well preserved and extremely interesting. The 333 panels of religious and astrological subjects are divided according to the months of the year: each represented by nine scenes in three tiers, with an allegory of the month together with its sign of the zodiac, planet and constellation, as well as the labours of the month and astrological illustrations. A touch screen, also in English, supplies details of the frescoes.

A door leads out to the long loggia (its vault charmingly painted with pomegranates) which overlooks the lovely Piazza delle Erbe.

THE MARKET PLACES

The two market places, Piazza della Frutta and Piazza delle Erbe, both have slightly raised pavements in the centre. In the former is a particularly good view of Palazzo della Ragione and the tall medieval tower known as Torre degli Anziani, and in the latter is a pretty fountain and at a corner two good Byzantine capitals which belong to the Palazzo del Consiglio (1283).

Close by, to the west, is a third picturesque market place, **Piazza dei Signori**, which is filled with a general market in the mornings on its raised pavement. Approached by a broad flight of steps is the **Loggia della Gran Guardia**, with arcades designed by Annibale Maggi in 1496 (it was completed in 1523). The **Palazzo del Capitanio**, built in the first years of the 17th century, has a tower adapted in 1532 by Giovanni Maria Falconetto to accommodate an astronomical clock dating from 1344 (the oldest in Italy). The palace (*usually open only on Wed, 10–12.30, or by appointment, T: 049 876382*) is on the site of the Carraresi castle: its 14th-century portico can be seen at no. 11 Via Accademia, now the seat of the Accademia Patavina di Scienze, Lettere ed Arti, which incorporates a chapel with frescoes of Old Testament scenes by Guariento dating from around 1360.

An archway leads beneath the clock tower into the Corte (or Piazza) del Capitaniato (*map Padua 3*), a pleasant square with ancient acacias. Here, behind the monument to the Paduan-born playwright and actor Ruzante (Angelo Beolco), the **Liviano** houses the arts faculty of the University, built in 1939 by Giò Ponti, with an entrance hall frescoed by Massimo Campigli. The building incorporates the Sala dei Giganti (*approached from the Corte Arco Valaresso, but not open regularly to the public, though it is sometimes used for concerts; for information, T: 049 827 3047*), with frescoes of famous men by Domenico Campagnola and Gualtiero and Stefano dell'Arzere (1539). These were painted over earlier 14th-century frescoes, including a fragment attributed to Altichiero showing Petrarch reading in his study, possibly drawn from life (Petrarch spent the last years of his life near Padua at Arquà).

THE DUOMO, BAPTISTERY & MUSEO DIOCESANO

In Piazza del Duomo (*map Padua 5*) is the palace which used to house the Monte di Pietà pawnbroker's (13th–14th century), remodelled with a portico by Giovanni Maria Falconetto in 1530. Now owned by a bank, it is used for exhibitions.

The interior of the **Duomo** (*closed 12–3.30*) dates from a reconstruction in 1552 by Andrea da Valle and Agostino Righetti to a design, much altered, of Michelangelo, and the chapels have paintings dating from that time or later. The sanctuary was redesigned (unfortunately rather pretentiously) by Giuliano Vangi in 1997.

The Baptistery (*open every day 10–6*) was built at the end of the 12th century and in 1378 the interior was entirely covered with wonderful frescoes by Giusto de' Menabuoi. They are his best work and one of the most interesting medieval fresco cycles in all Italy. In the dome is Christ Pantocrator surrounded by a host of angels and the Blessed; in the drum, scenes from Genesis; in the pendentives, the Evangelists; and on the walls, scenes from the lives of Christ and St John the Baptist. In the apse are illustrations from the Apocalypse, including the very memorable beast, just as described in Revelation 13: 'I saw a beast rise up out of the sea, having seven heads and ten horns, and upon his horns ten crowns, and upon his heads the name of blasphemy. And the beast which I saw was like unto a leopard, and his feet were as the feet of a bear, and his mouth as the mouth of a lion…and I saw one of his heads as it were wounded to death…'. The crowns in Giusto's interpretation are mitres. On the altar is a polyptych, also by Giusto.

The **Museo Diocesano** (*open 9–6 except Mon; summer opening hours subject to change; T: 049 8761924; combined ticket with the Baptistery*) is housed in the spacious Bishop's Palace (Vescovado). On the first floor is a hall with manuscripts and incunabula including many 15th-century codexes. On the third floor is the huge Salone dei Vescovi with portraits of one hundred bishops of Padua by Bartolomeo Montagna (early 16th century). The chapel of Santa Maria degli Angeli was built in 1495 and the small triptych by Jacopo Parisati da Montagnana dates from the same time. Another chapel, symmetrically placed off the Salone, has unusual simple frescoed decoration carried out a few years later (and only recently discovered). The rooms in between display reliquaries, and a Pietà also by Jacopo Parisati; works by Nicoletto Semitecolo (late 14th century); and two beautiful panel paintings of the Madonna, one by Giusto de' Menabuoi and the other by Paolo Veneziano. Also here are an early 14th century Cross in rock crystal and silver and a 13th-century gospel cover in Limoges enamel. Another series of rooms display works from the 16th–19th centuries: artists include Francesco da Bassano, Giovanni Battista Tiepolo, and Tiziano Aspetti (two bronze panels). There is also a collection of vestments.

THE OTHER CHURCHES AND *SCUOLE*

TO SAN MICHELE

Via Memmo leads west out of Prato della Valle past the **Torresino** (*map Padua 7*), a very eccentric church with an orange Neoclassical façade, turreted campanile and castellated drum. There are several villas in the square here. Take the cobbled Via Torresino and then diverge right on the pretty Via della Paglia, with its miniature portico. In this street Palladio lived as a young man from 1508–23. At the end, across a canal behind a wall, are the conspicuous buildings of a medieval castle transformed into a prison in 1808 (and in use up until 1992). Just to the left is the **Oratorio di San Michele** (*map Padua 7; open Tues–Fri 10–1, Sat and Sun 3 or 4–6 or 7*), all that remains of the ancient church of San Michele (documented as early as 970). It has frescoes (detached) by Jacopo da Verona dated 1397 including, above the arch, a charming domestic *Annunciation* scene which occupies the entire wall since it consists of three distinct episodes: on the left is the Angel, and in the middle a maid at work in the Virgin's house and orchard (with a chicken pecking at the ground). On the right is the portly Virgin Annunciate with a dog beside her asleep in his basket on the parquet floor, and a straw-seated chair (reminiscent of those painted by Van Gogh), and linen hanging up to dry, while the dove of the Holy Spirit flies in at the door.

The **Museo La Specola** (*map Padua 5; admission only by appointment at the Oratorio di San Michele for guided visits at weekends at 4 in Oct–April or at 6 in summer*). The very high tower (part of the castle which became a prison, *see above*) dominates this part of the town, in front of the Oratorio di San Michele. It was transformed into an observatory in the 18th century and has a small museum of astronomical instruments made in Padua in the 18th and 19th centuries. The view is remarkable.

SANTA MARIA DEI SERVI

This church in Via Roma (*map Padua 6*) has a long portico along its north flank. In the chapel to the left of the choir a wood Crucifix (varnished to look like bronze) was convincingly attributed to Donatello a few years ago and many scholars now believe it could well be by the great sculptor's hand. The church also contains, on the Baroque altar of the Madonna dell'Addolorata by Giovanni Bonazza, a statue of a *Madonna and Child* dating from around 1400 by Rainaldino di Francia.

SCUOLA DI SAN ROCCO

Map Padua 4. Open 9.30–12.30 & 3.30–7 except Mon.
Reached from one of the narrow lanes which lead north out of Piazza della Frutta, this is an attractive Renaissance building frescoed in 1525 with scenes illustrating the life of St Roch. Those on the right wall (some of them detached) are attributed to Domenico Campagnola and Girolamo Tessari. The scenes of later episodes in the saint's life on the left wall are by Gualtiero, born in Padua, and include a townscape of Padua, and St Roch dying in prison in the company of a dog. The last scene of his

funeral is attributed to Stefano dell'Arzere and is one of the most interesting. The 17th-century altarpiece is by Alessandro Maganza.

TO SAN FRANCESCO

In a little garden at the beginning of the pretty Via di San Francesco, lined on both sides by porticoes, is the so-called **Tomba di Antenore** (*map Padua 6*), the 'Tomb of Antenor', the Trojan prince whom Livy credits with the founding of Padua. When the skeleton of a large man was unearthed in the 13th century, it was supposed to be that of Antenor and so this marble sarcophagus was supplied for it and it was set up on short columns here. Beside it is another sarcophagus dating from 1309. Palazzo Zabarella in this street also dates from the 13th century, and is now used for exhibitions.

The church of **San Francesco** (*map Padua 6; closed 12–4*) was begun in 1416 and enlarged in the following century when the second south chapel frescoes by Girolamo dal Santo were painted. Two very fine large bronze reliefs from the funerary monument of the natural philosopher Pietro Roccabonella can be seen above the door into the sacristy and above the door in the south transept. They are by the great bronze-worker Il Riccio, who carried out most of his works in Padua, and his master Bartolomeo Bellano, probably one of Donatello's assistants. The Baroque altar in the south transept was designed by Giuseppe Sardi.

The parallel Via Cesare Battisti, to the north, is another pretty road with porticoes, typical of the old town.

VIA ALTINATE

The **Porta Altinate** (*map Padua 4*) is a gateway of the 13th-century town wall. The later walls, built by the Venetians in 1513–44, with a circumference of some 11km, survive and the two gates to the west, the **Porta Savonarola** and the **Porta San Giovanni**, were built by Giovanni Maria Falconetto, their design derived from ancient Roman architecture. Palazzo Melandri, at no. 18 Via Altinate, has a beautiful four-light window. **San Gaetano** was built in 1586 by Vincenzo Scamozzi. **Santa Sofia** (*beyond map Padua 4*), founded in the 9th century, is the oldest church in Padua. It was rebuilt in the 11th-12th century in a style which recalls earlier churches of the Exarchate of Ravenna. The apse is particularly remarkable.

THE SCUOLA DEL CARMINE

In an unattractive modern area across the river towards the railway station is the church of the Carmine (*map Padua 2–4*), next to which is the Scuola del Carmine (*only open Tues and Thur 10–6*). It dates from 1377 but has 16th-century frescoes of the life of the Virgin by Giulio and Domenico Campagnola and Stefano dell'Arzere, notably the *Meeting of St Anne and St Joachim*.

THE COMMONWEALTH WAR CEMETERY

West of the centre is a small Commonwealth war cemetery with over 500 graves. (*For details see www.cwgc.org. To get there, leave by Porta Savonarola and continue straight along Via Vicenza and Via Chiesanuova. Turn right up Via della Biscia.*)

PADUA PRACTICAL TIPS

INFORMATION OFFICES

IAT offices at the railway station and at Caffé Pedrocchi (*www.turismopadova.it*).

The **Padova Card** is a combined ticket (available valid for 48hrs or 72hrs) which gives free entrance to the main museums and monuments of Padua, plus free travel on the tram and the city buses. It can be purchased from the Information Office at the railway station or at the Musei Civici Eremitani.

GETTING AROUND

A **tramline** with services every few minutes traverses the city north–south from the railway station, with convenient stops at Eremitani (for the Scrovegni Chapel), Ponti Romani (for Palazzo della Ragione, market places and Caffè Pedrocchi), Santo and Prato della Valle.

By train: Padua is well connected by rail. Direct services go to Venice, Vicenza, Rovigo, Monselice, Bassano del Grappa and Castelfranco.

By bus: Services throughtout the province are run by SITA (*T: 049 8206844*). ACTV bus no. 53 links Padua to Venice via the towns of the Brenta.

By boat: For boat trips on the Brenta Canal, see p. 63.

WHERE TO STAY

€€€ **Donatello.** A luxurious hotel overlooking the Santo; with a restaurant with a pleasant summer terrace. *Via del Santo 102, T: 049 875 0634, hoteldonatello.net. Map Padua 6.*

€€ **Majestic Toscanelli.** An old-established hotel family run in a little square near Piazza delle Erbe, with 32 simply furnished rooms (and garage). *Via dell'Arco 2, T: 049 663244, toscanelli.com. Map Padua 6.*

€ **Al Santo.** In one of Padua's loveliest old arcaded streets leading to the Santo. Very simple, with parquet floors, but reasonably priced. Restaurant. *Via del Santo 147, 049 8752131, alsanto.it. Map Padua 6.*

WHERE TO EAT

€€ **Ai Porteghi.** A traditional *trattoria* which serves Paduan specialities. Closed Sun, midday Mon. *Via Cesare Battisti 105, T: 049 660746, trattoriaaiporteghi.com. Map Padua 6.*

€€ **Antico Brolo.** A small, old-established restaurant in a historic building in the city centre. Also a pizzeria. Tables in the garden in summer (enclosed in winter). Closed midday Mon. *Corso Milano 22, T: 049 664555, www.anticobrolo.it. Map Padua 3.*

€€ **Belle Parti.** Near Piazza dei Signori, serving innovative cuisine. Closed Sun. *Via Belle Parti 11, T: 049 875 1822, ristorantebelleparti.it. Map Padua 4.*

CAFÉS AND CAKE SHOPS

Pedrocchi (*see p. 82*) is one of the most famous cafés in all Italy. **Graziati**, Piazza dei Frutti 40 (*open every day;*

map Padua 4), has excellent snacks and is famous for its *millefoglie*. The **Lilium** pasticceria on Piazza del Santo (*corner of Via del Santo; map Padua 6*), with its old-fashioned interior, is good for chocolate and the Dolce di Sant'Antonio. Good snacks (and the *Dolce di Sant'Antonio; see below*) can be bought at the simple bakery in Via Cappelli just out of Piazza del Santo (*map Padua 6*).

MARKETS

Daily food markets open in the morning except Sun (and all day on Sat) in Piazza delle Erbe and Piazza della Frutta (which also has delicacies). Piazza dei Signori has a general market open in the mornings, and there is a large weekly market on Sat in Prato della Valle.

LOCAL SPECIALITIES

Dolce di Sant'Antonio is a delicious cake (or large bun) studded with candied fruits.

FESTIVALS AND EVENTS

Festival dei Solisti Veneti, Classical music concerts in Paduan churches, May–Sept. *Villeggiando*, concerts and theatre in villas around Padua, May–Sept. *Notturni d'Arte*, music and theatre in museums, May–Sept. *Teatro Estate*, theatre festival, Aug. *Stagione Concertistica*, classical music, Oct–March. *Rassegna del Jazz Italiano*, jazz festival, Nov–Dec. Festival of St Anthony on 13 June, and *Padova del Medioevo* on the first Sun in Oct, both with processions, pageantry, etc. University graduation ceremonies take place regularly, when the newly dubbed 'doctor', usually crowned with 'laurels', is fêted in the streets by an army of friends in fancy dress chanting '*Dottore, Dottore....*' and sometimes drenching him or her—and the onlookers—with water or worse.

The Euganean Hills

T he Euganean Hills (Colli Euganei; *map Veneto East A2*) are an unexpected sight: a small group of low humps rising abruptly from the plain southwest of Padua. Geologically speaking, they are lacoliths, formations that occur when magma forces its way to the surface through a double layer of rock, causing the upper layer to erupt as a hump-backed hill. Covered with chestnut woods, Colli Euganei are now protected as a regional park, and have pleasant paths for walking. The vineyards produce a good white wine. The hot thermal springs, rich in minerals, have been well-known since Roman times and the spa towns here are still much visited. Other highlights include the pretty little town where Petrarch spent the last years of his life, and the historic towns of Este and Montagnana. It was at Este that Shelley wrote his *Lines Written among the Euganean Hills*, about the healing power of nature and landscape:

Many a green isle needs must be
In the deep wide sea of Misery,
Or the mariner, worn and wan,
Never thus could voyage on...

THE SPA TOWNS

Abano Terme is the most famous spa in the Euganean Hills, and its numerous hotels are open in the season (March–Oct), with thermal pools offering mud therapy effective especially against rheumatism and arthritis. The town has some interesting early 19th-century buildings designed by the Venetian architect Giuseppe Jappelli (whose most famous work is the Caffè Pedrocchi in Padua). **Montegrotto Terme** has more parks and extensive remains of ancient Roman baths as well as a small Roman theatre. A less grand and rather old-fashioned spa is **Battaglia Terme**, with a park also laid out by Jappelli.

ABBAZIA DI PRAGLIA
This huge abbey (*shown by a monk every 30mins, summer Tues–Sun 3.30–5.30; winter 2.30–4.30*) is approached by a beautiful, tree-lined driveway. A Benedictine foundation of 1080, rebuilt in the 15th and 16th centuries, it is still active and the monks are renowned for their skill in restoring books. The church (Santa Maria

Assunta) was built between 1490 and 1548, probably to a design by the great Venetian sculptor and architect Tullio Lombardo; the Romanesque campanile is a remnant of the original building. The vaulted Latin-cross interior has 16th-century Venetian paintings, a 14th-century wooden crucifix over the high altar, and frescoes in the apse by Domenico Campagnola. The parts of the monastic buildings open to visitors include two very fine 15th-century cloisters and the large refectory with ceiling paintings by Giovanni Battista Zelotti, 18th-century carved woodwork and a *Crucifixion* frescoed by Bartolomeo Montagna (1490–1500).

VILLAS & GARDENS

In a wonderful position in the wooded hills above Luvigliano (*map Veneto East A2*), surrounded by vineyards and fields, is the Villa Olcese, known as the **Villa dei Vescovi** (*open Wed–Sun 10–sunset, villadeivescovi.it*). It was built in 1535–42 for the Bishop of Padua, Francesco Pisani, under the direction of Alvise Cornaro by Giovanni Maria Falconetto, and continued by Andrea da Valle in 1567. Both Giulio Romano and Vincenzo Scamozzi were involved in the project. On three sides it has open loggias overlooking the lovely landscape. It contains frescoes by the Netherlandish artist Lambert Sustris (1545), who also worked in Padua. The garden is being replanted.

In 1570 Andrea della Valle was also involved in the construction of the **Castello del Catajo** (*open Tues, Sun and holidays 2.30–6.30; summer 3–7, castellodelcatajo. it*), just north of Battaglia Terme off Via Maggiore. He built it for Pio Enea degli Obizzi, a captain of the Venetian army, and the contemporary frescoes by Giovanni Battista Zelotti on the first floor depict the exploits of members of the Obizzi family, including one who accompanied Richard I of England on the Crusades, and another who perhaps fought for Edward III at Neville's Cross. When the building was altered in the 17th century, part of the beautiful garden was created with numerous fountains.

At **Valsanzibio** (*map Veneto East A2*) is the **Villa Barbarigo**, built in the mid-17th century for the Venetian nobleman Zuane Francesco Barbarigo. Its lovely garden (*open March–Nov 10–1 & 2–sunset*) survives from that time, with numerous pools and fountains, as well as a box maze, and statues.

Further afield, at **Bagnoli di Sopra** (*map Veneto East B3*), monastic buildings were transformed in the 17th century by Baldassarre Longhena into the **Villa Widmann Borletti**, with a fine garden (*only open Thur 3–6*) decorated with statues by Antonio Bonazza (1742). Carlo Goldoni stayed here with Ludovico Widmann in the 1750s and put on several performances of his plays in the little theatre (the great playwright dedicated his *La Bottega del Caffè* to Ludovico).

At **San Pelagio/Due Carrare** (*map Veneto East B2*) the Villa Zaborra (really a castle) has an 'Air Museum' (Museo dell'Aria; *open March–Nov Wed and Thur 9–1, Fri and Sat also 2.30–6.30, Sun 10–7; in winter only Sun 10–5*). Here the famous eccentric poet and nationalist Gabriele d'Annunzio, who served as a daredevil pilot in the Italian air force and had urged his country to go to war with Austria, planned his flight to Vienna in 1918. This was followed by the Italian victory over Austria at Vittorio Veneto, and a year later by d'Annunzio's flight to Fiume, which he managed to seize for Italy. The history of these notorious exploits is illustrated, and the museum also provides a broad panorama of air 'transport' from the experiments of Leonardo da Vinci to the era of space travel.

ARQUÀ PETRARCA

This delightful little medieval *borgo* (*map Veneto East A2*), the 'soft quiet hamlet' of Byron's *Childe Harold* (Canto IV), is in a pretty position in the Euganean Hills, where numerous *giuggiole* trees grow. This ancient Asian plant, *ziziphus jujuba*, produces an orange fruit, more or less the size of an olive and rich in Vitamin C, which is harvested in early October (when a festival is celebrated here in its honour). In 1868 the village added the name of the poet Petrarch to its ancient name, since he lived here for the last four years of his life, and died here in 1374. Born in the Tuscan town of Arezzo, he spent the 1360s between Padua and Venice, and when appointed canon of Monselice was given a little house here which he restored (*it is at the top of the village and is usually open 9–12.30 and sometimes in the afternoon, but always closed on Mon*). It was altered in the 16th century, when some paintings were added with scenes from Petrarch's most famous works including the *Canzoniere*, probably the most imitated collection of love poems in Western literature. Petrarch was a great Humanist and his verse is an extremely rational and modern analysis of his sentiments and ideas. The visitors' book has Byron's signature: he came here in 1818 while staying in Este (*see below*). In the lower part of the village is the church, outside which is Petrarch's plain sarcophagus of red Verona marble, with an epitaph composed by himself: FRIGIDA FRANCISCI LAPIS HIC TEGIT OSSA PETRARCE; SUSCIPE VIRGO PARENS ANIMAM; SATE VIRGINE PARCE. FESSAQ IAM TERRIS CELI REQUIESCAT IN ARCE. ('This stone covers the cold bones of Francesco Petrarca; receive his spirit, O Virgin mother; O thou born of the Virgin, pardon him. Now weary of the earth, may he find repose in the citadel of Heaven.')

MONSELICE, ESTE & MONTAGNANA

Rising on the southeast slopes of the Colle Euganei, **Monselice** (*map Veneto East A2–A3*) was a Roman settlement, a Lombard *gastaldato* in 602, a free commune, a seigniory, and finally a Venetian dominion. Today it is an active industrial and agricultural centre. It takes its name (literally, 'mountain of flint') from the small mound of debris dug from the quarry that twice served to pave Piazza San Marco in Venice. The castle stands at the top of the hill, the town at the bottom, the monuments along a road and walkway that wind between the two along the slopes.

In the lower town, on the east side of Piazza Mazzini, is the medieval Torre Civica, with a fine loggia and crenellated parapet. From the square, Via del Santuario climbs past the 16th-century Monte di Pietà, with a small loggia, to the **Castello Cini** (*open April–Nov Tues–Sun, on the hour at 9, 10, and 11 and in the afternoon at 2, 3 and 4, or 3, 4 and 5, castellodimonselice.it*). It has an 11th- or 12th-century core, but was enlarged in subsequent centuries. The interior houses a collection of paintings, sculpture, weapons, Renaissance furniture, tapestries, and in the Sala del Camino Vecchio, a monumental fireplace shaped like a tower. An antiquarium has finds from the five Lombard tombs, dating from the mid-7th century, discovered on the hillside.

Continuing along Via del Santuario you soon come to the 16th- and 17th-century **Villa Nani-Mocenigo**, with a wall decorated with curious 18th-century statues of dwarves, which also line the spectacular terraced staircase. Just a little further on is the **Duomo Vecchio**, dedicated to St Justina, a Romanesque-Gothic church of 1256 with a 12th-century campanile and a three-part façade with a rose window, smaller mullioned windows, and a 15th-century porch. Within are frescoes and altarpieces by minor 15th-century Venetian painters. At the end of the avenue stands the **Villa Duodo**, by Vincenzo Scamozzi (1593), enlarged in the 18th century, when the façade and the monumental staircase to the formal garden were added. It now belongs to the University of Padua and can only be seen from the outside. Its grounds include the cypress-shaded Santuario delle Sette Chiese, entered from the 18th-century Piazzale della Rotonda, a scenic balcony behind the Duomo Vecchio. The sanctuary comprises six chapels designed by Scamozzi after 1605, containing paintings by Palma Giovane, and the church of San Giorgio, octagonal outside and elliptical within.

At the top of the hill stands the ruined **Rocca** (*open for guided visits only from April–Oct, ask at the Castello Cini*), a keep built by Ezzelino da Romano, tyrant of Padua, for the Emperor Frederick II in 1239 and enlarged by Padua's subsequent ruling family the Carraresi. Recently restored, it contains a little museum with finds from the site and a panoramic terrace. On the east slope of the hill is the old church of San Tommaso, which conserves some 13th-century frescoes.

ESTE

This little town, at the southern edge of the Colli Euganei (*map Veneto East A3*), was a centre of the ancient Veneti before it became the Roman Ateste. Later it was the stronghold of the Este family, who were afterwards dukes of Ferrara, and from 1405 Este was under Venetian dominion. The huge battlemented Carraresi castle dates mainly from 1339, and its impressive walls enclose a public garden. Here in the 16th-century Palazzo Mocenigo is the **Museo Nazionale Atestino** (*open daily 8.30–7.30*), founded in 1888 to house finds from excavations in the area, and opened here in 1902. The Roman section is on the ground floor, and includes a fine bronze head of Medusa (1st century AD). The pre-Roman section, on the first floor, has prehistoric collections related to the ancient Venetic civilisation, with Bronze Age finds and burial artefacts from the early Iron Age. The Benvenuti situla (c. 600 BC) is decorated with bronze reliefs. A *Madonna and Child* by Cima da Conegliano is also displayed here.

Behind the castle (Via Cappuccini) are the lovely parks of several villas, including the **Villa Kunkler**, occupied by Byron in 1817–18. Shelley composed *Lines Written Among the Euganean Hills* while watching the sun rise and set from here.

The **cathedral of St Tecla**, a medieval church rebuilt in 1690–1708 by Antonio Francesco Gaspari, has an 18th-century campanile built on an 8th-century base. In the elliptical interior there is a large painting of *St Tecla Freeing Este from the Plague*, by Giambattista Tiepolo (1759).

From here Via Garibaldi and Via Alessi bear southwest to the church of **Santa Maria delle Consolazioni** (or Santa Maria degli Zoccoli, 1504–10), with a campanile of 1598. The Cappella della Vergine contains a magnificent Roman mosaic pavement excavated nearby.

On the other side of town (about 500m away) are the Romanesque church of **San Martino**, with a campanile of 1293 (leaning since 1618), 18th-century sculptures and two altarpieces by Antonio Zanchi; and the 15th-century basilica of **Santa Maria delle Grazie**, rebuilt in the 18th century, which contains a Byzantine *Madonna* of the early 15th century, venerated as miraculous. Other interesting monuments are the 16th-century **Palazzo del Principe**, by Vincenzo Scamozzi, who also designed the façade of the church of San Michele; **Villa Cornaro** (now Benvenuti), with a 19th-century park designed by Giuseppe Jappelli; the 18th-century **Villa Contarini**, known also as the Vigna Contarena; the **Palazzo del Municipio**, also dating from the 18th century; and the octagonal church of the **Beata Vergine della Salute** (1639), with two octagonal *campanili* flanking the apse.

About 5km southwest of Este, off the SP15, is the **Abbazia di Santa Maria delle Carceri** (*open for guided tours Sat 3–6.30 and Sun 11–12 & 3–7, abbaziadicarceri.it*). Founded in the 11th century, it includes an octagonal church of 1643, remains of a 12th-century Romanesque cloister and a larger 16th-century Renaissance cloister and a library.

MONTAGNANA

The magnificent medieval walls which surround the entire small town of Montagnana (*map Veneto East A3*) are among the best preserved in all Italy. They were built by the rulers of Padua, Ezzelino da Romano and the Carraresi, between the 12th and 14th centuries and are nearly two kilometres in circumference. They are particularly impressive since at their foot there is a park on the site of the moat, which in the days of Venetian domination (after 1405) was turned into grassy fields where hemp was grown (and 'spun' along the walls) for use in ships' riggings for Venice's great fleet.

There are just four gates, the best preserved of which are the Rocca degli Alberi or Porta Legnano, dating from 1362, with a fortified bridge and tower, and the Porta Padova. This is adjoined by the 13th-century **Castello di San Zeno** and the tall **Mastio di Ezzelino** with the Museo Civico (*open for guided tours Wed, Thur and Fri at 11; Sat and Sun every hour from 10.30 or 11, and from 3 or 4–5 or 6*). The contents include Bronze and Iron Age finds (9th–8th centuries BC) from a local prehistoric site, and material from tombs and inscriptions dating from the 1st century AD when there was a Roman *vicus* (village) here. There is also a collection of medieval ceramics.

Palazzo del Municipio, an austere building with rusticated portico, was designed in 1538 by Michele Sanmicheli (but later remodelled). The Sala del Consiglio has a coffered ceiling of 1555.

The **cathedral of Santa Maria**, in the large, central Piazza Vittorio Emanuele, was built in a transitional Gothic-Renaissance style between 1431 and 1502 on the site of an 11th-century structure of which a few traces remain. The brick façade, with three little bell turrets, has a doorway which was probably added in 1530 by Jacopo Sansovino (the carved figure of the Madonna is by Antonio Minello). The tall, early Renaissance interior, a single aisle with barrel vaulting, has a large fresco of the *Assumption of the Virgin* in the apse, attributed to Giovanni Buonconsiglio, a protagonist of the Venetian school, who is known to have lived here from 1505 until 1513 (there is an altarpiece also by him on the south side). Other frescoes probably by his hand are on the west wall of the north transept and on the inside of the façade. On the high altar, in a stone frame, is a huge *Transfiguration* signed and dated 1556 by Veronese.

Close to the walls is the church of **San Francesco**, a 14th- and 15th-century edifice altered in the 17th century, with a tall 15th-century campanile. It contains a *Transfiguration* by the school of Veronese (clearly inspired by the autograph work in the cathedral), and a *Madonna* by Palma Giovane.

Just outside the walls, across the moat from the Porta Padova, stands the **Villa Pisani Placco** (*no admission*), the central part of which was designed by Andrea Palladio. It was built around 1560. The two main elevations have a double central order of Ionic and Corinthian columns terminating in a pediment. Also noteworthy are the splendid frieze with bucranic metopes and the harmonious ground-floor atrium, with statues of the *Seasons* by Alessandro Vittoria (1577).

EUGANEAN HILLS PRACTICAL TIPS

GETTING AROUND

By train: Trains from Padua for the spa towns stopping at Abano Terme (6mins), Terme Euganee-Abano–Montegrotto (10–12mins) and Battaglia Terme (15mins). The spas can also be reached by train from Rovigo (c. 20mins). Trains to Monselice from Padua in c. 20mins, from Rovigo in c. 15mins, from Venice in c. 50mins. For Este and Montagnana, there are a few direct trains from Padua; others require a change at Monselice. Trains from Rovigo and Venice also require a change at Monselice.

By bus: Buses run by APS (*www. apsholding.it*) numbered T and AT link Padua station to Luvigliano. Bus M goes to Abano and Montegrotto. Other buses go to Este in c. 55mins, via Battaglia Terme and Monselice. Buses from Padua station also go to Valsanzibio and Arquà Petrarca (c. 1hr) via Abano and Montegrotto. For

Montagnana, change at Este. Praglia (for the abbey) is served by buses from Padua on the Teolo, Vò and Noventa Vicentina routes (journey time to Praglia c. 25mins). Buses from Padua also serve Bagnoli di Sopra in c. 1hr.

WHERE TO STAY

ABANO TERME (*map Veneto East A2–B2*) Abano and the smaller spa towns are equipped with numerous big hotels, mostly comfortable with thermal pools (some of them only open April–Nov). They include €€€ **Trieste e Victoria**, a well-established, typical elegant spa hotel with lovely gardens and thermal pool (*Via Pietro d'Abano 1, T: 049 866 5100, hoteltriestevictoria. com*); and €€ **Terme Columbia**, modern and efficient, with a thermal pool (*Via Augure 15, T: 8594788, abanosite.it*).

MONTAGNANA (*map Veneto East A3*) €€ **Aldo Moro.** In the historic centre of this magnificently walled town. First opened in 1940, it has a pleasant old-fashioned atmosphere with chandeliers and an elegant restaurant (closed Mon) which has good fish and a wide selection of regional wines. *Via Guglielmo Marconi 27, T: 0429 81351, hotelaldomoro.com.*

TEOLO (*map Veneto East A2*) € **Alla Posta.** In wooded countryside. From 1870 to 1911 there was a staging post here for the Padua mail, and this simple hotel (with restaurant) is its successor. A sound choice if you are looking for somewhere very reasonable to stay and which is not a spa hotel (it is about 12km west of Abano Terme). Very advantageous half board or full board terms available. *Via Roma 20, T: 049 9925877, hotelallaposta.com.*

WHERE TO EAT

ARQUÀ PETRARCA (*map Veneto East A2*) €€ **La Montanella.** Old-established restaurant with a terrace and garden. Closed Tues evening and Wed. At the entrance to the village. *Via dei Carraresi 9, T: 0429 718200, montanella.it.*

MONSELICE (*map Veneto East A2–A3*) €€ **La Torre.** Traditional dishes prepared with considerable skill. Closed Sun evening and Mon. *Piazza Mazzini 14, T: 0429 73752.*

MONTAGNANA (*map Veneto East A3*) €€ **Aldo Moro.** See hotel above.

Teolo (*map Veneto East A2*) € **Al Sasso.** *Trattoria* serving delicious regional dishes. Closed Wed. *Via Ronco 11, Località Castelnuovo, T: 049 992 5073.*

FESTIVALS AND EVENTS

Autumn is the time when most of the local festivals take place: the Palio of Montagnana (a horse race outside the walls) is held on the first Sun in Sept with celebrations with fairs and markets which last a week. The *Giostra della Rocca* is a popular festival in costume at Monselice, and in the same month the *Settembre Euganeo*, with cultural events, is held in Este. Jujube festival in Oct at Arquà Petrarca.

LOCAL SPECIALITIES

Arquà Petrarca is known for its olive oil. Monastic products, including honey, liqueurs and herb teas, are produced and sold at the Abbazia di Praglia.

Rovigo & the Po Delta

The southeastern Veneto encompasses the lower course of the River Po, a place rich in natural and human history. This is the last alluvial plain of the great river, which begins in the northwestern corner of Italy and flows toward the Adriatic bearing tons of silt from its Alpine sources and depositing it along its way, 'filling in' the sea more and more every year. The delta of the Po is Italy's most extensive wetland, a permanent home to dozens of animal species and a stopping place for migratory birds.

ROVIGO

A walled town in the 12th century, Rovigo (*map Veneto East A3–B3*) was taken by the Venetians in 1482, and remained under their control until the fall of the Republic in 1797. Though its main street is no longer paved with water (the River Adigetto was covered over to form the Corso del Popolo in the 1930s), the town still has a Venetian atmosphere.

In the central Piazza Vittorio Emanuele II is the attractive 16th-century Palazzo del Municipio and the library of the Accademia dei Concordi, founded in 1580. In Palazzo Roverella, begun in 1474 on a design attributed to Biagio Rossetti, is the **Pinacoteca dei Concordi** (*open 9–7 except Mon; concordi.it and palazzoroverella. com*). Its fine collection of paintings (begun in 1833) is particularly representative of Venetian art from the 15th–18th centuries. It includes a *Madonna* by Giovanni Bellini, and *St Lucy and Stories from her Life* by the little-known Quirizio da Murano (dated 1462), as well as 17th-century works by Sebastiano Mazzoni, and 18th-century portraits by Alessandro Longhi and Tiepolo. Important exhibitions are also held here. At the other end of the piazza is the Gran Guardia, built for the Austrians in 1854 by Tommaso Meduna. Just off the southern corner of the piazza is Palazzo Roncale, a fine building by Sanmicheli (1555).

To the north is **Piazza Garibaldi**, with an equestrian statue of the hero himself by Ettore Ferrari, and the Caffè Borsa. The Camera del Commercio encloses the well-preserved Salone del Grano, built in 1934 with a remarkable glass barrel vault, while the Teatro Sociale has a Neoclassical façade dating from 1819.

Via Silvestri leads out of the square past the church of **San Francesco** (with sculptures by Tullio Lombardo) to Piazza XX Settembre, at the end of which is **La Rotonda**, or Santa Maria del Soccorso, a centrally-planned octagonal church surrounded by a portico, built in 1594 by the little-known architect Francesco Zamberlan. The campanile was designed by Baldassare Longhena in the 17th century. The very fine interior decoration, which survives intact from the 17th century, consists of a series of paintings celebrating Venetian officials with elaborate allegories: the lower band includes five by Francesco Maffei (*see below*) and others by Pietro Liberi. Above stucco statues (1627) is another cycle of paintings by Antonio Zanchi, Pietro Liberi, Andrea Celesti and others. The dome was painted in 1887.

FRANCESCO MAFFEI

Often overlooked as an artist, Maffei's style is usually described as being fluidly, typically Baroque, with all the opulence that that implies, tempered by the recherché exaggeration of Mannerism. What critics often fail to pinpoint is the nervous, haunting quality that pervades all his work. In his own day he was called a painter 'not of dwarves but of giants…whose style stupefied everyone'. Maffei (1605–60) worked in Vicenza for most of his career, with occasional forays to other cities, of which Rovigo is a notable example. His best works are either religious or allegorical, particularly those that show the apotheosis or glorification of local dignitaries (such as his *Glorification of the Podestà Giovanni Cavalli* in La Rotonda in Rovigo). By dint of rapid, bird-like brushstrokes and an unpredictable use of colour, Maffei invests his works with a bizarre, other-worldly atmosphere. He died of plague in Padua.

THE POLESINE

This flat area west of Rovigo, between the Adige and Po rivers, is traversed by numerous canals. At **Fratta Polesine** (*map Veneto East A3–B3*), facing a bridge over a canal, is Villa Badoer (*open July–Oct Tues–Sun 10–12 & 3.30–6.30*), built by Palladio in 1556 for the Venetian nobleman Francesco Badoer. It is enclosed by an attractive brick wall and preceded by a green lawn with two fountains and two 19th-century magnolia trees. The outbuildings are linked to the house by curving porticoes, and a wide flight of steps leads up to the villa with an Ionic portico and temple pediment. The empty interior is interesting for its remarkable plan (the service rooms and servants' quarters are on a lower level) and for the damaged contemporary frescoes by the otherwise unknown Giallo Fiorentino. Beside the villa is the Villa Molin (Grimani Avezzù), a fine building in the Palladian style, and there are several other interesting late 17th- or early 18th-century villas nearby.

Lendinara (*map Veneto East A3*) has a few fine palaces and an exceptionally tall campanile beside its cathedral, built in 1797. It was the birthplace of a hero of the Italian Risorgimento Alberto Mario, who is commemorated in a monument here, while a plaque on his house gratefully records the remarkable exploits of his wife, the Englishwoman Jessie White.

JESSIE WHITE MARIO

Born in 1832 and nicknamed by the Italians 'Miss Uragano' ('Hurricane Jessie'), White devoted her life to the cause of Italian independence and later to the amelioration of social conditions amongst the poor of the nation. She accompanied Garibaldi on many of his campaigns (she was with him and the Thousand when they set sail from for Palermo from Genoa in 1867, and she organised an ambulance service on their way back to Naples). Trained as a doctor (a profession from which women were still officially barred), she earned her living as a writer, journalist and teacher. She got to know Giuseppe Mazzini in London and Genoa (where in 1857 she had been arrested and imprisoned for four months—but it was there that she met her future husband, Alberto Mario). She helped raise money for the Republican cause, and after Unification she travelled to Naples and Sicily to document and bring to the attention of the press the appalling conditions of the inhabitants and the workers in the sulphur mines. She died in Florence in 1906 but her ashes were brought to Lendinara to be buried in the cemetery beside her beloved husband, who predeceased her.

Badia Polesine (*map Veneto East A3*) has remains of the abbey of Vangadizza, founded in the 10th century and enlarged in the 11th. The attractive 12th-century campanile stands near two 12th-century tombs. All that remains of the church (destroyed by Napoleon) is the drum of the domed chapel, which contains painted decoration attributed to Filippo Zaniberti and interesting stuccoes of the Cardinal Virtues. There is a picturesque irregular cloister. The Museo Civico Baruffaldi (*only open on Thurs 9–12*) contains 12th–17th-century ceramics. The Teatro Sociale dates from 1813.

THE PO DELTA

The Po is the longest river in Italy (652km). Its source is at Piano del Re (2050m) in Piedmont, on the French border, and it is joined by numerous tributaries (including the Ticino and the Adda) as it crosses northern Italy from west to east through Lombardy and the Veneto on its way to the Adriatic. The wide open plain—the largest in Italy—through which it runs and which separates the Alps from the Apennines, is known as the *pianura padana*. In the late Middle Ages the Po was navigable, and one of the principal waterways of Europe. In 1599 the Venetian Republic carried out major works of canalisation in the delta area in order to deviate the course of the river south to prevent it silting up the Venetian lagoon. It now reaches the sea by seven different channels: the largest (which carries 60 percent of its waters) is called the 'Po di Venezia'. The delta formed by this operation is the largest area of marshland in Italy. Sadly, the waters of the Po are extremely polluted. Studies have shown that the river feeds hundreds of tons of arsenic into the Adriatic every year, and according to European Union regulations, none of its waters should be used for drinking, swimming or irrigation.

Despite this depressing fact, however, the flat open landscape of the delta, with wide views over the reedy marshes and numerous wetlands (known as *valli*), is remarkably beautiful, whether in typical misty weather or on clear autumnal days. Rice and sugar beet were once intensely cultivated here, and some attractive old farmhouses survive, although most of them have been abandoned.

The marshes have interesting birdlife, counting some 350 species, including cormorants, herons, egrets, grebes and blackwinged stilts. Despite opposition from naturalists, the shooting season is still open from Sept to Jan. Pila and the Po della Pila have important fisheries, and all over the delta area eels, bass, carp, tench, pike and grey mullet are caught. Clams (a new clam was imported into the delta in the early 1980s from the Philippines) and mussels are also cultivated here.

Very few boats (apart from those of the fishermen) venture into the delta area, for many of the channels are only 1–2m deep. A few characteristic bridges of boats and ferries survive. The whole Polesine area has been subject to disastrous floods since the 19th century.

Adria (*map Veneto East B3*), the ancient capital of the Polesine, gave its name to the Adriatic Sea (to which it is now joined only by canal). The excellent Museo Archeologico (*open daily 8.30–7*) contains evidence of the city's Graeco-Etruscan origins. The earliest finds from the upper Polesine date from the 11th–9th centuries BC. There are also very fine Greek red- and black-figure ceramics, beautiful Roman glass (1st century AD), and gold and amber objects. Nearby is the 17th-century church of Santa Maria Assunta, which incorporates some Roman masonry. Across the Canal Bianco is the cathedral, which has a little 6th-century Coptic bas-relief and a crypt with remains of Byzantine frescoes.

Loreo (*map Veneto East B3*) is built on a canal and has a parish church by Baldassare Longhena. **Rosolina**, further east, is on the Via Romea, in parts a post-war revival of the long-decayed Roman Via Popilia, which ran down the Adriatic coast from Venice to Ravenna.

Porto Tolle (*map Veneto East C3*) stands on the Isola della Donzella, the largest island on the delta. The island used to have *valli* with fisheries, but was reclaimed after a flood in 1966 and now has rice fields. The southern part of the island is occupied by the Sacca di Scardovari, an attractive lagoon lined with fishermen's huts and boats. Mussels and clams are cultivated here, and it is inhabited by numerous birds. On its shores is a tiny protected area illustrating the typical vegetation of the wetlands that once covered this area. The easternmost island on the delta, the Isola di Batteria, is gradually being engulfed by the sea. It is no longer inhabited and is the only oasis on the delta. At the end of the delta is a lighthouse built in 1949 on land only formed some hundred years ago.

For Chioggia, see p. 59.

ROVIGO & THE PO DELTA PRACTICAL TIPS

GETTING AROUND

By train: There are frequent trains from Rovigo to Badia Polesine (c. 30mins) calling at Fratta Polesine and Lendinara. Trains from Rovigo also go to Rosolina (c. 45mins) via Adria and Loreo. Rail services also link Rovigo with Venice (60–90mins) and Padua (c. 40mins), and there are a few through trains to Verona Porta Nuova (c. 2hrs). Trains link Rovigo and Chioggia in just over 1hr.

By bus: For Porto Tolle, there are buses from Rovigo main bus station. Journey time c. 90mins via Adria and Loreo. Buses also link Rovigo with Badia Polesina (c. 35mins) via Lendinara.

WHERE TO STAY

LOREO (*map Veneto East B3*) €€ **Cavalli.** In the heart of the Polesine. With restaurant, renowned for its risotto and seafood. Closed Mon. *Riviera Marconi 69, T: 0426 369868, www.albergocavalli.it.*
ROVIGO (*map Veneto East A3–B3*) €€ **Villa Regina Margherita.** In an Art-Nouveau style building, with restaurant. *Viale Regina Margherita 6, T: 0425 361540, hotelvillareginamargherita.it.*
TAGLIO DI PO (*map Veneto East C3*) € **Tessarin.** Simple but comfortable. With restaurant. *Piazza Venezia 4, T: 0426 346347, hotel-tessarin.com.* There are hotels of all categories at the holiday resorts of Albarella and Rosolina Mare.

WHERE TO EAT

ARIANO NEL POLESINE (*map Veneto East B3*) €€ **Stella del Mare.** There are good fish restaurants in the delta area (although mostly quite pricey). This one at Ariano (località Gorino Veneto) is frequented by those who appreciate excellent, simply cooked fish. With a garden, at the delta of the Po di Goro, which divides the Veneto from Emilia Romagna. Closed Mon and Tues at lunch. Best to book. *Via Po Superiore 36, T: 0426 388797, ristorantestelladelmare.com.*
LUSIA (*map Veneto East A3*) € **Trattoria al Ponte.** A good choice for a simple meal, at Lusia, northeast of Lendinara. *Via Bertolda 27, T: 0425 669177, trattoriaalponte.com.*
PORTO TOLLE (*map Veneto East C3*) €€ **Da Brodon.** *Trattoria* renowned for its rice and fish dishes. Closed Mon. *Località Ca' Dolfin, T: 0426 384240.*
ROVIGO (*map Veneto East A3–B3*) €€ **Tavernetta Dante** (dai Trevisani). A well-known place to eat. Tables outside in summer. Closed Sun. *Corso del Popolo 212, T: 0425 26386.*

At Rovigo there are also many wine bars where you can have a Venetian *ombra*, a good glass of wine with delicious snacks (*cicchetti*).

LOCAL SPECIALITIES

At various markets in the Po Delta you can see the local catch of fish (in the mornings at Donada and Scardovari; and in the afternoons at Pila).

Vicenza

Vicenza (*map Veneto West D2*) is an extremely beautiful and well preserved small town in a pleasant position beneath the foothills of the green Monti Berici. Palladio (*see below*), who settled here in 1523, practically rebuilt it in his distinctive classical style, and established its fame to such an extent that it has been greatly admired by travellers since the 18th century. His most important buildings here are the Basilica and the Teatro Olimpico, but there are also numerous fine palaces by him (or inspired by him). Vicenza is a particularly pleasant place to visit. It is very peaceful, has excellent railway links, and it is just a short walk from the station to the centre of town. From the centre it is also easy to reach (on foot) two of the most important villas in the entire Veneto: La Rotonda, Palladio's architectural masterpiece, and the Villa Valmarana, with its joyous frescoes carried out some two centuries later by Giambattista and Gian Domenico Tiepolo.

ANDREA PALLADIO

Andrea di Pietro della Gondola (1508–80), nicknamed Palladio (from Pallas, the Greek goddess of wisdom) by his patron, the poet Giangiorgio Trissino (1478–1550), designed villas, palaces and churches throughout the Veneto in a Classical style that would profoundly change the face of the region and inspire numerous imitations. His *Quattro Libri*, or *Four Books on Architecture*, became a manual for later architects, especially in England and the United States. In the engraved illustrations for this treatise, Palladio noted the significant dimensions of his buildings, linking together their plan, section and elevation in a series of proportional relationships. The seemingly easy elegance that distinguishes Palladio's designs was, in fact, the result of his careful calculation of such proportional relationships. In applying these systems of numerical progression, which were often associated with contemporary musical harmonic theory, to the spatial relationships of a building, Palladio succeeded in creating the pleasing visual harmonies that characterise his architecture.

HISTORY OF VICENZA

The Roman municipium of *Vicetia*, the successor of a Gaulish town, was destroyed during the barbarian invasions, but traces of its theatre survived. It rose to importance again in the later Middle Ages and became a free *comune*. The Della Scala of Verona took control of the city after 1314, but from 1404 until the end of the Venetian Republic it placed itself firmly under the protection of the Serenissima.

The Venetian dialect word *contrà* (or *contrada*) is still used instead of 'Via' in the older districts of the town, and a surprising number of grand Venetian Gothic palaces survive. After a turbulent period, together with the rest of the Veneto, in the early 19th century Vicenza joined united Italy in 1866, but suffered much damage during the Second World War. Vicenza today is a busy town, home to numerous small companies (and some large ones), with a particular focus on textiles, leather and metalworking (including gold). The Colli Berici region produces DOC wines.

PAINTERS IN VICENZA
Vicenza's churches are full of interesting paintings by lesser-known artists influenced by the great Venetian school of painting. Alessandro Maganza (1556–c. 1630) was the son of an erudite painter Giovanni Battista, who was a close friend of Palladio and his patron Trissino. So it was natural that Alessandro was called in to work on the decoration of Palladio's Villa Rotonda here. Paintings by him can also be seen in Santa Corona, the Duomo, and the Basilica of Monte Berico. Giulio Carpioni, who died in Vicenza in 1678, carried out a number of paintings for Santi Felice e Fortunato, although he is best remembered for his genre paintings (one of which is preserved in the Museo Civico). Giovanni Battista Pittoni (1687–1767) was a well-known contemporary of Giambattista Tiepolo and his historical and mythological were also popular outside Italy. There is an altarpiece by him in Santa Corona (and in the Duomo you can see a painting by an ancestor, Girolamo).

CORSO PALLADIO, TEATRO OLIMPICO & PALAZZO CHIERICATI

At the entrance to the town stands the massive **Porta Castello** (*map Vicenza 3*), a fragment of a stronghold built by the Della Scala rulers of Verona but destroyed in 1819. In Piazza Castello, just inside the gate, are three huge columns of **Palazzo Breganze**, designed by Palladio in the early 1570s: he built only these two bays of what would have been a palace on a colossal scale.

CORSO PALLADIO
The handsome Corso Palladio (*map Vicenza 3*) is the principal street of Vicenza, with many fine palaces, and fashionable clothes shops. At the beginning, at no. 13 on the left, is **Palazzo Thiene Bonin Longare**, apparantly designed by Palladio but probably continued by Vincenzo Scamozzi, with a good atrium and courtyard (and garden beyond). Opposite **Palazzo Capra**, transformed into shops, preserves its portal commissioned from Palladio in the 1540s: it has pilasters rather than free-standing columns, and these also decorate the window above the balcony. Further on, the handsome Neoclassical façade on a high plinth of the church of **San Filippo Neri** was built in 1824 by Antonio Piovene on a design by Ottone Calderari. It contains a good 18th-century organ made by the Favorito brothers. Beyond the Palazzo Thiene (no. 47) in pink and peach pastel colours (it was once a 15th-century Venetian

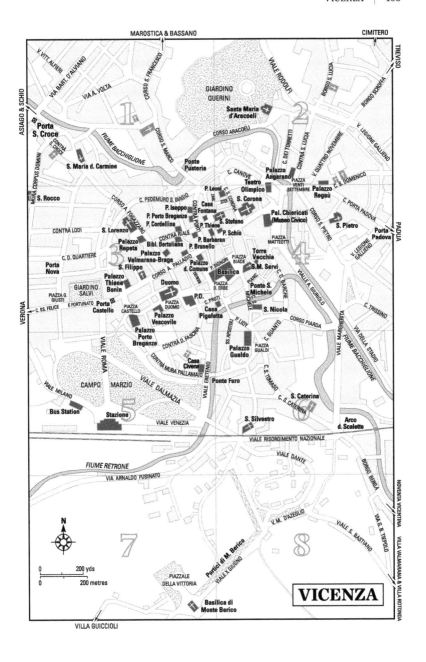

Gothic palace and now has a modern interior), is the much better-preserved Palazzo Brunello (no. 67), painted in a deeper red, with its portico over the pavement and an interesting courtyard. It has two little balconies and roundels with reliefs of Roman emperors in profile over the central window on the *piano nobile*. Contrà do Rode leads under **Palazzo Pojana**, also by Palladio, and beyond is the huge Palazzo del Comune, the Town Hall, with its flags, formerly a private palace, begun by Vincenzo Scamozzi in 1592 but only finished in 1662. It has a massive columned portico extending over the pavement, and classical columns in the courtyard. **Palazzo da Schio** (no. 147) is known as the Ca' d'Oro since it resembles a 15th-century Venetian Gothic palace. Its brick exterior has four little balconies and two grand windows on the *piano nobile* and floor above. It has a handsomely carved arch at its entrance, and archaeological fragments are preserved in the portico. Slightly set back from the road is another Neoclassical church façade, that of San Gaetano.

The Corso now begins to descend slightly and loses its pleasant paving. Beyond the raised garden railing of Santa Corona is the tiny **Casa Cogollo**, which has two engaged Ionic columns beneath two Corinthian pilasters above. Above the entrance are two reliefs of winged figures. There is a well in the tiny courtyard. This was traditionally thought to have been built by Palladio for Pietro Cogollo, but is not now usually attributed to him.

TEATRO OLIMPICO

Map Vicenza 2–4. Open 9–5 (or later in summer) except Mon; for information see www.museicivicivicenza.it. Behind the statue in Piazza Matteotti is a gate into a walled garden which belongs to Palazzo del Territorio, which was part of a medieval castle, the rebuilt tower of which survives. Across the garden, which has a number of architectural fragments and ancient sculpture, an inconspicuous door gives access to the theatre.

The famous Teatro Olimpico was designed by Palladio for the Accademia Olimpica, an academy founded in 1555 for drama performances, of which Palladio was a distinguished member. Building only began the year of his death (1580) and so it fell to Scamozzi to complete it. The opening play, performed in 1585, was Sophocles' *Oedipus Rex*. Goethe saw the theatre in 1786 and found it 'inexpressibly beautiful'.

Beyond the room used by the Academy, and a vestibule where some of the tiny oil lamps designed by Scamozzi to light the scenery are displayed, visitors are first directed downstairs where there is a gallery illustrating the history of the theatre, before emerging through a door onto the large stage. The shallow *cavea*, derived from Vitruvian models, is surmounted by a peristyle of Corinthian columns (which was the place from which the audience originally entered the theatre). It still has its tiered wooden seating and you can sit and admire the classical *frons scenae*, built of wood and stucco, its architecture derived from ancient Roman buildings. In the niches are statues of distinguished academicians by Agostino Rubini and Domenico Fontana, and reliefs of the Labours of Hercules adorn the attic storey. Scamozzi designed the remarkable fixed scenery of three streets lined with noble palaces leading away from the stage in perfect perspective, towards a brilliant blue sky.

From the exit, keep left along the cobbled Stradella del Teatro Olimpico to return to Piazza Matteotti.

MUSEO CIVICO

Map Vicenza 4. Usually open 9–5 except Mon. T: 0444 222811, www.museicivicivicenza. it. Entrance in Piazza Matteotti.

The huge porticoed **Palazzo Chiericati Valmarana** is an excellent example of Palladio's early work, erected in the 1550s or 1560s, although the façade was only completed a century later. It is now home to the Civic Museum.

The atrium and entrance hall are handsome oval rooms with niches and apses beneath pronounced cornices. The room on the left has a very fine ceiling fresco of the *Chariot of the Sun* by Domenico Brusasorci. The chimney piece has an ingenious (deliberately broken) stone frame. The adjoining room also has a good ceiling by Battista Zelotti and statues of Francesco Sforza and his wife, Bianca Maria Visconti, dating from around 1494. Here you can see a tiny Palladian spiral staircase.

The excavations which were carried out during restoration work are open in modernised underground rooms.

Highlights of the display on the main floor include a *Transition of the Virgin,* signed and dated 1333 by Paolo Veneziano; *Calvary* by Hans Memling; paintings by Bartolomeo Montagna; a stucco relief of the *Madonna and Child* by Jacopo Sansovino; *A Miracle of St Augustine* by Tintoretto; the *Three Ages of Man* by Van Dyck; an exquisite small *Madonna and Child* in a beautiful landscape surrounded by scenes from the life of Christ attributed to Jan Brueghel the Elder; and works by Giambattista Tiepolo and his son Gian Domenico. The museum also owns 33 drawings by Palladio.

Arranged in three rooms on the top floor (with very interesting wood panelled ceilings) is a collection donated to the city by Giuseppe Roi (1924–2009). It consists mostly of small paintings, drawings and engravings of all periods, beautifully displayed. In the first room are works by Giorgio Morandi, Ardengo Soffici, Giambattista Tiepolo (drawings and an oil painting of a merchant), Telemaco Signorini (a very small Scottish landscape), a scene in Lazio attributed to Corot and a tiny painting of the port of Naples by Giuseppe de Nittis. In the second room are engravings by Manet, works by Medardo Rosso and a charcoal portrait by John Singer Sargent. The last room has a little *Holy Family* by Garofalo and a *Deposition* painted on slate by Brusasorci.

PIAZZA DEI SIGNORI & THE BASILICA

Piazza dei Signori (*map Vicenza 3–4*) is a dignified square graced by two huge columns standing on high, elaborate bases, one bearing the Redeemer (1640) and the other the Lion of St Mark (1520), a clear statement of Vicenza's loyalty to the Venetian Republic. At one corner of the piazza rises the unusually tall and slender **Torre di Piazza**, erected in the 12th century but heightened with additional storeys in 1311 and again in 1444. Opposite the magnificent Basilica (*described below*) is the **Loggia del Capitaniato**, commissioned from Palladio in 1571 by the town council as part of the residence of the Venetian governors. Between the three arches on the façade are four giant semi-columns in brick which reach to the height of the attic story. The stucco decoration by Lorenzo Rubini illustrates the Venetian victory at Lepanto in the same year. Beside it is the long façade of the Monte di Pietà pawnbroker's: the left wing dates from 1500 and the right wing from 1553–7, and they are separated by the church of San Vincenzo, by Paolo Bonin (1614–17).

THE BASILICA

The huge hall in the interior is open 10–6 except Mon. It is now used for exhibitions. The terraces at the top of the building can also usually be visited at the same time.

This splendid building is one of Palladio's masterpieces, and it was he who first called it a 'basilica' to illustrate his intention of creating a Classically-inspired public building for use as the town hall and law courts, in the tradition of an ancient Roman basilica. The nucleus of the building is the medieval Palazzo della Ragione, the Palais de Justice. In 1549 Palladio was called in to replace a double exterior loggia of 1494 which had partly collapsed. He had the ingenious idea of surrounding the building entirely with two open colonnaded galleries, Tuscan Doric below and Ionic above, crowned with a balcony terrace decorated with statues. The project was only completed in 1617, but Palladio's original design was adhered to nevertheless. Built in bright local limestone, the completed building shows Palladio's admiration for ancient Roman architecture and his skill in giving a new shell to an essentially Gothic core. Restoration of the building was completed in 2012.

Stairs lead up to the loggia and one of the three entrances to the huge Gothic hall of the Palazzo della Ragione, with a remarkable beamed ship's keel roof. The 13th-century building on this site was destroyed by fire in 1444 and this beautiful hall was rebuilt by Domenico da Venezia in 1460. When exhibitions are in progress it is unfortunately very difficult to appreciate the true grandeur of this huge space.

By a door off the loggia, a modern spiral staircase (or a lift) ascend to the terrace at the top of the building behind the statues. Here you can see from close up the lovely pink and white chequered exterior of the building with its round windows below the green roof (there are charming little empty niches at the corners). The view over the rooftops takes in the towers and campanili of the town, as well as Palladio's high green dome of the cathedral tribune, and his Villa La Rotonda on the hill of Monte Berico.

In the porticoes beneath the basilica, the quaint old wooden shop windows and shop signs have been preserved, even if today they don't always correspond to the merchandise for sale inside.

PIAZZA DELLE ERBE AND SANTA MARIA DEI SERVI

The Basilica stands between Piazza dei Signori and **Piazza delle Erbe**, a market square with a medieval brick prison-tower connected to the Basilica, which is very well seen from here. On one side of the piazza is an interesting medley of houses with a portico supported on columns of all shapes and sizes. In the adjacent Piazza delle Biade, **Santa Maria dei Servi** has nine statues on its façade. It is a Gothic church of 1407 enlarged at the end of the century. On the first south altar, beside a pretty little carved doorway, is a lovely altarpiece of the *Madonna and Sts Sebastian and Roch* (with an angel musician below) by Benedetto Montagna. The second north altar is an early 16th-century Lombardesque work with statues and stone reliefs.

THE DUOMO & MUSEO DIOCESANO

The **Duomo** (*map Vicenza 3; open 10.30–11.45 & 3.30–6*) was rebuilt after it had been all but destroyed in 1944, but the beautiful tall Renaissance **tribune** at the east end (begun in 1482), with a high dome (not visible in the interior) on a Palladian design added at the end of the 16th century, survived the bombs, and remains an extraordinary sight. The façade dates from the same century and the brickwork is patterned with pink lozenges and clover leaves on a white ground beneath a very unusual crowning frame at the top. The sturdy detached campanile was built in the 11th century on a ruined Roman building.

There is a raised sanctuary in the broad **interior**, and a pink balustrade in front of the side chapels. The third south chapel has 17th-century stuccoes and statues and paintings by Alessandro Maganza. In the fourth chapel (on the right wall) is a *Transfiguration* by Girolamo Pittoni. In the fifth chapel is a gold-ground polyptych of the *Dormition of the Virgin* by Lorenzo Veneziano (mid-14th century).

In the tribune, the high altar against the east wall is beautifully decorated with precious marbles and *pietre dure* by the local workshop of Pedemuro, where Palladio worked as a young man (some scholars believe he may have helped to make this altar, which would have been his very first work). On either side the twelve 17th-century paintings, in a pretty framework which follows the shape of the apse, are by local artists including Andrea Celesti, Pietro Liberi and Antonio Zanchi.

The chapel at the end of the north side has 16th-century funerary monuments with busts attributed to Alessandro Vittoria. The sixth chapel on this side dates from the early 17th century. In the fifth chapel is a 15th-century polychrome relief. The altarpiece and frescoes in the fourth chapel are the work of Bartolomeo Montagna. The crypt, with its four massive columns, also has a 15th-century polychrome relief and sarcophagi.

MUSEO DIOCESANO (PALAZZO VESCOVILE)
Map Vicenza 3. Open 10–1 & 2–6 except Mon.
The well displayed Diocesan Museum occupies the Bishop's Palace, which also had to be rebuilt after 1944, although the charming courtyard-loggia of 1494 survived. The **ground floor** has finds from the Roman city, including a 4th-century sarcophagus with a very early representation of the Adoration of the Magi. Medieval sculpture includes a very unusual 8th-century sarcophagus in the form of a trough with an inscription. There is a lovely cope with pairs of parrots dating from the early

13th century, probably derived from a Persian design. A whole room is given over to a display of 14th-century illuminated antiphonals and codexes.

On the landing are the sword and spurs from a knight's tomb in the Duomo (1412). The paintings on the **upper floor** include *San Bernardino* (early 16th century) and 17th-century works by Alessandro Turchi. In the corridor is a painting of *Christ in Glory between Franciscan Saints* by Baciccia. One room has a display of Church silver and a statuette of the Madonna in gilded silver dating from around 1386.

Underground rooms have a great miscellany of works, including an alabaster relief by the 15th-century English school, finds from excavations in the Hebrew city of Hebron, and a fascinating collection of Coptic crosses from Ethiopia. Here also can be seen remains of medieval buildings on this site.

At no. 6 Piazza del Duomo is the entrance to the **Criptoportico Romano** (*only open on Sat and the 2nd Sun of the month from 10–12*). It was probably part of a 1st-century Roman residence.

SANTA CORONA

Map Vicenza 4; open 9–12 & 3–6 except Mon.
Just out of Piazza Matteotti at the end of Corso Palladio, Contrà Santa Corona leads up past a garden to the important church of Santa Corona. It is early Gothic in style (1261) with a Renaissance east arm of 1489. The lovely bright interior was restored in 2009–12. It takes its name ('Holy Crown') from the story that in 1259, King Louis IX of France donated a thorn from Christ's Crown (which had come to France as booty from Constantinople) to the Blessed Bartolomeo da Breganze of Vicenza. This church was built specifically to house the precious relic.

NORTH SIDE
There are some interesting altarpieces here. The second one **(A)**, by Bartolomeo Montagna, has the unusual subject of Mary Magdalene with Sts Jerome, Paula, Augustine and Monica, with large predella scenes below; the third altarpiece of the *Charity of St Anthony* **(B)** is by Leandro Bassano; the fourth altar **(C)** has a late Gothic votive image of the Virgin with an early 16th-century landscape view of Vicenza by Fogolino. The fifth altar **(D)** was beautifully carved in 1501 by Girolamo Pittoni (on a design by Rocco da Vicenza) to contain a superb late work by Giovanni Bellini, the *Baptism of Christ*. The group of three female figures on the left have wonderfully coloured robes, and an orange parrot assists from a rock. In the background is a wonderful mountainous landscape.

On the wall of the **north transept (E)** there is a late 14th-century painting of the *Derision of Christ* by Tentorello.

EAST END
Visitors are allowed up into the **sanctuary (F)** to see the beautiful high altar made in 1669. It is inlaid with pietre dure with fruits and flowers and has three panels

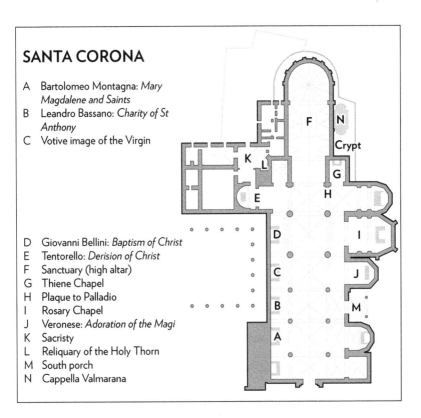

SANTA CORONA

A   Bartolomeo Montagna: *Mary Magdalene and Saints*
B   Leandro Bassano: *Charity of St Anthony*
C   Votive image of the Virgin

D   Giovanni Bellini: *Baptism of Christ*
E   Tentorello: *Derision of Christ*
F   Sanctuary (high altar)
G   Thiene Chapel
H   Plaque to Palladio
I   Rosary Chapel
J   Veronese: *Adoration of the Magi*
K   Sacristy
L   Reliquary of the Holy Thorn
M   South porch
N   Cappella Valmarana

illustrating the Last Supper, Resurrection, and Ascension (with views of Vicenza and the Basilica below). Above is a marble tabernacle and on the balustrade is more exquisite marble inlay with birds and animals. You can also go behind the altar to see the choir stalls, which have fine wooden inlay dating from the end of the 16th century.

On the right of the sanctuary is the **Thiene Chapel (G)**, with two splendid Gothic family tombs and an altarpiece by Giovanni Battista Pittoni (1723). On the wall outside is a sculpted wood Crucifix dating from the 13th century.

A plaque on the nave pillar **(H)** records the **burial of Palladio** here in 1580; his remains were removed in the 19th century to the Cimitero Maggiore (*just beyond map Vicenza 2*).

SOUTH SIDE

The Rosary Chapel **(I)** was sumptuously decorated in the early 17th century by Giovanni Battista and Alessandro Maganza. In the third chapel **(J)** there is a **painting by Veronese**, a very crowded *Adoration of the Magi*. The eccentric dramatic scene includes the 'stable' supported by Veronese's familiar huge classical columns, and the kings are accompanied by a mounted soldier in shining armour.

It was painted in 1573 at the same time as another similar work of the same subject now in the National Gallery in London.

SACRISTY AND CHAPTER HOUSE
Through a door in the north transept there is access to the sacristy **(K)**, with a pretty vaulted ceiling. In a little niche outside, fitted with cupboard doors, the exquisite gold **reliquary of the Holy Thorn (L)** dating from the 14th century is to be displayed. In the cloister you can see the Chapter House, which has 17th-century statues.

In the **south porch (M)** there is an interesting tomb decorated with an elephant and pyramid, dating from around 1430.

Off the crypt is the beautiful **Cappella Valmarana (N)**, designed by Palladio. It has a strikingly simple design with two lateral apses with two roundels above for the windows and two Corinthian columns flanking the altar (and four Corinthian capitals in the four corners beneath the cornice).

MUSEO NATURALISTICO ARCHEOLOGICO
In the two cloisters of the former convent of Santa Corona, behind a Neoclassical façade of 1823, is the Museo Naturalistico Archeologico of the Museo Civico (*open Tues–Sun 9–5, later in summer; entrance at no. 4 Contrà Santa Corona*). Upstairs, arranged in the monks' cells, is the Natural History collection, and geological material (with special reference to the Monti Berici). Downstairs are finds from the site of the Roman theatre of Vicenza and Lombard material, as well as Iron Age finds from the province, including reliefs of the 5th century BC.

THE PALACES NORTH OF CORSO PALLADIO

This lovely area of the old town has numerous interesting palaces in its quiet streets.

On the west side of Contrà Santa Corona is **Palazzo Leoni Montanari** (*map Vicenza 4; now owned by a bank, the ground floor is used for exhibitions. Open 10–6 except Mon*). The palace was remodelled in the late 17th century by two wealthy merchants, Giovanni Montanari and Nicolò Leoni, and has interesting architectural elements (some of which were added in 1808). Beyond the androne, with its carved dragons above the archway, is the lovely courtyard, and the staircase is decorated with elaborate stuccoes and statues by Angelo Marinali and paintings by Louis Dorigny. The huge hall on the *piano nobile*, with its five doors, has painted tapestries and stuccoes, and the Galleria della Verità has a very elaborate stucco ceiling with a painting by Giuseppe Alberti. The Loggia d'Ercole is also profusely decorated with stuccoes. The paintings include works by Canaletto and Pietro Longhi and two lovely small landscapes by Francesco Guardi. There are also paintings by Francesco Zuccarelli, Luca Carlevarijs, and a fine view of Venice's Grand Canal by Michele Marieschi. On the floor above there is a very interesting display of a large collection of icons, considered by some to be the most important in existence outside Russia. It is introduced by a 19th-century iconostasis which incorporates painted doors from the late 16th century. The display is by subject rather than by date (and well labelled also in English): some of the most interesting works include a small view of the Council of Nicaea, painted in the late 15th century, and the *Ascension of Elijah* dating from the 13th century.

Contrà Santo Stefano leads to Contrà Zanella, where the church of **Santo Stefano** (*map Vicenza 4; open only in the morning*) contains a painting by the great Venetian painter Palma Vecchio. Opposite is **Palazzo Negri de Salvi**, dating from the 12th century but altered in the 15th century, next to the brick Gothic **Casa Fontana**, with a balcony and two grand central windows on the two upper floors.

The huge **Palazzo Thiene** (now owned by a bank) was probably begun on a design by Giulio Romano in 1542 and may have been continued by Palladio after Giulio's death in 1546 (although it remained unfinished). The splendid entrance portico, with four delightful 'spongy' columns and architectural fragments displayed on the walls, leads into the cobbled courtyard. Here you can see the two sides attributed to Palladio and on the third side, a portico of four columns from the early Renaissance palace, which is incorporated into the structure. In the interior there is a very fine stuccoed ceiling by Alessandro Vittoria.

Stradella di San Gaetano (renamed Stradella della Banca Popolare) leads past the east flank of Palazzo Thiene (with Palladio's façade 'wrapped' round the corner into the lane) to emerge in the lovely peaceful Contrà Porti, with more interesting palaces. Here can be seen the Renaissance façade of Palazzo Thiene (no. 12), with rustication, and a fine portal with roundels in relief and remains of frescoes at the top, dating from 1489 by Lorenzo da Bologna. Opposite is **Palazzo Montano Barbaran**, where the **Palladio Museum** was opened in 2012 (*map Vicenza 3; open 10–6 except Mon*). It is also the seat of the Centro Internazionale di Studi di Architettura Andrea Palladio. The handsome entrance portico has paired columns and many of the rooms contain fine late 16th-century ceilings, though only one of them is lit, the Salone dei Cesari by Andrea Vicentino (1580–3), with stucco and busts in gesso by Agostino Rubini. The (rather disappointing) Palladio Museum, arranged in these rooms, consists of models of the great architect's works and loud videos with experts describing his life and influence.

At no. 8 Contrà Porti (towards Corso Palladio) is the Gothic Palazzo Cavallini. In the other direction, at no. 15, a plaque records the death here in 1529 of Luigi da Porto, author of the story of 'Romeo and Juliet'. Next to it is **Palazzo Porto Breganze** (no. 17), a Venetian Gothic building with a Renaissance doorway, and the magnificent 15th-century Palazzo Colleoni Porto (no. 19), with a loggia overlooking a little garden. Adjoining is **Palazzo Iseppo Da Porto** (no. 21), with a lovely androne, built by Palladio in 1548 but now being converted into apartments.

TO SAN LORENZO

On Contrà Riale (*map Vicenza 3*), in the former 17th-century monastery buildings of San Giacomo, is the historic **Biblioteca Bertoliniana**, left to the city in 1702 by Giovanni Maria Bertolo. On the right is **Palazzo Cordellina**, also owned by the library and used for exhibitions. Built by the Vicentine Ottone Calderari, it has a good androne in Palladian style.

Contrà Riale ends in the busier Corso Fogazzaro, with shops. To the right it leads past **Palazzo Repeta** (no. 49), built in the first decade of the 18th century by Francesco Muttoni. This palace stands on the corner of the piazza in front of the church of **San Lorenzo** (*map Vicenza 3; open 7–12 & 3.30–7*). The splendid marble portal by Andriolo de Santi dates from the mid-14th century. The lovely interior has huge columns and a vaulted nave and aisles. The two stoups date from 1939. Above the west door is the very unusual 18th-century monument to Giovanni Battista da Porto, and at this end of the north aisle a monument to the architect Vincenzo Scamozzi, with his bust. At the east end of the south aisle, between the windows, is a *Deposition* by Luca Giordano. In the south transept, the altar of the Santissima Trinità, made for the Pojana family, has sculptures dating from 1456, and a fresco above painted at the end of the 15th century. In the sanctuary hangs a 15th-century wood Crucifix, and opposite two paintings by Francesco Pittoni there are two more monuments to members of the Da Porto family, one of them, recording the brothers Leonardo, Ludovico and Pietro, attributed to Palladio (1555). In the chapel to the left of the sanctuary are three statues signed by Antonino Veneziano in 1443, and an interesting large (but very ruined) detached fresco of the *Martyrdom of St Paul* attributed to Bartolomeo Montagna. There is yet another Da Porto monument here. The sacristy is entered through a door on either side of which are paintings attributed to Pittoni, and a door leads out to the 15th-century cloister, with its well dating from the previous century. At the end of the north aisle is a prettily carved altar thought to be by the workshop of Pedemuro, and in a niche in the centre of this aisle is a ruined 14th-century fresco of the Marys beneath the empty Cross.

PALAZZO VALMARANA-BRAGA

This *palazzo* (Corso Fogazzaro 16; *map Vicenza 3*) by Palladio (1565) has giant pilasters uniting two storeys of the building, and a handsome portico. It was badly damaged in the War but has recently been restored by the family who live here (*visits by appointment: palazzovalmaranabraga.it*). On the ground floor, the Studiolo has an exquisite ceiling with gilded stuccoes by Lorenzo Rubini and paintings by Giovanni Battista Zelotti (1567–8) and its original floor, and on the upper floor there are paintings by Giulio Carpioni and portals designed by Francesco Muttoni.

THE SOUTHERN DISTRICTS NEAR THE RETRONE RIVER

The ornate, 15th-century **Casa Pigafetta** (*map Vicenza 3–4*), with three charming balconies on the top storey, a French motto on the façade, and a lovely old entrance arch, stands in the pedestrian lane of the same name. On the adjacent house, a plaque records Antonio Pigafetta (1491–1534), who was born in Vicenza and formed one of Magellan's company on his circumnavigation of the globe in 1519–22.

Further downhill, facing the river and with a portico over the pavement, the long white **Casa Civena** (now a clinic; *map Vicenza 5*) was probably the first palace to be built by Palladio (in 1540–6), and it still bears an inscription to his patron Trissino. Only the central bays are original, since it was altered in the 18th and 19th centuries.

Ponte Furo leads over the river, with a good view left of the green roof of the Basilica and the Torre di Piazza, and (right) of Monte Berico. In a widening of the road, in Contrà Santi Apostoli, the curve of the house fronts follows the shape of the Roman Theatre, the ruins of which once stood here and were drawn by Palladio.

From the castellated Porton del Luzo, a 13th-century gateway, continue along Contrà Porton Luzo past a very unusual house with brick columns above a rusticated ground floor, to an irregular piazza with a few trees and the huge long façade of the **Palazzi Gualdo**, dating from the 15th–16th centuries, decorated with square reliefs and with a good courtyard. Beside it, the Stradella del Pozzetto leads out of the piazza past the Contrà Paolo Lioy, where you can see the charming little Gothic Casa Caola. The river is recrossed over the lovely hump-backed **Ponte San Michele** (1620), its cobbled way only open to pedestrians. Just before the bridge, in this peaceful corner of the town, is the oratory of **San Nicola** (*map Vicenza 4; open Thur 10–12, Sat 3–6*). The 17th-century interior has canvases by Francesco Maffei (*see p. 99*) and ceiling paintings which are the last work by his contemporary Giulio Carpioni. At the foot of the bridge, on the corner of Contrà Piancoli, is the **house where Goethe stayed** in 1786, when he came to Vicenza to admire the works of Palladio (plaque).

GOETHE ON VICENZA

Standing face to face with these magnificent buildings, which Palladio created, and seeing how already they are debased by men's mean and squalid requirements, one realises that most of them were conceptions that went far beyond the power of those who commissioned them to execute. How poorly adapted are these splendid products of a superior mind to the lives of ordinary men!   *Italian Journey (19th September 1786)*

OUTSIDE PORTA CASTELLO

From outside Porta Castello, Corso San Felice leads west, away from the centre of the town. It passes the railings and 17th century-entrance gate of the delightful **Giardino Salvi** (*map Vicenza 3; open all day*), which was first laid out as a botanical garden. At one end of an L-shaped canal you can see the Loggia Valmarana, a villa in Palladian style built over the water in 1592. At the other end of the canal, here spanned by several bridges, is a loggia by Baldassare Longhena (1649).

SANTI FELICE E FORTUNATO

Beyond map Vicenza 3, about 1km from Porta Castello, approached along a busy narrow road, but well worth visiting. Open 9–11.30. Usually closed in the afternoon.

The first church of Santi Felice e Fortunato was a palaeochristian edifice, probably dating from the Constantinian era (4th century) and enlarged under Theodosius in the following century. The present structure is in effect the third church on this site, dating from a reconstruction in the 10th century (and with 12th-century alterations).

In the little **courtyard** outside there are a number of ancient sarcophagi, including one with palaeochristian symbols and an inscription. In front of the church façade stands a strange pillar called the Colonna di San Gallo, with a carving of horsemen dating from 1300. The very curious fortified **campanile**, with a clock, dates from 1166. The church has an ancient **portal** with very early fresco fragments showing two angels of the Resurrection blowing their trumpets as the dead emerge from their tombs, dating from some time before 1154.

The basilican **interior** was restored in the 20th century, when the Baroque decorations were destroyed. In several places in the nave and aisle, 4th–5th-century mosaic pavements from the palaeochristian church have been revealed beneath the modern floor. On the south wall are three large, framed 18th-century paintings and an altarpiece by Giulio Carpioni. At the end of the nave is a stone statue of the *Madonna della Misericordia* by Antonino Veneziano (c. 1452). In the raised sanctuary a 2nd-century sarcophagus serves as high altar and in the apse are good frescoes by Giulio Carpioni. At the end of the north wall is a finely carved 15th-century tabernacle. On this wall there are three more large paintings by Carpioni, and an altarpiece by Alessandro Maganza.

Off the sacristy is an ancient domed cruciform chapel, or **martyrium**, probably dating from the 5th century, extremely interesting for its architecture, and with traces of mosaics, though it was sadly over restored a few years ago.

The charming little **crypt** has a curving wall, set up on which is an ancient 4th-century stele with an inscription relating to the two brothers Felix and Fortunatus (Felice e Fortunato) who were martyred in Aquileia during the persecutions of Diocletian. Their relics, neatly tied up in small bundles, are displayed behind an old grate.

Outside the church is a little **Museo Lapidario** (*usually only open Tues and Fri mornings, but the walls are made of glass so you can see most of the contents from the outside*), which protects some of the Roman, palaeochristian and Lombard carvings as well as sarcophagi from the church. One sarcophagus, complete with its lid, has symbolic pagan heads of the Four Seasons. The medieval sculpture includes a pair of 12th-century lions and there are six 18th-century wood busts of abbots.

MONTE BERICO, VILLA VALMARANA & VILLA LA ROTONDA

The green hillside of Monte Berico, conspicuous from all parts of the town with its basilica and two important villas, has been largely preserved from modern buildings, and is best reached on foot (the pleasant walk takes about 1hr 30mins).

For the Basilica take Viale Eretenio along the river from Ponte Furo (map Vicenza 5–6), and then Viale X Giugno which crosses the railway and soon meets the long flight of steps which ascends the steep hillside beneath the Portici. This monumental portico with chapels was designed by Francesco Muttoni in the 18th century. There is a good view (east) of Villa La Rotonda from just below the basilica.

For **Villa Valmarana** and **Villa Rotonda** there is an alternative route from Ponte San Michele, along Contrà Pozzetto, and then Contrà San Tommaso and Contrà Santa Caterina to the Arco delle Scalette (*map Vicenza 6*), designed by Palladio. Here begins Via Massimo d'Azeglio and then (left) Via San Bastiano, which continues uphill to the two villas.

BASILICA DI MONTE BERICO

The Basilica (*map Vicenza 7; closed 12.30–3.30*) stands on the site of a sanctuary, erected on the spot where two apparitions of the Virgin occurred in the 15th century. It is still a pilgrim shrine (with a festival on 8 Sept). It was rebuilt, apart from the campanile, by Carlo Borella in 1688–1703, although Lorenzo da Bologna's facade of 1476 was re-erected alongside the present south front. It contains a lovely *Pietà* by Bartolomeo Montagna (1500). In the **refectory** is the *Supper of St Gregory the Great*, a superb huge painting by Veronese dating from 1572. The great Venetian painter was clearly fascinated by the subject of festive repasts, and around this time he painted the subject many times, whether as a Last Supper, a Marriage at Cana, a Supper in the House of Simon or a Supper in the House of Levi. All the scenes are set in a majestic columned portico and include numerous figures of grandly-dressed Venetians, as well as servants and animals. This painting, over 8m by nearly 5m, was hacked into 32 pieces by Austrian soldiers in 1848, in retaliation for a rebellion of the Veronese against Austrian rule. It was restored at the expense of the emperor Franz Joseph. Also here is a *Baptism of Christ* by Alessandro Maganza.

Piazzale della Vittoria, beside the church, built as a memorial of the First World War, commands a magnificent view of the mountains that once marked the front line (*see p. 184 for more on WWI in this part of Italy*). Viale X Giugno continues beyond the basilica to the **Villa Guiccioli**, built at the end of the 18th century by Gianantonio Selva, with a beautiful park (*beyond map Vicenza 7; open 9–dusk except Mon*). The villa houses the **Museo del Risorgimento e della Resistenza** (*open 9–1 & 2.15–5 except Mon*).

VILLA VALMARANA

From the Basilica, Villa Valmarana can be reached on foot by following the Portici downhill, and (halfway down) taking Via Massimo d'Azeglio to the right, from which there is a good view of Vicenza. Just beyond a Carmelite monastery, the narrow cobbled Via San Bastiano (*map Vicenza 8; closed to through traffic*) diverges right. It leads downhill past a charming dovecote to (15mins) Villa Valmarana, called 'ai Nani' from the dwarves that decorate its garden wall (*open 9 March–4 Nov 10–12.30 & 3–6 except Mon; at other times check the website: villavalmarana.com. There is a café*). The villa was purchased by Giustino Valmarana in 1715 and is still owned by the family. It is famous for the superb frescoes in the *palazzina* by Giambattista Tiepolo, dating from 1757, with scenes from the *Iliad* and *Aeneid*, as well as from the epic poem *Gerusalemme Liberata* by Tiepolo's contemporary Torquato Tasso, and the romantic *Orlando Furioso*, published in 1532 by Ludovico Ariosto. The *foresteria* was decorated with delightful pastoral scenes by Tiepolo's son Gian Domenico.

VILLA LA ROTONDA

The stony path (Stradella Valmarana) on the right beyond Villa Valmarana continues downhill to the white Villa La Rotonda, also now a Valmarana villa (*open at the time of writing 15 March–3 Nov daily except Mon 10–12 & 3–6 (exterior only); interior shown on Wed and Sat, at the same times. But it is best to check the website, as times are subject to frequent change: villalarotonda.it.*)

Built as a belvedere for Paolo Almerico on this charming hilltop site, the villa has a central plan consisting of a circular core within a cube. The four classical porticoes complete its symmetry. Crowned with a remarkable low dome, its design is reminiscent of the Pantheon in Rome. Begun c. 1551 by Palladio, it was taken over at his death by Vincenzo Scamozzi and finished in 1606 for the Capra family. The Villa La Rotonda had a profound influence on the history of architecture and was copied in numerous buildings, including Chiswick House, London. The domed central hall was frescoed at the end of the 17th century by Louis Dorigny, and the *piano nobile* painted by Anselmo Canera, Bernardino India and Alessandro Maganza. The *barchessa* was designed by Vincenzo Scamozzi.

VICENZA PRACTICAL TIPS

INFORMATION OFFICE

Piazza Matteotti 12 (*map Vicenza 4*), T: 0444 320 854, *vicenzae.org, visitpalladio.com, provincia.vicenza.it.* The **Biglietto Unico Museum** card can be purchased at the Teatro Olimpico. Valid for three days, it allows free admission to Vicenza's museums.

GETTING AROUND

By train: There are frequent trains to Vicenza from Verona (25mins or 1hr on the slow Regionale services), Padua (16mins or 30mins), Treviso (70mins) and Venice (45mins or 90mins).

WHERE TO STAY

€€ **Due Mori.** A very pleasant hotel in an excellent position in the old centre between Corso Palladio and Piazza Signori. It has a *dépendence* across the road which has a lovely roof-top terrace. *Contrà Do Rode 24, T: 0444 321886, hotelduemori.it. Map Vicenza 3.*
€€€ **Campo Marzio.** In a modern building in the large public garden between the train station and Corso Palladio. Parking facilities. *Viale Roma 21, T: 0444 545 700, hotelcampomarzio. com. Map Vicenza 5.*
€ **Cristina.** A simple hotel, well run by a pleasant family. Not in the centre—it

is outside Porta Castello—but good value. *Corso Santi Felice e Fortunato 32, T: 0444 323751, hotelcristinavicenza.it. Map Vicenza 3.*

WHERE TO EAT

€€ Antico Ristorante agli Schioppi. Traditional dishes with ingredients typical of the Veneto. Just off Corso Palladio. Closed Sun and Mon at lunchtime. *Piazza Castello 24, T: 0444 543701. Map Vicenza 3.*

€€ Scudo di Francia. Just a few steps from the Basilica, offering classical Vicentine cuisine. *Contrà Piancoli 4, T: 0444 323 322. Map Vicenza 4.*

€ Righetti. A very inconspicuous restaurant, though right in the centre of town, frequented by locals. Excellent quality and reasonably priced regional dishes. You set your own table, and go to the counter to order, and pay at the desk at the end. There is also seating outside in the piazza in good weather. Closed Sat and Sun. *Piazza Duomo 3, T: 0444 543135. Map Vicenza 3.*

WINE BARS AND CAFÉS

Perhaps the best wine bar is **Bere Alto** in Contrà Pedemuro San Biagio (*map Vicenza 3*), though there are numerous others. **La Meneghina** café (*Contrà Cavour 18*) first opened in 1791 (the street leads down to Piazza dei Signori past the flank of the Palazzo del Comune; *map Vicenza 3*). It has a lovely little interior, and a very welcoming owner. **Pasticceria Sorarù**, in Piazza dei Signori, has plenty of seating outside.

MARKETS

A market is held all over the centre of town on Thur.

FESTIVALS AND EVENTS

Festival of the Madonna di Monte Berico, Sept 8.

LOCAL SPECIALITIES

The vineyards on the Colli Berici produce renowned wines. A symbol of the town is dried stockfish, *bacalà alla vicentina*, cooked in various ways (and spelt thus, instead of with two 'c's as in Venice. An annual festival dedicated to this delicacy is held at Sandrigo (*map Veneto West D2*), and here there is a local confraternity which celebrates the fish, introduced from Norway into the region when fresh fish was hard to come by. See baccalaallavicentina.it.

The Veneto Villas

Most of Palladio's villas in the Veneto (and many from later periods) are to be found in the province of Vicenza and are listed below. The names of the villas change with each new owner, but they generally also carry the name of the original proprietor. They are scattered widely over the province, often in remote areas outside small towns (where available, street addresses have been given in the description below to help with their location, as signposting is generally poor). Many of the villas are privately owned and thus closed to the public (except with special permission), but the exteriors and gardens are often their most important features, since they are usually surrounded by farm buildings and sometimes by extensive parks. Others are open as *agriturismo* hotels or are used for events. Opening times change frequently and accessibility varies; it is therefore advisable to consult their websites or the information office in Vicenza before starting a tour.

THE VILLAS OF THE VENETO

The province of Vicenza is particularly rich in villas of the famous *ville venete* type. These were built from the 15th century onwards by rich noble Venetian families who were anxious to invest in land on the *terraferma* and contribute to its fertility by the construction of canals and irrigation systems. In the early 16th century Palladio invented an architecture peculiarly fitted to these prestigious villas, which he saw both as places of repose and as working farms. He derived their design in part from the villas of the ancient Romans and used Classical features in their construction. He took particular care in the siting of his villas, sometimes on low hills or near canals, and almost always surrounded by gardens and farmland. The distinctive service wings are known as *barchesse*. The name comes from the boat houses which were provided for the earliest villas on the Brenta Canal.

Numerous villas by Palladio survive in the province. In the 17th and 18th centuries many more villas were constructed, some of these particularly interesting for their interiors and frescoes (including some by Tiepolo and his son Gian Domenico). Architects of importance who succeeded Palladio include Vincenzo Scamozzi (1552–1616), who was born in Vicenza, and who completed a number of Palladio's buildings here, although he also worked extensively in Venice and other parts of the Veneto. Other architects influenced by Palladio were Antonio Pizzocaro, Francesco Muttoni and Giorgio Massari. Orazio Marinali was responsible for the statuary in many of the gardens.

The most important villas (but by no means all of them) are listed below by period. *See also www.villevenete.net and vicenza-unesco.com.*

VILLAS BY PALLADIO ON THE OUTSKIRTS OF VICENZA

CRICOLI
Villa Trissino Trettenero. Designed (1531–38) by Palladio's first patron, Gian Giorgio Trissino, the architect worked here as a young man. *Strada Marosticana 6, beyond map Vicenza 1.*

BERTESINA
Villa Gazzotti Grimani Curti. An early work by Palladio (1542–43) which is interesting for its façade, but only the central hall and loggia remain from the original design. *Via San Cristoforo 23; T: 0444 542360. Open by appointment daily 9–12 & 2.30–6.30, vicenza-unesco.com. Map Veneto West D2.* On the estate, surrounded by a huge park, is **Villa Ghislanzoni Curti**, built in 1764, and now an *agriturismo* (*villaghislanzoni.it*).

VILLAS BY PALLADIO NORTHEAST OF VICENZA

VIGARDOLO DI MONTICELLO CONTE OTTO VI
Villa Valmarana Bressan. Begun in 1541 by Palladio, this is an austere building with a typical entrance. Recent restoration work has revealed remains of frescoes. *Via Vigardoletto 33; T: 337488693. Open only by appointment. Map Veneto West D2.* There is no evidence that this village directly influenced Jefferson's choice of the name Monticello for his home in Virginia, but Jefferson certainly owned Palladio's *Four Books on Architecture*, and considered it his 'Bible'.

QUINTO VICENTINO
Villa Thiene. Dated around 1545, this villa was left unfinished by Palladio. *Via IV Novembre 4; T: 0444 584 211. Open Mon–Fri 9.30–12.30, Mon and Thur also 5.30–6.30. Map Veneto West D2.*

BOLZANO VICENTINO
Villa Valmarana Scagnolari Zen. Designed around 1563 by Palladio for Giovanni Francesco Valmarana, but left unfinished and altered later (and seriously damaged in the Second World War). The pretty little chapel was added in 1615. In the garden are numerous 18th-century statues by Francesco Marinali the Younger. *Via Ponte 3, Località Lisiera. No admission. Map Veneto West D2.*

VILLAS BY PALLADIO SOUTH AND WEST OF VICENZA

BAGNOLO
Villa Pisani Ferri Bonetti. One of Palladio's most beautiful villas, recently well restored, begun in 1540 (the loggia was added around 1560). The main entrance has rusticated arches beneath a pediment, and the villa is surrounded by farm buildings. *Via Risaie 1; T: 0444 831 104. The piano nobile, cellars, and garden can be visited by appointment. villapisani.net. Map Veneto West C3.*

NEAR AGUGLIARO

Villa Saraceno. Begun by Palladio between 1545 and 1555, and surrounded by farm buildings. Owned and very well restored by the Landmark Trust of Great Britain (*apartments to rent*). *Open 1 April–31 Oct on Wed at 2–4; at other times by appointment; T: 0444 891 371. landmarktrust.org.uk. Map Veneto West D3.*

POIANA MAGGIORE

Villa Poiana. Built in 1555 by Palladio, with a typical Palladian arch over the entrance. It has contemporary frescoes by Bernardino India and Anselmo Canera and stuccoes by Bartolomeo Ridolfi. The frescoes in the atrium are attributed to Giovanni Battista Zelotti. It is one of the architect's very best works and is still in a rural setting. *Via Castello, T: 0444 323014. Open April– Sept Wed–Fri 10–1 & 2–6; weekends 10–6. www.villapoiana.it. Map Veneto West C3.*

VANCIMUGLIO

Villa Chiericati da Porto Rigo. Built in 1554, almost certainly by Palladio (but left unfinished), with an Ionic portico. *Via Nazionale 1; T: 0444 387 076. The exterior and garden are usually open. Map Veneto West D2.*

VILLAS BY PALLADO NORTH OF VICENZA

CALDOGNO

Villa Caldogno Nordera. Built around 1545, and generally attributed to Palladio, with frescoes dating from the same century by Gianantonio Fasolo and Battista Zelotti. *Via Zanella 3; www.comune.caldogno.vi.it Open March–Oct Fri 3–6, Sat 9–12. Map Veneto West C2.*

LUGO DI VICENZA

Villa Godi Malinverni. One of the earliest known works by Palladio (1540–2). The piano nobile was frescoed in the 16th century by Giovanni Battista Zelotti. A wing of the palace has a representative collection of 19th-century Italian paintings. *Via Palladio 44; T: 0445 860 561, villagodi. com. Open March–May and Oct–Nov 2–6; June–Sept 3–7. Map Veneto West C1–D1.* **Villa Piovene** (Porto Godi). Also at Lugo. Palladio is thought to have built the central core in around 1539, with an Ionic pronaos, and in the 18th century Francesco Muttoni added the two porticoes on either side and the long central flight of steps up through the garden, which has statues by Orazio Marinali or his workshop. It is surrounded by a large park which is open every day from 2–6 or 7. *Via Palladio 51, vicenza-unesco.com. Map Veneto West C1–D1.*

Famous villas by Palladio elsewhere in the Veneto are Villa Badoer at Fratta Polesine, Villa Barbaro at Maser near Asolo, Villa Emo at Fanzolo di Vedelago, Villa Foscari (La Malcontenta), close to Venice, Villa Pisani at Montagnana and Villa Cornaro at Piombino Dese.

LATER 16TH-CENTURY VILLAS

NEAR AGUGLIARO
Villa Saraceno delle Trombe. Designed in 1550 by Sanmicheli. *Via Finale 10; T: 0444 891084. The exterior can be visited from March–Oct on Wed 10–12.30 & 1.30–3. Map Veneto West D3.*

GRISIGNANO DI ZOCCO
Villa Ferramosca-Beggiato. Designed by Gian Domenico, the father of the more famous Vincenzo Scamozzi, around 1568, with a Palladian style loggia and pediment. *Via Vittorio Veneto, Località Barbano; T: 347 722 4056. Open by appointment). Map Veneto West D2–D3.*

LONGA (NEAR SCHIAVON)
Villa Chiericati Lambert. Built in 1590 (but altered in the 19th century), with 16th-century frescoes attributed to Pozzoserrato, and surrounded by a park. It is now the seat of Showa, a Japanese musical academy. *Map Veneto West D2.*

LONIGO
Palazzo Pisani (now the Town Hall, where exhibitions are also held) is a very grand mansion of 1557. On the outskirts stands the Rocca, or Villa Pisani (1576), a charming work by Vincenzo Scamozzi (recalling Palladio's Villa Rotonda). *Via Rocca 1, T: 0444 831625. Open by appointment, April–Oct. Map Veneto West C3.*

SANDRIGO
Villa Sesso Schiavo Nardone. Built by a follower of Palladio in 1570, with contemporary frescoes by Giovanni Antonio Fasolo. *Via San Lorenzo 5; villasessoschiavo.it. Open by appointment. Map Veneto West D2.*

VILLAVERLA
Villa Verlato. Built in 1576 by Vincenzo Scamozzi, it has the appearance of a *palazzo* and contains frescoes by the little-known Girolamo Pisani and Giovanni Battista Maganza. *Piazza del Popolo 1; T: 348 351 9260. Open by appointment. Map Veneto West C2.*

17TH-CENTURY VILLAS

LONGARE
Villa da Schio. Three buildings on a hillside in the hamlet of Costozza, near Longare, surrounded by a lovely garden which features sculptures by Orazio Marinali. He worked in the stone quarries of Costozza nearby which had supplied building stone to the Romans as well as Palladio. The **Villino Garzadori**, built in 1690, has frescoes by Louis Dorigny. *Piazza da Schio 2; T: 0444 555099. Now run as an agriturimso, but the park is open Tues–Sun 10–2 & 4–7, in winter 10–2. costozza-villadaschio.it. Map Veneto West D2.*

CASTELGOMBERTO
Villa da Schio Piovene. Built in 1666, probably by Antonio Pizzocaro. It has 18th-century additions and is surrounded by a garden with statues by the workshop of Orazio Marinali. Inside are three early works by

Giambattista Tiepolo. The chapel dates from 1614. *Via Villa 147. Garden open April–Oct by appointment, villadaschio. com. Map Veneto West C2.*

COLZÈ
Villa Colzè Feriani. Rebuilt in the 17th century, with a chapel containing sculptures by Orazio Marinali. There is pleasant but simple *agriturismo* accommodation on the estate (*T: 0444 636039, agriturismovillaferiani.it*). *Map Veneto West D2.*

VILLAVERLA
Villa Ghellini. Built in 1664–79, this is the most important work of Antonio Pizzocaro. *Via Sant'Antonio 6; T: 0445 856073. Open Mon–Fri 10–12 & 3–5 or 4–6; Sat 10–12. Map Veneto West C2.*

THIENE
Villa Beregan Cunico (Ca' Beregane). Built in 1639 by Antonio Pizzocaro, it has an exceptionally long low façade with numerous windows. *On the road between Thiene and Vicenza. Only open by appointment, T: 0445 360923. Map Veneto West C2.*

BREGANZE
Villa Diedo Basso. Built in 1664–84, with later additions. Breganze is known for its wines (including the justly famous Maculan Fratte, a red made from Cabernet and Merlot grapes grown on the sunny slopes to the north), which can be purchased at the beautiful modern Maculan Cellars in the village. *Map Veneto West D1–D2.*

18TH-CENTURY VILLAS SOUTH AND WEST OF VICENZA

ALTAVILLA VICENTINA
Villa Valmarana Morosini. Built by Francesco Muttoni in 1724, now a hotel (*see overleaf*).

NEAR MONTEVIALE
Villa Loschi Zileri Motterle. Attributed to Francesco Muttoni and Muttonio Massari, surrounded by a fine park with exotic trees. The staircase and *salone* have the earliest frescoes by Tiepolo (1734) outside Venice. *Via Zileri 1, Località Biron. Now the studio of a firm of architects, and only open by appointment; T: 0444 570141, 0444 964190; studiomotterle. com. Map Veneto West C2.*

MONTECCHIO MAGGIORE
This picturesque village and legendary stronghold of the 'Montagues' of *Romeo and Juliet*, has two restored Scaligeri

castles. Just outside, owned by the Province, is the **Villa Cordellina Lombardi**. Built by Giorgio Massari (1735), it has very fine frescoes (1743) by Giambattista Tiepolo in the central hall. *Via Lovara 36, open April–Oct Tues–Fri 9–1, Wed, Thur, Sat and Sun also 3–6; T: 0444 908112. Map Veneto West C2.*

SAREGO
Villa da Porta 'La Favorita'. Built by Francesco Muttoni in 1714–15. *Località Monticello di Fara; T: 0444 421 201. Open by appointment. villalafavorita. com. Map Veneto West C3.*

ORGIANO
Villa Fracanzan Piovene. Built in 1710 and attributed to Francesco Muttoni, with an interesting garden (and *barchessa*). *Via San Francesco*

2; T: 0444 874589. Open April–Oct for guided tours on Sun and holidays 3–7; otherwise by appointment. www. villafracanzanpiovene.com. Map Veneto West C3.

MONTEGALDA
Castello Grimani Sorlini. A 12th-century castle adapted as a villa in the 18th century, with a fine park decorated with statues by the workshop of Orazio Marinali. *Via Castello 21; not open regularly; see fondazionesorlini.com. Map Veneto West D3.*

18TH-CENTURY VILLAS NORTH OF VICENZA

DUEVILLE
Villa Da Porto Casarotto. Built by Ottone Calderari in 1770–76. *Via Da Porto 89, villadaportocasarotto.com. Map Veneto West D2.*

THIENE
Castello di Thiene (also known as Palazzo Porto-Colleoni). A late Gothic Venetian castle which was the residence of the Porto family. It may have been begun by Domenico da Venezia and was completed in 1476.

It is fully furnished and was frescoed around 1570 by Giovanni Antonio Fasolo and Giovanni Battista Zelotti, who together decorated many other villas in the Veneto. It has a charming chapel and a magnificent stable block dating from the late 17th or early 18th century, attributed to Francesco Muttoni. It is surrounded by a public park. *Via Garibaldi 2. Open only Sun and holidays March–Nov at 3, 4 and 5, www.castellodithiene.com. Map Veneto West C1–C2.*

VENETO VILLAS PRACTICAL TIPS

GETTING AROUND

The best way to explore the villas around Vicenza is by car. However, it is possible to get to most villages by local buses run by Ferrovie Tramvie Vicentine. Consult their website (*www.ftv.vi.it*) for details of routes and timetables. There are trains from Vicenza to Dueville (15mins) and Thiene (30mins).

VILLAS OFFERING ACCOMMODATION

NB: These are mainly agriturismi or villa rentals offering accommodation for longer stays, the accommodation is mostly modern and in the outbuildings, but offers a fun chance to stay on a Palladian or Palladian-type estate. See veneto-agriturismo.it.

NEAR AGUGLIARO (*Map Veneto West D3*)
Villa Saraceno. Beautifully restored

and appointed. Sleeps 12. *T: 0444 891371. landmarktrust.org.uk.*
ALTAVILLA VICENTINA (*Map Veneto West C2*)
€ **Hotel College Valmarana Morosini**. Fifty very simply furnished modern rooms, with fabrics seemingly either in bright red or bright blue. Breakfast is included in the price. *Via Marconi 97, T: 0444 573988, www. collegevalmarana.it.*
BERTESINA (*Map Veneto West D2*)
Villa Ghislanzoni Curti. Six apartments in the *barchesse* and outbuildings. *Via San Cristoforo 73, T: 347 5232100, villaghislanzoni.it.*
COLZÈ (*Map Veneto West D2*)
Villa Colzè Feriani. Two guesthouses in the former outbuildings accommodating up to 12 guests. *Via Borgo 16, T: 0444 636039, agriturismovillaferiani.it.*
LONGARE (*Map Veneto West D2*)
Villa da Schio. In the village of Costozza. Two-bedroom apartment for weekly rental (other options by agreement). Restaurant (closed Mon). *Piazza da Schio 2; T: 0444 555099, 340 485 4568, costozza-villadaschio.it.*

WHERE TO EAT

CALDOGNO (*Map Veneto West C2*)
€ **Trattoria Molin Vecio**. In an old 16th-century watermill in beautiful countryside. Very interesting food, also for those on special diets. Excellent lunchtime menu of just one course designed especially if you need to get back to work. Reasonable prices. Closed Tues. *Via Giaroni 116, T: 0444 585168, molinvecio.it.*
ALTAVILLA VICENTINA (*Map Veneto West C2*)
€€ **Trattoria Leoncino**. Family

run with local recipes, mostly meat but including the ubiquitous *bacalà alla vicentino. T: 0444 572032, www. trattorialeoncino.com.*
€ **Trattoria Montrosso**. Pleasant place to eat with sound cooking. *Via Roma 76, T: 0444 371362, trattoriamonterosso.it.*
SANDRIGO (*map Veneto West D2*)
€€ **La Trattoria di Palmerino**. Family run and specializing in *bacalà*. Closed Tues evening and Wednesday. *T: 0444 659034, palmerino.eu.*
€€ **Antica Trattoria Due Spade**. An old-established restaurant. *Via Roma 5, T: 0444 659948, duespade.com.*

FESTIVALS AND EVENTS

The region is particularly famous for its cuisine and throughout the year there are food and wine festivals everywhere: pea (*bisi*) festival at Longare in May; a watermelon festival at Lonigo in July; *bacalà* and polenta festival at Thiene in late Oct, and a mushroom festival in June and Sept also at Thiene. Sandrigo is the birthplace of the 'Venerable Confraternity of *bacalà alla vicentina*'(salt cod simmered in milk) and celebrates it with a festival in Sept.

LOCAL SPECIALITIES

Local products are on sale at Lugo di Vicenza for the *Festa di San Giovanni* (around 24 June). The typical cured *salame* produced around Vicenza is called *soprèssa*. The wines of the Breganze region are particularly well known, where blends of local cultivars such as the white Garganega or the red Corvina Veronese, Rondinella and Molinara, are used to produce good red and white wines.

Bassano del Grappa & Marostica

S ituated where the Brenta River emerges from the hills, **Bassano del Grappa** (*map Veneto West D1*) is a pleasant town of arcaded streets and old houses, many of which still have faded frescoes on their façades. The town is famous as the home of a family of well-known painters—the da Ponte, called Bassano after this, their birthplace (*see below*). It is also visited for its famous wooden bridge across the Brenta, designed by Palladio. The town's name comes from the nearby Monte Grappa (1775m), where the Italian and Austro-Hungarian armies clashed in a series of terrible battles in 1917–18. Ernest Hemingway came here as a Red Cross volunteer in October 1918, during the final days of the Grappa campaign, an experience which provided much of the inspiration for *A Farewell to Arms*. Bassano is also known, coincidentally, for its grappa, the spirit distilled from grape skins (though the name of the spirit has no etymological link with that of the mountain).

THE BASSANO FAMILY

There were four main members in this prominent family of Venetian painters. Francesco da Ponte the Elder (c. 1475–1539) worked in Bassano and painted in a rustic style, using soft colours like those of the Bellini. His son Jacopo (c. 1510/18–1592) the most famous of the family, rose to prominence in late-Renaissance and early-Baroque Venice. His religious paintings, lush landscapes, and scenes of everyday life show the influence of fashionable contemporaries such as Parmigianino. A pioneer of the genre scene and one of the first painters to be interested in peasants and animals, his Biblical characters are represented as real yokels, and he often pays more loving attention to the ox and the ass than to the human characters. Jacopo had four painter sons: Francesco, Gerolamo, Giovanni Battista and Leandro. Leandro and Francesco achieved fame and some fortune in Venice. Leandro was even given a noble title by the doge. Francesco worked a lot with his father, but his life ended in tragedy: he threw himself to his death from a top floor window at the age of 44.

THE TOWN CENTRE OF BASSANO

The northernmost part of the historic centre, including the 15th-century cathedral (with paintings by the Bassano), stands inside the walled complex of the Castello

Superiore, which dates to 900–950 but was enlarged and fortified in the 13th, 14th and subsequent centuries, when the town was successively under the rule of the Ezzelini, the Visconti of Milan, and, after 1404, of Venice. A tower of the old fortress serves as the base of the campanile. The area to the south of this, occupied in part by the 14th-century Castello Inferiore, developed around three adjacent squares, Piazzetta Monte Vecchio and the more recently renamed Piazza Garibaldi and Piazza Libertà.

In Piazza Garibaldi stands the former Franciscan church of **San Francesco**, a Romanesque-Gothic building with an elegant vestibule of 1306 and a graceful campanile. It has remains of 15th-century frescoes and, in the apse, a painted wooden Crucifix of the 14th century. A door on the right of the porch leads to the **Museo Civico** (*open Tues–Sat 9–7, Sun and holidays 10.30–1 & 3–6*), housed in the former Franciscan friary with its beautiful 17th-century cloister. The diverse collection includes: archaeological finds from Bassano and the region; a collection of ancient Greek and Italic vases (with some very fine volute kraters); a Crucifix by Guariento and works by the Vivarini; a room devoted to the sculptor Canova and another with a comprehensive collection of works by Jacopo Bassano, offering the best overview of his work anywhere in the world. Paintings by Jacopo's sons are also on display.

FROM PIAZZA LIBERTÀ TO THE RIVER
Piazza Libertà, near Piazza Garibaldi, has the Loggia del Comune (1582) with a fresco of *St Christopher* ascribed to Jacopo Bassano, and two 18th-century buildings, the Palazzo del Municipio and the church of San Giovanni Battista.

Piazzetta Monte Vecchio, which was the main square of the city in the Middle Ages, is lined with fine old palaces, most notably the 15th-century Palazzetto del Monte di Pietà, with inscriptions and coats of arms on the façade. Just off the square is Via Bartolomeo Gamba, which leads downhill to the **Ponte degli Alpini**, the famous covered wooden bridge across the River Brenta, which retains the form designed for it by Palladio in 1569. The river is subject to sudden floods, and the bridge has had to be rebuilt many times: it has been proved over the centuries that only a wooden structure (rather than stone) can survive the force of the water. The bridge takes its current name from the Alpini regiment, who crossed it numerous times during the campaigns on Monte Grappa in the First World War. The regiment was also responsible for rebuilding the bridge after the Second World War. The view upstream is extremely picturesque, with the wooded mountains rising above the clustering red roofs of the town, the foaming water of the river and the houses on the riverfront, all well preserved. The best view of the bridge itself is from the far side, from a lane which leads left beside a little garden on the banks of the river.

Just as you enter the bridge from Via Gamba, on the left, is **Nardini**, a characteristic little bar, with a grappa distillery of 1769. You can sample grappa here, and buy bottles to take home. They will tell you that Hemingway often popped in for a shot. Back on Via Gamba, in the Poli distillery, is the **Museo del Grappa**, also offering the chance to taste and buy, illustrating the history of grappa and its production (*open daily 9–7.30; poligrappa.com*). At the far (west) end of the bridge, entered through the Taverna al Ponte, is the small **Museo degli Alpini**, with photographs and other memorabilia (*Via Angarano 2; open Tues–Sun 8.30–8*).

Also on the river (east bank, south of the bridge) is the lovely 18th-century **Palazzo Sturm** (*open Tues–Sat 9–1 & 3–6, Sun and holidays 10.30–1 & 3–6*), which houses two museums. The entrance is through the attractive Neoclassical courtyard overlooking the river. The entrance hall (1765) has frescoes by Giorgio Anselmi in Bolognese Baroque style, including a *Fall of the Giants* and other allegories. The **Museo della Ceramica** exhibits a collection of ceramics illustrating the production of Italian manufactures, including local ware from Bassano, Nove and Vicenza. Beyond a belvedere (now enclosed) overlooking the river is the delightful little Sala dell'Alcova, which preserves its original 18th-century Rococo decoration intact, including exquisite inlaid woodwork and painted Old Testament scenes by the Treviso-born artist Gaetano Zompini. The **Museo Remondini** (named after a family of local printers) illustrates the history of typography. Its highlights, in the Sala del Tesoro, include drawings, prints and engravings by a variety of artists, including Mantegna and Dürer. They are exhibited in rotation because of their fragility.

VILLA CA' ERIZZO LUCA

In the northern part of town, close to the river, is Villa Ca' Erizzo Luca, a beautiful frescoed villa which was used as the headquarters of the Red Cross during the First World War. Hemingway stayed here in 1918 together with his fellow volunteers, including John Dos Passos. The villa is now open as a museum, with some good photographs (*Via Ca' Erizzo 35; at the top of Via Gamba turn left, keep straight along Via Margnan and Via San Sebastiano, which turns into Via Ca' Erizzo; villacaerizzoluca.it*).

VILLAS IN THE ENVIRONS OF BASSANO

On the western outskirts of Bassano, at Sant'Eusebio, is the **Villa Angarano Bianchi-Michiel**, built in the late 17th century by Domenico Margutti, perhaps to a design by Longhena, the great Venetian Baroque architect. The *barchesse* are on an older plan by Palladio. It belongs to the five Bianchi-Michiel sisters, who make wine here.

In the southern outskirts of Bassano, east of the river, is the **Villa Rezzonico-Borella**, its corner towers reminiscent of a medieval castle, though it was built in the early 18th century and is attributed as an early work to Longhena. It has a fine park and garden. Napoleon stayed here in 1796, at the time that his troops, under Massena, defeated the Austrians near Bassano (*Via Ca' Rezzonico 68, visits by appointment, T: 0424 220672 or 348 5646447, villarezzonicoborella.com*).

A road leads northeast out of Bassano to **Romano d'Ezzelino** (*map Veneto West DI*) with the 17th-century Ca' Cornaro, which has an orangery by Vincenzo Scamozzi (*exterior viewable by appointment; see www.villevenete.net*). Nearby is **Mussolente**, with the Villa Negri Piovene on a low hill approached by a long flight of steps from the Asolo road, and flanked by two porticoed outbuildings.

MAROSTICA

Marostica (*map Veneto West D1*), a stronghold of the Ezzelini in the 12th–13th centuries, was rebuilt in 1311–86 by the Scaligeri. It came under Venetian control in 1404 and remained faithful to the Republic from then onwards. Today it is a charming old fortified townlet preserving its medieval ramparts, which connect the lower castle on the piazza with the upper castle on the green hillside above. It has a particularly pleasant climate, and excellent cherries are grown in the surroundings. Its biennial chess game with human combatants has become a famous spectacle. The delightful Piazza Castello, with the stone chessboard on which the game is played, has a superb view of the ramparts climbing the green hillside to the upper castle. The battlemented Castello Inferiore (*open daily 10–12 & 2.30–6*) in the piazza was built by the Scaligeri in the early 14th century and restored in 1935. There are a beautiful well and an ancient ivy in the courtyard; stairs lead up to the loggia with a catapult reconstructed in 1923. The Sala del Consiglio was frescoed in the 17th century. Chessboards are provided for the public at the other end of the piazza, in a loggia beneath a bank building (matches are often played here at weekends).

Via Sant'Antonio leads past the church of **Sant'Antonio**, which contains an altarpiece by Jacopo Bassano and his son Francesco (1574), to the 17th-century church of the Carmine. A path leads up the green hillside to the **Castello Superiore**, also built by the Scaligeri, but ruined by the Venetians in the 16th century (it can also be reached by road).

South of the town is **Nove**, known for its ceramics. The Antonibon family were active here from 1727 producing majolica and porcelain, examples of which can be seen in the Museo Civico in Palazzo de Fabris (*open Tues–Sat 9-1, Sun 3-7*). On the Brenta at **Cartigliano** is the eccentric, unfinished Villa Morosini Cappello on Piazza della Concordia (now owned by the municipality), truly an extraordinary sight. It was begun in 1560 probably by the engineer Francesco Zamberlan, who was a friend and collaborator of Palladio, and is best known for La Rotonda at Rovigo. The remarkable trabeated Ionic colonnade that surrounds the *piano nobile* may have been added in the 17th century. In the parish church, the Chapel of the Rosary is decorated with frescoes (1575) by Jacopo Bassano and his son Francesco, and has an altarpiece by Bartolomeo Montagna.

THE ALTOPIANO DEI SETTE COMUNI

Bassano and Marostica lie at the foot of the Altopiano dei Sette Comuni—a plateau c. 1000m above sea level that takes its name from seven townships (Asiago, Enego,

Foza, Gallio, Lusiana, Roana and Rotzo; *map Veneto West C1–D1*), united from 1310–1807 in an autonomous federation. The inhabitants of the plateau are of Germanic origin (the Cimbri) and the area is both a winter and summer resort. **Recoaro Terme** is a well-known spa with ferruginous springs. **Asiago**, near the centre of the plateau, was the scene of bitter fighting in the First World War.

BASSANO & MAROSTICA PRACTICAL TIPS

GETTING AROUND

By train: There are direct services to Bassano del Grappa from Padua (65mins) and Venice (90mins); other routes involve a change at Cittadella or Castelfranco Veneto. The nearest station to Marostica is Bassano del Grappa.

By bus: There are frequent services between Bassano del Grappa and Marostica (15mins). Buses from Bassano bus station, just west of the railway station, also serve Cartigliano via Nove, and there are services for Asiago too (90mins), though these often require a change at Thiene. For Recoaro Terme, the best solution is to take a bus from Vicenza main bus station (c. 80mins). There are buses roughly every hour between Bassano del Grappa and Vicenza (journey time c. 1hr) and frequent direct services between Marostica and Vicenza. These are all run by Ferrovie Tramvie Vicentine (www.ftv.vi.it).

WHERE TO STAY

BASSANO DEL GRAPPA (*Map Veneto West D1*)
€ Hotel Al Castello. At the top of the old town, a simple, old-fashioned place with basic comfort, good prices and a warm welcome. Parking. *Via Bonamigo 19 (Piazza Terraglio), T: 0424 228665, hotelalcastello.it.*

MAROSTICA (*Map Veneto West D1*)
€€ La Rosina, 4km outside Marostica in the hills of the Valle San Floriano. A delightful place run by the grandchildren of Rosina. With good restaurant. *Contrà Marchetti 4, T: 0424 470360, larosina.it.*

WHERE TO EAT

BASSANO DEL GRAPPA (*Map Veneto West D1*)
€€ Trattoria El Piron. A family restaurant in business for many years, serving Veneto cuisine right in the heart of town. *Via Zaccaria Bricito 12 (off Via Gamba), T: 0424 525306, elpiron.altervista.org.*

€€ Trattoria Ostaria Al Borgo. Well-established restaurant serving local dishes made with local ingredients, including (in season) the famous asparagus. Closed Wed and midday Sat. *Via Margnan 7, T: 0424 522155.*

MAROSTICA (*Map Veneto West D1*)
€ Osteria Madonnetta. A wine bar which has been popular since 1904, which serves good food and has all the best local wines. Closed Thurs. *Via Vajenti 21, T: 0424 75859, www.osteriamadonnetta.it.*

NOVE (*Map Veneto West D1*)
€ **Trattoria Da Agnese**. Well worth seeking out. *Via Pedalto 23 (south out of town, on the road to Crosara), T: 0424 474400.*

LOCAL SPECIALITIES

Bassano is particularly known for its white asparagus (asparago bianco di Bassano DOP), which has its own festival in April. White wine made from the Vespaiolo grape, grown in the Breganze region southwest of Marostica, is also a local speciality. Grappa is for sale all over Bassano, and can be tasted at the historic Poli and Nardini distilleries. For cocktails, try Palazzo delle Misture (*Salita Ferracina 8*). Good cheeses available all over the region include Asiago and Grana Padana. Nove is well known for its ceramics, and Marostica for its cherries (and straw hats).

MARKETS

There is a weekly market on Tues in Piazza degli Scacchi in Marostica.

FESTIVALS AND EVENTS

Bassano celebrates its famous asparagus in April. At Marostica a famous chess game (*Partita a Scacchi*), in which the whole town participates, takes place every two years (even years) on a Fri, Sat and Sun evening in early Sept. The tradition commemorates a duel fought in 1454 between Rinaldo d'Angarano (black) and Vieri da Vallonara (white) for the hand of Lionora, daughter of Taddeo Parisio, the local Venetian governor. Vieri won the first match, and white still wins every game today, although a different game from the history of chess is chosen to be re-enacted each year. The herald who conducts the event speaks in Venetian dialect. At the end of the game the wedding takes place, with some 500 participants in 15th-century costume—flag-throwers, drummers, medieval musicians and a host of attendants. The game is held at 9pm (also at 5pm on the last day) and tickets should be bought by June. In odd years, when the 'players' are sent abroad to perform the game, an international chess festival is held in the town. *Information from the Associazione Pro Marostica, Piazza Castello 1, T: 0424 72127, www.marosticascacchi.it.*

Also in Marostica a cherry festival is held on the last Sun in May. Rotzo, in the Altopiano dei Sette Comuni, is famed for its potatoes and holds a potato festival in late Aug or early Sept.

Verona

Verona (*map Veneto West B3*) is one of the most attractive large towns in northern Italy. The wide pavements of its pleasant streets, made out of huge blocks of the local red marble, give the town an air of opulence. The birthplace of Catullus and perhaps Vitruvius in the 1st century BC, Verona has impressive Roman remains including the famous amphitheatre known as the Arena (which is extremely well preserved) and its ancient theatre on the hillside above the river. It has an unusually high number of very beautiful large Romanesque and Gothic churches, the finest of which is the basilica of San Zeno. Many of them have very colourful frescoes and their lovely works of art are mostly by skilled local artists.

Romeo and Juliet was set in Verona, and their are several 'shrines' associated with Juliet: as Shakespeare himself declared:

'[...] while Verona by that name is known,
There shall no figure at such rate be set,
As that of true and faithful Juliet.'

The Della Scala family, who ruled the town from the late 13th century, are commemorated by their sumptuous tombs and their castle, Castelvecchio, now a museum. The Piazza dei Signori and the adjoining Piazza delle Erbe are two of the finest squares in Italy, and there are lovely peaceful narrow streets nearby in the loop of the river Adige, which is an important feature of the town. Verona's historic prosperity is derived from the fact that it stands at the junction of two main traffic arteries: from Germany and Austria to central Italy, and from Piedmont and Lombardy to the Veneto and Friuli-Venezia Giulia. It is well equipped to receive hundreds of thousands of visitors every year and is especially crowded in summer during the opera season, when performances are held at the Arena.

HISTORY OF VERONA

Originally a Bronze Age settlement, Verona became a Roman colony in 89 BC and flourished under the Roman emperors. In the early Middle Ages a succession of Ostrogoths, Lombards and Franks chose Verona as their seat, before it became an independent *comune* in 1107. Family feuds within the city (on which the story of Romeo and Juliet is based) were settled by the tyrant Ezzelino da Romano, who ruled the city (at times together with Padua) from 1231 until his death in battle in 1259. A year later Mastino Della Scala transformed his office of *podestà* into a more powerful role and his family retained exclusive control of the government of the city as a *signoria* for the next 120 years. Their reigns, especially that of Cangrande I, from 1311 to 1329, saw the power of Verona greatly increase in the Veneto. The splendid Castelvecchio, with its bridge over the Adige, was built by the Della Scala, and they are also recorded in their elaborate monuments grouped together in a grand enclosure beside their palace in Piazza dei Signori. For a few years after the Della Scala, Gian Galeazzo Visconti of Milan took control of the city, but by 1405 Verona had chosen to become part of the Venetian Republic; it remained under her protection until the downfall of the *Serenissima* in 1797. Just one year later, armed rebellion against the French (the '*Pasque Veronesi*') brought retaliation in which much of the city was destroyed. In the 19th century the city passed back and forth between the hands of the French and the Austrians before it was ceded to Austria at the Congress of Vienna and so was forced to become an Austrian stronghold during the Italian wars of independence. In 1866 it finally joined united Italy.

During the Second World War the city suffered considerably from bombing, and the bridges were all blown up. In the Castelvecchio in 1944, Mussolini's puppet Republican government staged the trial of Count Galeazzo Ciano, Mussolini's son-in-law, who had been a Fascist minister but later became a leading opponent of the *Duce* (the court ordered Ciano's execution).

ART AND ARCHITECTURE IN VERONA

The great church of San Zeno is one of the outstanding achievements of Romanesque architecture in Italy. The architect Michele Sanmicheli (1486–1559) designed some important buildings for this, his native town. But it is in the field of painting that Verona is especially interesting, for the numerous works in its churches and museums by local artists, most of them little-known elsewhere. Interestingly the greatest painter born in the town, Paolo Caliari, always known as Veronese, left no works of great importance here since he was active almost entirely in Venice. But nevertheless it is clear to see how much he was influenced as a young man by Verona's local school of painting.

Altichiero was the most important painter at work in northern Italy in the second half of the 14th century: although he was born in Verona, most of his best surviving works are now in Padua. However, there are frescoes by him here in the two most important churches of Sant'Anastasia and San Fermo (as well as in Santa Maria della Scala).

The most famous painter who lived in the town in the early 15th century was **Pisanello**. Although we know he decorated a number of palaces, his remarkable fresco of *St George* in Sant'Anastasia is one of the very few by him to have survived (another, but in very poor condition, can be seen in San Fermo). Fewer than ten paintings can today be attributed to him, but one of the loveliest can be seen in the Castelvecchio museum. He was clearly fascinated by naturalistic details and the Gothic world of chivalry, and painted with the care of a miniaturist. He is best known for the numerous exquisite small bronze medals and plaquettes he made which can be seen in museums all over the world.

Pisanello's near contemporaries Giovanni Badile and Stefano da Zevio both also painted charming joyful Madonnas (now preserved in the same room in the Castelvecchio museum), as well as carrying out frescoes in Sant'Anastasia and San Fermo (Badile died young, but also produced frescoes for Santa Maria della Scala).

Numerous native artists were at work in the town in the later 15th century: among them perhaps the most influential was Domenico Morone, whose frescoes in the library of the convent of San Bernardino (now called the Sala Morone) are considered his best works. His son Francesco also carried out frescoes in Sant'Anastasia. Francesco Bonsignori was at work at the same time as Domenico in San Bernardino (and his works can also be seen in the Castelvecchio museum). Numerous successors of Domenico include Francesco Torbido (altarpiece in San Zeno and frescoes in the Duomo), Antonio Badile (San Nazaro e Celso), and Giovan Francesco Caroto, all of them born in the 1480s. Badile has been recognised as Veronese's earliest master, and Caroto was perhaps the ablest of these painters and the best represented in the town (Castelvecchio, San Fermo, San Giorgio in Braida, Santa Maria in Organo, San Francesco, San Paolo and Sant'Eufemia). Girolamo dai Libri, also born in the late 15th century, was one of the most talented Veronese followers of Domenico Morone: he earned his second name (*Libri*, books) from his skill as an illuminator of manuscripts. His paintings, which often incorporate beautiful landscapes, can be seen in Sant'Anastasia, San Giorgio in Braida and three other churches in the town.

In the early 16th century artists of the '*maniera*' included Caroto's pupil Domenico Brusasorci, who was at work on frescoes in Santo Stefano, Santa Maria in Organo and Sant'Eufemia. His son Felice, who was particularly skilled in portaiture, also left altarpieces here, and the one in San Giorgio in Braida must have influenced Veronese. Domenico's near contemporary Paolo Farinati is well represented with altarpieces and frescoes (San Giovanni in Fonte, San Giorgio in Braida and the Museo degli Affreschi).

The Olivetan monk Fra' Giovanni da Verona, born in the city in 1457, left his masterpiece here: the magnificent intarsia choir stalls in Santa Maria in Organo. Such was their fame that he was then called to work in the Vatican.

PIAZZA BRÀ & THE ARENA

The huge Piazza Brà (*map Verona Right 11*; Veronese dialect for *braida*, from the German *breit*, meaning 'wide') is the best-known piazza in Verona, mostly closed to traffic and with a garden in the centre. It is particularly spacious and three of its sides are occupied by three monumental buildings, one dating from ancient Roman times (the amphitheatre) and the other two from the Neoclassical period. On the fourth side is an exceptionally wide pavement called the **Liston**, which has a series of cafés and restaurants, popular and lively almost all day long, and, in the centre, **Palazzo Malfatti**, with a high rusticated portico and a balcony on the first floor. It was built by Verona's greatest native architect, Michele Sanmicheli, towards the end of his life in 1555.

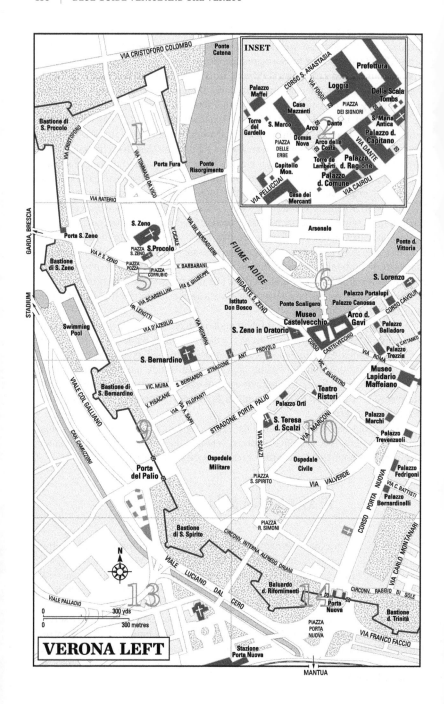

VIA CRISTOFORO COLOMBO

Ponte
Catena

INSET

Prefettura

CORSO S. ANASTASIA

VIA FOGGE

Palazzo
Maffei

Loggia

Casa
Mazzanti

Della Scala
Tombs

PIAZZA
DEI SIGNORI

Torre
del
Gardello

S. Marco

Arco
Dante

S. Maria
Antica

Domus
Nova

Palazzo d.
Capitano

PIAZZA
DELLE
ERBE

Arco della
Costa

VIA DANTE

Capitello
Mon.

Torre de
Lamberti

Palazzo
d. Ragione

Palazzo
d. Comune

VIA CAIROLI

Casa dei
Mercanti

VIA PELLICCIAI

Bastione di
S. Procolo

VIA CRISTOFORO

1

Porta Fura

Ponte
Risorgimento

FIUME ADIGE

Arsenale

Ponte d.
Vittoria

VIA TOMMASO DA VICO

VIA RATERIO

GARDA, BRESCIA

S. Zeno

V. CICALE

VIA DEL BERSAGLIERE

Porta S. Zeno

PIAZZA
S. ZENO

S.Procolo

RIGASTE S. ZENO

6

S. Lorenzo

STADIUM

VIA P. S. ZENO

Bastione
di S. Zeno

PIAZZA
POZZA

PIAZZA
CORRUBIO

5

V. BARBARANI

VIA S. GIUSEPPE

VIA SCARSELLINI

Istituto
Don Bosco

Ponte Scaligero

Palazzo Portalupi

Palazzo Canossa

CORSO CAVOUR

VIA LENOTTI

Museo
Castelvecchio

Arco d.
Gavi

Palazzo
Balladoro

VIA D'AZEGLIO

VIA ROSMINI

S. Zeno in Oratorio

CORSO CASTELVECCHIO

VIA ROMA

Palazzo
Trezza

CATTANEI

Swimming
Pool

ANT   PROVOLO

VIA S. SILVESTRO

Museo
Lapidario
Maffeiano

S. Bernardino

VIC. MURA

VIA S. BERNARDO STRADONE

V. PISACANE

VIA FILOPANTI

Teatro
Ristori

Palazzo
Marchi

VIALE COL. GALLIANO

Bastione di
S. Bernardino

VIA SAFFI

STRADONE PORTA PALIO

Palazzo Orti

VIA MARCONI

Palazzo
Trevenzuoli

CAN. CAMUZZONI

9

S. Teresa
d. Scalzi

VIA SCALZI

Palazzo
Fedrigoni

Ospedale
Militare

Ospedale
Civile

VIA C. BATTISTI

Porta
del Palio

PIAZZA
S. SPIRITO

VIA   VALVERDE

CORSO PORTA NUOVA

Palazzo
Bernardinelli

10

PIAZZA
R. SIMONI

Bastione
di S. Spirito

CIRCONV. INTERNA ALFREDO DRIANI

N

VIALE LUCIANO DAL CERO

VIALE PALLADIO

13

0   300 yds

0   300 metres

Baluardo
d. Rifornimenti

14

Porta
Nuova

CIRCONV. RAGGIO DI SOLE

VIA CARLO MONTANARI

Bastione
d. Trinità

PIAZZA
PORTA
NUOVA

VIA FRANCO FACCIO

Stazione
Porta Nuova

VERONA LEFT

MANTUA

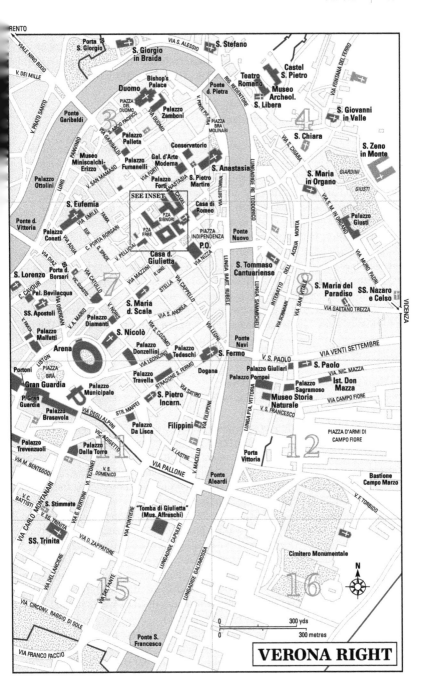

VERONA RIGHT

The **Portoni della Brà**, a battlemented archway of 1389, stands astride the busy Via Porta Nuova, the entrance to the city from the south (and the railway station). It fittingly bears an inscription with Romeo's desperate affirmation: 'There is no world without Verona walls,' after Friar Laurence had tried to comfort him:

'Hence from Verona art thou banished:
Be patient, for the world is broad and wide.'

The archway adjoins the huge Doric **Palazzo della Gran Guardia**, begun in 1609 by Domenico Curtoni for military use (and completed some two centuries later by Giuseppe Barbieri). It is now an exhibition venue. Even more imposing is the huge Neoclassical **Palazzo Municipale**, also by Barbieri, the Town Hall of Verona.

The Amphitheatre, always known as the **Arena** (*map Verona Right 7; open 8.30–7.30pm; Mon 1.30–7.30*) was built around AD 100 and is very well preserved: it is the third largest Roman amphitheatre to survive, after the Colosseum and the one in Capua. An earthquake in 1183 destroyed all but four arches of the outermost arcade, but the inner arcade of two orders superimposed is almost complete with its 74 arches (the Colosseum has 80). Splendid vaulted passageways open into the cavea, where the 44 tiers of seats can accommodate some 22,000 spectators (they were restored in the 16th century after the stone had been pillaged for building material in the Middle Ages). The performance here of *Aida* in 1913 set a new standard for the production of operatic spectacle, and the Arena still hosts a popular opera festival in the summer.

MUSEO LAPIDARIO MAFFEIANO

Map Verona Left 10. Entrance just outside the Portoni della Brà. Open 8.30–2 except Mon.

Founded in 1716 by the dramatist Scipione Maffei (1675–1755), this was one of the first public museums in Italy. It is housed around a courtyard with a magnificent porch at one end, with six huge Ionic columns, built in 1604 by Domenico Curtoni. Curtoni, who was clearly influenced by Palladio, designed this building to be seen in conjunction with his Palazzo della Gran Guardia (*see above*) along the line of the medieval walls. At that time the courtyard was already used to display ancient inscriptions. The porch served as an entrance to the Teatro Filarmonico, rebuilt in 1716 by Francesco Bibiena, where Mozart played in 1770. Francesco came from a family of architects particularly well known as builders of theatres, and by this time he had already built theatres in Vienna and Nancy. This one had to be reconstructed in 1969 (when it was given a new entrance on Via Roma) after destruction during the War and again by fire. The low Roman Doric porticoes on either side of the courtyard were added in 1745 to display the lapidary collection (the scale was destroyed in the 20th century by the addition of the two floors above).

There is a lift to the first floor, where some 100 Greek inscriptions from Smyrna, the Cyclades, Attica and the Peloponnese, ranging in date from the 5th century BC to the 5th century AD, constitute the best collection of its kind in Italy. Displayed on its own by the far window overlooking Piazza Brà is a fragment from a sepulchral stele of a seated woman in relief dating from the 5th century BC. On the second floor is Roman material from the Veneto and Etruscan cinerary urns. Through a glass door you can see the walkway over the Portoni della Brà.

Outside in the courtyard, the Etruscan urns set into the wall of the entrance porch by Maffei in the 18th century are still in place, and in the porticoes are more inscriptions.

MUSEO DI CASTELVECCHIO

Map Verona Left 6. Entrance from the drawbridge on the Corso Castelvecchio. Open 8.30–7.30; Mon 1.30–7.30.

This magnificent castle, built by Cangrande II della Scala in 1354, was used throughout the following centuries as a citadel, and after the fall of Venice as barracks. It was opened as a museum in 1925 and after War damage was imaginatively recreated by Carlo Scarpa. The details of his work throughout the museum bear close study and this is perhaps the place where you can best appreciate his style and skill in inventing (simple) ways of displaying works of art in order that they can be viewed to best advantage.

A drawbridge leads into the lovely **courtyard**, with a water garden designed by Scarpa and eleven medieval inscriptions relating to the Della Scala family.

THE DELLA SCALA DYNASTY

The Della Scala family, or Scaligeri, ruled Verona during the 13th and 14th centuries. The founder of the dynasty was Mastino I, 'the Mastiff', who became *podestà* (chief magistrate) after the death of the tyrant Ezzelino da Romano in 1259. He converted the position into a hereditary one, and named himself *capitano del popolo*. A faction of disaffected nobles plotted his downfall, and in 1277 he was assassinated in the Piazza dei Signori. The greatest of the Scaligeri was Mastino's grandson, Cangrande I, the 'Great Dog', who inherited the title in 1311. Cangrande was the archetypal medieval Italian ruler: ruthless warrior and tyrannical overlord, yet at the same time a cultured patron of the arts. He supported the Ghibelline faction (the imperial party) against the Guelphs (the papal party), and harboured Dante, who had been exiled from Florence for his political views. Cangrande conquered Padua, Treviso and Vicenza. His nephew Mastino II brought Verona to the zenith of her power, capturing Brescia and Parma. But he was cursed with a line of cruel and murderous heirs. Their lust for conquest led the powerful city states of Florence and Venice to make a pact against them, and gradually much of Verona's territory was lost again. When Gian Galeazzo Visconti, Duke of Milan, made an assault on Verona, the last of the Della Scala fled the town under cover of darkness, on 19th October 1387. They were never to rule in Verona again. Their great castle remains, however, filled with extraordinary works of art. And around the ceiling cornices of many of the rooms, you can still see frescoes of the family emblems: the ladder (*scala*) and the spotted dog (*can* or *mastino*).

Ground floor of Castelvecchio

The first six rooms in a straight row, connected by arches, have a splendid display of sculpture. The **early medieval pieces** include a small *arca* with interesting high reliefs depicting the story of the lives of the two saints Sergius and Bacchus, who served in the Roman army in Syria but, when they refused to join in pagan sacrifices, were condemned to death, one to be beaten and the other to be beheaded. This little tomb for their relics was commissioned by a Benedictine abbot in 1179 from an unknown sculptor: the abbot is shown kneeling as he is presented to Christ enthroned by the two saints (on one of the short sides). Also here is a magnificent silver plate with a battle scene, a set of spoons and gold jewellery, all dating from the Lombard period (6th–7th centuries AD). The next rooms have lovely **14th-century statues**, including St Cecilia (with long pigtails and holding her attribute, a portable organ) and Santa Libera, a polychrome statuette with the same hairstyle: both are thought to be by the same sculptor. The Crucifixion group in Room 4 has a strikingly ugly figure of Christ, with his mouth open and deformed legs. In Room 5 is a damaged but delightful relief of the young St Martin and the beggar, thought to be by a Tuscan sculptor (1436).

Upper floor

Room 7 contains 13th–14th-century frescoes and the treasures found in Via Trezza in Verona in 1938: the **precious jewels** dating from the 14th century include a bejewelled gold star. The sword and belt were found in the tomb of Cangrande I. Room 8 has **frescoes by Altichiero and his workshop**. The panel paintings in Room 9 include a polyptych in a lovely frame, the only signed work known by Turone di Maxio (1360) and 30 delightful Biblical scenes (from the *Creation* to the *Coronation of the Virgin by Christ in Heaven*) painted in Verona in the mid-14th century. Also here are works by Tommaso da Modena. Room 10 is the only room in the castle which preserves its original painted wall decorations. Here are displayed some of the masterpieces of the collection: three Madonnas on easels: *Madonna del Roseto* by Stefano da Zevio (the Madonna literally immersed in a bed of roses), *Madonna della Quaglia* by Pisanello (the Madonna shown with exceptionally long hair, also in a garden, inhabited by quails) and a third by Michele Giambono (although damaged, the Madonna has particularly striking eyes). Also here is *St Jerome in the Desert* by the Venetian painter Jacopo Bellini.

The long **Salone della Reggia**, overlooking the Adige, has another work by Jacopo Bellini (*Christ on the Cross*) and sweet works by Giovanni Badile, and the *Death of the Virgin*, a damaged work by Giambono. Off the end of this room, the small Room 12 contains **Flemish works** including (on an easel) a *Crucifixion* by Lucas van Leyden.

Stairs designed by Scarpa lead up past remains of frescoes on the walls. In the room to the right are three very beautiful **Venetian Madonnas**: one in a maroon cloak and with a curly haired Child by Giovanni Bellini; another thought to be by Bellini's workshop; and one by Alvise Vivarini, displayed on an easel. The *Crucifixion* (with a donor) is by Cristoforo Canozzi da Lendinara, and the two paintings of St Catherine and Veneranda are by Carpaccio. Room 14 contains **works by Francesco Morone**, son of Domenico the influential Veronese painter. In Room 15 the *Madonna and Child* by Francesco Bonsignori is very unusual and in a lovely frame. Room 16 is devoted to **Liberale da Verona** (also known as a very fine miniaturist). The long hall has works by Liberale's pupil Giolfino and in the little room at the end are two more masterpieces: Mantegna's *Holy Family* and Carlo Crivelli's *Madonna della Passione*. Arms and armour are displayed in Room 19.

Continue through two doors out onto the magnificent **battlements**, with their swallowtail (or 'Ghibelline') merlons and views of the old bridge across the river and into the clock-tower. From here you can see the 14th-century statue of Mastino II and the **equestrian statue of Cangrande I**, both horse and rider fully armed, and strikingly displayed by Scarpa on an elevated concrete stand. Modern stairs lead down past Cangrande into Room 20, with works by Cavazzola (Paolo Morando), including the *Deposition* with a very fine landscape: he was a Veronese follower of Domenico Morone. Room 21 has 16th-century works by Giovan Francesco Caroto and Girolamo dai Libri, both influenced by Liberale da Verona. Room 22 has **works by Tintoretto and Veronese** (Verona's greatest painter but who left very few of his works in his native city), and in Room 23 Domenico Brusasorci is well represented. The last rooms have works dating from the 17th and 18th centuries, including some by Giambattista Tiepolo and Pietro Longhi.

Approached through the south wing of the castle (or from outside it) is the very fine **Ponte Scaligero** (only open to pedestrians), which was built at the same time as the Castelvecchio by Cangrande II. After its destruction in the Second World War, it was very well reconstructed, using the original materials.

SAN ZENO

Map Verona Left 5. There is a pleasant peaceful walk along the river from the Castelvecchio past the little 13th-century church of San Zeno in Oratorio, to Piazzetta Portichetti. Here Via Bereo Barbarani leads into Piazza Corrubbio, recently smartened up, which adjoins Piazza San Zeno. The entrance to the church is usually on the left of the façade. Open 8.30–6, Sun and holidays 12.30–6.

San Zeno is one of the most beautiful Romanesque churches in northern Italy. It was begun in 1120 and completed some 100 years later. The apse was rebuilt in 1398. It has wonderful 12th-century sculpture on the facade and the bronze doors, and a superb painting by Mantegna adorns the high altar.

Exterior of San Zeno
The façade has a magnificent circular window which depicts the Wheel of Fortune. It is the work of Brioloto (c. 1200), an artist who worked on a number of buildings in Verona. The lovely band of twin arches is continued round the south side. Flanking

BASILICA DI SAN ZENO

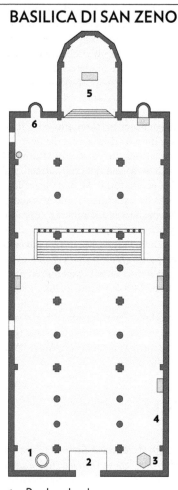

1 Porphyry bowl
2 Bronze doors
3 Painted Cross
4 Altarpiece by Torbido
5 Presbytery (Mantegna triptych)
6 Smiling St Zeno

the doorway are five tiers of fascinating reliefs in very good condition with scenes from the Old and New Testaments by two sculptors known simply as Maestro Nicolò and Maestro Guglielmo (1138): on the right, the lowest one shows Theodoric hunting a stag which leads him headlong into Hell; above are the *Creation of Adam*; the *Creation of the Animals*; the *Creation of Eve* and the *Temptation*; and at the top the *Expulsion from Paradise* and *Cain and Abel*. On the left, the lowest panel shows a group of mounted knights and foot soldiers in a battle; the panel above is divided into a series of scenes: the *Visitation, Annunciation*, the Virgin before the Nativity, the *Annunciation to the Shepherds* with their sheep, and the Magi preparing for their journey to Bethlehem; above is the *Adoration of the Magi*, the *Presentation in the Temple*, and the Angel with Joseph; above again, the *Flight into Egypt* and *Baptism of Christ*; and at the top the *Garden of Gethsamene, Betrayal of Judas* and the *Crucifixion*. The doorway itself, dating from the same date and by the same sculptors, has a porch supported on marble lions with a polychrome lunette of St Zeno. St Zeno, Verona's patron saint, is apparently buried in the crypt of the church, and prayers are left for him here.

The entrance to the church is usually through the lovely **cloister**, with coupled columns built in 1123.

Interior of San Zeno

The church has a raised presbytery and a trifoliate wooden ceiling which survives from 1386. Some of the piers have capitals from Roman buildings. Also from ancient Rome are the large **porphyry bowl (1)** and stoups at the west end (the font in pink marble dates from the 12th century). Here you can see the remarkable **bronze doors (2)** made for the entrance in the 12th century, with reliefs of scenes from the Old and New Testaments. The frames are decorated with masques, and two of them, especially large, served as door handles. Some of the reliefs are too high up to see clearly, but on the left door at eye level you can see Christ in Heaven and the Devil throwing sinners into the fire.

On the west wall, the **painted Cross (3)** is attributed to Lorenzo Veneziano (mid-14th century).

The **first south altarpiece (4)** is by the Veronese painter Francesco Torbido (1520), and the second is made up of 'knotted' columns of red marble resting on a lion and a bull.

In the **presbytery (5)** is a huge altarpiece in wonderful colours and excellent condition (in its original frame), which is one of the great works by Mantegna. The triptych, memorable also for its garlands which unite the three scenes (together with the pilasters with classical tondi in 'relief'), shows the Madonna with angel musicians and eight saints. The figures are depicted as if seen from a low viewpoint (the predella is a copy of Mantegna's wonderful original, now in the Louvre). It was painted between 1457 and 1459 in Padua after Mantegna had carried out the frescoes there in the church of the Eremitani, and the year before he moved to Mantua. The altarpiece clearly left a lasting impression on the local school of painting in Verona.

The frescoes in the apse behind and above the altarpiece are attributed to Martino da Verona (late 14th century). A 12th-century sarcophagus serves as high altar. On the balustrade are statues of Christ and the Apostles thought to be by a German sculptor working around 1250.

In the north apse **(6)** is a colossal polychrome seated **figure of St Zeno**, shown smiling, by a 13th-century sculptor.

The **crypt** has beautiful pink columns in various colours.

In the attractive piazza outside, with trees and a few *trattorie*, is the very fine brick **campanile** (1149) and a tower which survives from the former abbey (but which is popularly believed to be a relic of the 9th-century palace of King Pepin, son of Charlemagne). Also here is the church of San Procolo, founded in the 5th century (but usually kept locked).

SAN BERNARDINO

Some way south of San Zeno is the church of San Bernardino (1466; map *Verona Left 5*), entered through the cloister in front of the west façade, which has pretty carving round the portal. The first chapel on the south side has a barrel vault and was frescoed all over in the early 16th century by the local painter Giolfino. The altarpiece in the second chapel is by Francesco Bonsignori. The damaged frescoes in the fourth chapel are attributed to Domenico Morone and his son Francesco, and Domenico painted the organ doors in the north aisle. The chapel at the end of this aisle is entirely covered with 16th-century paintings in a gilded framework. Outside is a sculpted polychrome *Pietà*. On the right of the sanctuary is a vestibule and circular chapel, a very refined work by Michele Sanmicheli (1557). In the north aisle is a charming organ (1481) on a graceful bracket and a Baroque altar by Francesco Bibiena, better known as a theatre designer. The Sala Morone (entered from outside the church), with Domenico's best frescoes (1503), was closed for restoration at the time of writing.

PIAZZA DELLE ERBE & PIAZZA DEI SIGNORI

The delightful **Piazza delle Erbe** (*map Verona Right 7 and Verona Left 2, Inset*) occupies the site of the Roman forum, and the picturesque houses have numerous balconies. In the centre, paved with huge square blocks of red Verona marble, rise a Gothic column with a stone lantern; a monument made up of a group of four columns; an ingenious fountain dating from 1368 with a Roman statue known as the '*Madonna Verona*'; and a tall column set up in 1523 bearing the Lion of St Mark (a replacement made in 1886 after the original had been destroyed at the fall of the Venetian Republic). The square is always busy (there is a daily market) and there are a number of cafés and restaurants. The brick Casa dei Mercanti, with its battlements, was founded by Alberto della Scala in 1301 (and restored in the 17th century). The *Madonna and Child* in the niche is by Girolamo Campagna (1595). A bronze statue commemorates the victims of an Austrian bomb that fell on this site in 1915. By the Torre del Gardello (1370) is the handsome Palazzo Maffei (1668), crowned with a balustrade bearing six statues. The Casa Mazzanti, once a palace of the Della Scala, has a 16th-century frescoed façade and a terrace which runs the whole of its length. The Arco della Costa, named from a whale's rib hung beneath the vault, is next to Palazzo della Ragione, founded before 1193 but much altered in the 19th century, although the massive Torre delle Carceri survives. The 12th-century **Torre dei Lamberti** (84m high) is open daily (*8.30–7.30; stairs or a lift*) and there is a very fine view from the top. The Romanesque courtyard was given a monumental Gothic staircase in 1450, and the crowning lantern provided some ten years later.

PIAZZA DEI SIGNORI

The Arco della Costa leads into the very peaceful Piazza dei Signori (*map Verona Right 7 and Verona Left 2, Inset*) which was the centre of medieval civic life and has arches over all the streets by which it is entered. The monument to Dante was set up in 1865 and the celebrated café here is named after him (in winter it operates only as a restaurant). Beneath the level of the piazza and in Via Dante, Roman paving has been revealed. The lovely **Loggia del Consiglio**, with arcades, a pretty balustrade, and twin windows, is an elegant Renaissance building dating from 1493. The statues depict famous Romans born in Verona and the inscription records Verona's faithfulness to Venice and their mutual affection. Over the arch is a statue of the physician Girolamo Fracastoro (1559). The north wing of Palazzo della Ragione bears a ruined Lion of St Mark and the marble-faced Palazzo del Capitano has a crenellated tower and a portal by Sanmicheli (in the pebbled courtyard you can see another portal, this one very bizarre, dating from 1687). The Palazzo degli Scaligeri (now the Prefettura) has been restored to its original 14th-century appearance with a brick front and crenellations. Opposite, the handsome Domus Nova, reconstructed in 1659, stands beside an archway crowned with a statue of the dramatist Scipione Maffei (1756). Beyond it you can see the back of the Casa Mazzanti (its façade is described above, on Piazza delle Erbe) with an outside walkway and stair, and a lovely Renaissance well-head (ingeniously linked to various windows with iron rods).

THE DELLA SCALA TOMBS (OR ARCHE SCALIGERE)

An archway leads out of Piazza dei Signori to a little square with the church of Santa Maria Antica beside a locked railing which ever since the 14th century has protected the tombs of the Della Scala family. This 'royal enclosure' celebrates the family dynasty and was a statement of its power. The magnificent wrought-iron work is decorated with the repeated motif of a ladder (*scala*), their emblem. All the tombs date from the same century, when the Della Scala were the *signori* (lords) of Verona: they dominated much of the Veneto *terraferma*, and for a brief time even ruled as far away as Parma and Lucca. The two most elaborate monuments, by Bonino da Campione, are those of Mastino II (died 1351) and, in the opposite corner, that of Cansignorio (died 1375), his son. The very fine Gothic tabernacles decorated with numerous statues and columns protect the tombs with recumbent effigies, but the two rulers are also shown as proud figures on horseback crowning the summits. The carving on the tomb of Cansignorio is particularly fine. Against the wall of the church is the plain tomb of Mastino I, the first of the Della Scala dynasty, assassinated a few steps away in Piazza dei Signori in 1277. Protected by a low roof is the tomb of Giovanni (who died in 1359) by Andreolo de' Santi. Nearby is the sarcophagus with bas reliefs of Bartolomeo, Mastino's nephew. He gave refuge to Dante after the Bianchi faction of the Guelph party in Florence had accused the great poet (who had taken part in the government of the city) of fraud and corruption at a time when he was absent from Florence in Rome, and when he failed to return to defend himself he was sentenced death, so decided never to return to his native city. He stayed in Verona under Bartolomeo's protection until the latter's death in 1304, and the great poet praises him in his *Paradiso* for this courtesy.

Over the side door of the church is the tomb of Cangrande I (died 1329), also by Bonino da Campione (with a copy of the original equestrian statue now in the Castelvecchio). Cangrande I was the most famous member of the family because of his significant conquests in northern Italy. He, too, features in Dante's *Paradiso* since he also gave hospitality to the exiled poet here between 1312 and 1318, and he is remembered by Dante for his '*magnificenze*'.

Santa Maria Antica (*map Verona Right 7, and Verona Left 2, Inset; closed 12.30–3.30*) has a 12th-century campanile and a lovely early Romanesque interior with a red marble bishop's throne on the right wall of the sanctuary.

Via Cappello leads out of Piazza delle Erbe past the entrance at no. 23 to the courtyard of the so-called **Casa di Giulietta** (*map Verona Right 7; open 8.30–7.30, Mon 1.30–7.30*). This is one of the most visited places in Verona because of its (spurious) associations with Juliet Capulet. Shakespeare's *Romeo and Juliet*, set in Verona, tells the story of Juliet Capulet (the anglicisation of Cappelletti) and Romeo Montague (Montecchi), an adaptation of a tale by the 16th-century novelist Luigi da Porto. The legend of a feud between the two families is apocryphal; in fact, it is probable that the clans were in close alliance. The romantic balcony (which only dates from 1935) overlooks the courtyard, and an entire wall at the entrance has been provided for visitors' signatures. The interior of this restored 13th-century house still has fine wooden ceilings on the top floor, where there is a ship's keel roof. There is also a bronze statue of the fictional heroine (touching its breast will supposedly bring you a new lover. The house infuriated Arnold Bennet: 'I am [determined] somehow to vent my rage at being shown Juliet's house, a picturesque and untidy tenement, with balconies certainly too high for love, unless Juliet was a trapeze acrobat, accustomed to hanging downwards by her toes. This was not Juliet's house, for the sufficient reason that so far as authentic history knows, there never was any Juliet.'

SANT'ANASTASIA

Map Verona Right 3–4; open March–Oct 9–6, Sun and holidays 1–6; Nov–Feb 10–5, Sun and holidays 1–5.
Sant'Anastasia is the largest church in Verona and a very fine Gothic building. It was begun in 1290 but work continued on it throughout the following two centuries. It is particularly interesting for its frescoes.

The unfinished **façade**, with its stripes of pink white and grey, has two sculptured panels on the right of the door with episodes from the life of St Peter Martyr. Born in Verona, he became a Dominican in 1221 and was famous as a preacher (one of the scenes shows him addressing a crowd of worshippers). He was stabbed to death by heretics on the road between Como and Milan in 1252 (the other scene records his martyrdom) and the following year he became the first Dominican saint. The church is dedicated to him. The quaint relief over the double doors bears six scenes from the *Annunciation* to the *Resurrection*. The graceful tower supports an eight-sided spire.

Interior of Sant'Anastasia
The huge interior is unusually bright and the vaults of the nave and aisles covered with very colourful frescoes against a white ground. The splendid pink, white and grey pavement dates from 1462. The massive columns are made of red Veronese marble. The **stoups** are supported by two life-like crouching figures: that on the left **(1)** carved in 1495 by Gabriele Caliari, father of the great Venetian painter Paolo (Veronese).

The **first south altar (2)** has a marble screen designed by Michele Sanmicheli with statues by Danese Cattaneo (1565). The next two have fine 15th-century frescoes but they are too high up to see clearly, and marble statues by Orazio Marinali.

The **south transept (3)** has a wonderful altarpiece by the Veronese painter Girolamo dai Libri of the *Madonna and Child Enthroned between St Thomas Aquinas and St Augustine*.

In the second chapel to the right of the sanctuary **(4)** is a carved wood altar and ancona. On the right wall is a superb large **fresco by Altichiero**, dating from the last decade of the 14th century which shows three members of the Cavalli family presented by their patron saints to the Madonna (a fragment). The tomb of Federico Cavalli has a fresco by Stefano da Zevio.

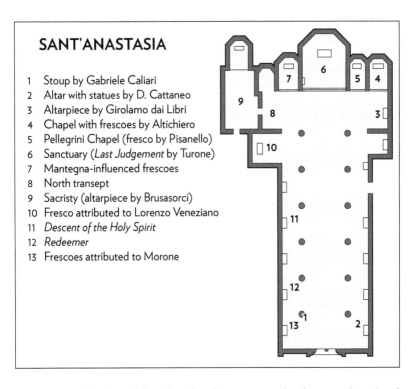

SANT'ANASTASIA

1 Stoup by Gabriele Caliari
2 Altar with statues by D. Cattaneo
3 Altarpiece by Girolamo dai Libri
4 Chapel with frescoes by Altichiero
5 Pellegrini Chapel (fresco by Pisanello)
6 Sanctuary (*Last Judgement* by Turone)
7 Mantegna-influenced frescoes
8 North transept
9 Sacristy (altarpiece by Brusasorci)
10 Fresco attributed to Lorenzo Veneziano
11 *Descent of the Holy Spirit*
12 *Redeemer*
13 Frescoes attributed to Morone

The **Pellegrini chapel (5)**, to the right of the sanctuary, has four apostles painted on either side of the entrance arch attributed to the school of Mantegna. The good Gothic family tombs here incorporate fine frescoes dating from the late 14th century. Wilhelm von Bibra, ambassador of Cologne to the Vatican, who died in 1490 is shown in an effigy, fully armed. The altarpiece of the *Madonna and Child with Saints* is by Lorenzo Veneziano, and includes portraits of the two donors Mastino II Della Scala and his wife Taddea. The terracotta reliefs of the life of Christ are by Michele da Firenze (1435).

Very high up on two sides of the entrance arch is a very damaged but famous fresco by Pisanello, a delightful scene of St George at Trebizond. The saint is about to mount his grey charger (memorably seen from behind, while his attendant's horse is shown full face to the viewer) and the princess appears between them in profile. As Berenson lamented, this work was carried out 'with no thought for the spectator on the floor of the church'! The **Sanctuary (6)** has a *Last Judgement* dating from around 1360 by Turone on the right wall and on the left wall 15th-century frescoes (difficult to see) by Michele Giambono around to the tomb of Cortesia Serego, a general who served under Antonio della Scala, who is shown in an equestrian statue of 1429 by the Florentine sculptor Nanni di Bartolo. Nanni was a pupil and collaborator of Donatello's and first introduced the vogue for works in terracotta in the Veneto (he also produced a sculpture for a tomb in San Fermo).

The chapel to the left of the sanctuary **(7)** has 15th-century frescoes by a painter influenced by Mantegna, and the next chapel has earlier frescoes, also interesting.

In the **north transept (8)** are early 15th–century frescoes attributed to Bonaventura Boninsegna. Above them are three framed paintings dating from the 15th–16th century by Paolo Farinati, Alessandro Turchi, and Liberale da Verona, and on the left wall, also in a frame, *Three Saints* by Francesco Morone.

The **sacristy (9)** retains its original 15th-century stained glass, and stalls dating from the end of the same century. On the right wall are two 18th-century paintings by Antonio Balestra and a 16th-century altarpiece by Felice Brusasorci.

The **fifth north chapel (10)** dates from 1596 and has a detached fresco attributed to Lorenzo Veneziano, and paintings by the 17th century Veronese school. The organ by Domenico Farinati (1705) stands over the north door. At the sumptuous fourth altar **(11)** is the *Descent of the Holy Spirit*, by Nicolò Giolfino (1518), surrounded by statues of saints and the Redeemer (above is a fresco by Francesco Morone). The second chapel **(12)** has a painting of the *Redeemer above Sts Erasmus and George*, also by Nicolò Giolfino, and the first chapel **(13)** has polychrome statues and more frescoes, also by Francesco Morone.

Outside, above the former convent gate, is the Gothic tomb of Guglielmo Castelbarco, who died in 1320. The little 14th-century church of **San Pietro Martire** is used for exhibitions.

Via Abramo Massalongo leads past the Neoclassical façade (1807) of the Conservatorio into Via del Duomo, from which the tall tower of the Duomo is conspicuous.

THE DUOMO & MUSEO MINISCALCHI-ERIZZO

The Romanesque exterior of the **Duomo** (*map Verona Right 3; open 10–5, Sun and holidays 1.30–5. San Giovanni in Fonte is closed in winter*) survives from its rebuilding around 1120, notably the two porches, and apse. At the main entrance, two griffins support the columns and the carving is signed by Maestro Nicolò, the sculptor who also worked at the church of San Zeno in the 1130s. In the lunette are polychrome Nativity scenes, and the two statues on either side of the door represent the paladins, Roland (identified by the name carved on his sword) and Oliver. The south porch has a double order of ancient Roman columns with finely-carved capitals, between which are reliefs of the story of Jonah and the Whale, and a lion. The magnificent apse, with delicate carving high up above the pilasters, also survives (it can be seen from Piazza Vescovile). The campanile was continued above its Romanesque base by Michele Sanmicheli (and the bell chamber only added in 1927).

Interior of the Duomo
The huge interior was covered with colourful frescoes in the 15th and 16th centuries, when the side chapels were constructed. The clustered pillars have interesting capitals. Round each chapel is a charming framework of sculptured pilasters and

architectural fretwork. The walls around the first three chapels on either side were decorated with architectural frescoes by Giovanni Maria Falconetto in 1503.

In the **south aisle**, the second chapel contains a small, crowded *Adoration of the Magi* by Liberale da Verona (showing the influence of Mantegna) surrounded by 16th-century paintings of four saints and the *Deposition* by Nicolò Giolfino, his pupil. By the nave pillar is a Romanesque marble stoup. The fourth domed chapel has extravagant Baroque decorations with six huge columns and stuccoes, ingeniously lit by two windows. The magnificent organ survives from the 16th century. At the end of this aisle is the lovely Cappella Mazzanti, with sculptured pilasters by Domenico da Lugo (1508): it protects the beautiful tomb of St Agatha, carved by a Campionese master (from Lake Lugano) in 1353. On the wall just to the right is the red tomb slab of Pope Lucius III, who died in Verona in 1185 (the face is damaged).

The graceful curved choir-screen at the **east end**, in pink and grey marble, was designed by Michele Sanmicheli in 1534. At the same time the dramatic frescoes in the choir were carried out by Francesco Torbido, thought to be on cartoons by Giulio Romano. The organ on the left is decorated with good paintings by Felice Brusasorci.

The Cappella Maffei in the **north aisle** has frescoes high up outside over the entrance and in the lunette by Giovanni Maria Falconetto, and sculptured pilasters as in the chapel opposite. The lovely predella here is by Michele da Verona. Outside the first north chapel is the tomb of Bishop Galesio Nichesola, who died in 1527, a fine work attributed to Jacopo Sansovino, who also designed the altar-frame in the chapel which encloses an *Assumption* by Titian, painted some 17 years after his much more famous painting of the same subject in the apse of the basilica of the Frari in Venice.

Off the north side of the Duomo is the entrance to a 12th-century vestibule with ancient columns, and part of the foundations of an early Christian basilica of the 4th century. **San Giovanni in Fonte** was built in the early 12th century, and the huge octagonal font hewn in the same century from a single block of marble has finely carved panels attributed to Brioloto. The fragmentary frescoes date from the 13th and 14th centuries, the painted Cross from the 15th century (attributed to Giovanni Badile), and the painting of the *Baptism of Christ* is by Paolo Farinati (1568). From the vestibule, steps lead up to the church of **Sant'Elena**, dating from the 9th century but restored in the 12th century, beneath which excavations have revealed remains of two early Christian basilicas (4th and 5th centuries), with fragments of mosaic pavements. The tombs of two early bishops have also been found here. The finely carved narrow stalls date from the 16th century and the altarpiece is by Brusasorci.

To the left of the façade of the Duomo, a passageway leads to the exterior portico of Sant'Elena and the charming Romanesque **cloister** with twin columns (in a two-storey arcade above one walk), also partly on the site of the 5th-century basilica, with remains in two places of a 6th-century mosaic pavement, one of which is polychrome.

In Piazza del Duomo an archway leads to the **Chapter Library**, founded by Archdeacon Pacificus (778–846), which has many precious texts and illuminated choirbooks dating from around 1368 and attributed to Turone.

Opposite the south door of the Duomo, a seated 14th-century figure of St Peter surmounts the doorway of San Pietro in Archivolto. Via Pietà Vecchia leads to

Piazza Vescovile with the magnificent Romanesque east end of the Duomo. The **Bishop's Palace** has an unusual exterior of 1502 with Venetian crenellations and a lovely portal decorated with statues including a delightful *Madonna and Child* attributed to Fra' Giovanni da Verona. The striped wall belongs to San Giovanni in Fonte (*described above*).

MUSEO MINISCALCHI-ERIZZO

Map Verona Right 3. Entrance at no. 2a Via San Mamaso; open Mon–Fri 11–1 & 3–7.
Palazzo Miniscalchi was given a monumental Neoclassical façade on Via Garibaldi in 1880, but the 15th-century building retains its façade on Via San Mamaso, with handsome marble windows and doorway, and its mural paintings dating from around 1580: it is one of the few palaces left in Verona which retains its exterior painted decoration, although once many palaces in the city had similarly decorated façades.

The house and its contents were left to a foundation in the 20th century by Mario Miniscalchi-Erizzo, and the eclectic collection formed by his family from the 17th to the 20th centuries is spaciously arranged in this their residence since the 15th century. In the first room is a collection of ivories, and in the dining room is a family portrait by Alessandro Longhi and a display of fine porcelain. A room with remains of 15th-century painted decoration on the walls (and Gothic windows and an old wood ceiling) has an 18th-century travelling desk in inlaid wood and a plate made in Urbino around 1519 which belonged to Isabella d'Este. A portrait by Sebastiano Bombelli shows Niccolò Erizzo and his five children. The two rooms on either side display a fine collection of small Renaissance bronzes, including works by Il Riccio, Tiziano Aspetti and Roccatagliata, as well as a plate with bronze reliefs and a copy of Michelangelo's *Moses*, both by Jacopo Sansovino. Beyond a room with a fireplace decorated with majolica from Faenza is a room with some curios which in the 16th century belonged to a Veronese collector who arranged them as one of the earliest known *Wunderkammers* in Italy. Two more rooms display arms and armour and toy soldiers, and archaeological material including Roman glass and 5th–4th-century BC bronzes, and small later Roman bronzes. Adjoining the chapel, with a lovely little 17th-century domestic altar in amber and ivory, is a small room with church silver and 15th-century ivory plaquettes. An 18th-century Venetian room contains Murano glass. The very fine collection of some 300 16th–17th-century drawings is displayed on a rotating basis.

SAN FERMO

Map Verona Right 7–8. Open 10–6, Sun and holidays 1–6; Nov–Feb 10–5, Sun and holidays 1–5).
A Benedictine church built from 1065 to 1138 survives below a second church rebuilt by the Friars Minor around 1313 in a Gothic style. On the façade is the tomb of Antonio Fracastoro, physician of the Della Scala, who died in 1368. The 15th-century porch on the north side protects a fine portal of 1363.

Interior of San Fermo

The broad interior, without aisles, has a very fine wooden ceiling of 1314 which has a frieze of portrait heads of 416 saints (not illuminated so difficult to see, but explained in a panel in the nave), and the various frescoes on the walls of the church mostly date from the same time. Over the west doorway **(1)** is a **fresco attributed to Altichiero or Turone**. On the south side, beyond the first altar, unfortunately very high up, is a delightful fresco of **angels by Stefano da Zevio (2)**. The marble **pulpit (3)** and the **tomb** of the donor, Barnaba Morano, in the adjoining chapel **(4)** were made by the same little-known sculptor, called Antonio da Mestre in 1306–1412. Outside is a lovely plain sarcophagus supported by two red marble oxen. The third altar has a painting by Francesco Torbido **(5)**.

The **choir (6)** has a curved screen of 1573 and wonderful frescoes on the ceiling of the sanctuary with symbols of the Evangelists and above the triumphal arch (including Guglielmo di Castelbarco offering the church to Prior Gusmerio), all dating from the early 14th century. The chapel to the left of the sanctuary **(7)** has an **altarpiece by Liberale da Verona** and 14th-century frescoes found a few years ago behind the altar. In a chapel off the north side **(8)** is a remarkable classical tomb on a very idiosyncratic design, in marble and bronze, made by Il Riccio around 1516 and perfectly preserved. It is the burial place of Girolamo and Marcantonio della Torre.

The elaborate **Lady Chapel** on the north side **(9)** has a good *Madonna and Saints* by Giovan Francesco Caroto. High up on the west wall is the **Brenzoni monument**

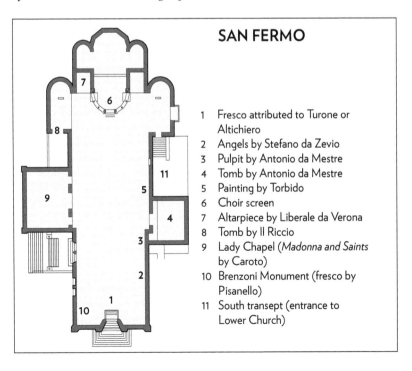

SAN FERMO

1   Fresco attributed to Turone or Altichiero
2   Angels by Stefano da Zevio
3   Pulpit by Antonio da Mestre
4   Tomb by Antonio da Mestre
5   Painting by Torbido
6   Choir screen
7   Altarpiece by Liberale da Verona
8   Tomb by Il Riccio
9   Lady Chapel (*Madonna and Saints* by Caroto)
10 Brenzoni Monument (fresco by Pisanello)
11 South transept (entrance to Lower Church)

(10) by Nanni di Bartolo (1439), with a very unusual sculpture of the *Resurrection of Christ* with the soldiers asleep at the tomb. It incorporates an exquisite *Annunciation* frescoed by Pisanello behind, with the Virgin shown in a Gothic chamber, and the angel with huge wings and long robes, but it is unfortunately in very bad condition.

From the south transept **(11)** a door leads down to the Romanesque **lower church**, with simple red decoration on the vaults.

THE LEFT BANK OF THE ADIGE

Although this part of the town has some very interesting monuments and churches, it is unfortunately very busy with traffic (since many streets on the right bank are pedestrian zones).

The prettiest part of the river is near the church of Sant'Anastasia (*map Verona Right 4*), where an attractive row of houses faces the river south to Ponte Nuovo. Parallel to the narrow road which skirts the river is Via Sottoriva, lined on one side by porticoes and Venetian-style houses. In the other direction Via Ponte Pietra leads north, with some fine palaces, including one (no. 23/a) with remarkable frescoes high up on its late 16th-century façade illustrating the various processes in cheese-making and in the butchering of pork. The very fine **Ponte della Pietra** (only open to pedestrians) is guarded by a picturesque tower. It was reconstructed after the War using part of the Roman and medieval masonry dredged up from the river.

Across the bridge is the venerable church of **Santo Stefano** (*map Verona Right 4; closed 12–4 and on Tues afternoons*), rebuilt in the 12th century with a raised sanctuary. In the first south chapel, built in 1620, is a painting of the *Forty Martyrs* by Orbetto. At the end of the south and north walls are monochrome frescoes by Battista del Moro. At the top of a broad flight of steps is a colossal seated statue of St Peter in tufo, a 14th-century work by a Veronese sculptor. Around the apse (with a stone episcopal throne) is an unusual raised gallery with 8th-century capitals and fragmentary remains of 12th-century painted decoration with animals. High up on the arches of both transepts are charming frescoes of angel musicians by Domenico Brusasorci. In the south transept is a 14th-century *Annunciation* and *Coronation of the Virgin* by Martino da Verona. In the vaulted crypt is a raised semicircular gallery.

There is a view of the Duomo across the river, the battlemented tower of the Bishop's Palace, and the pretty little loggia of the chapter library.

SAN GIORGIO IN BRAIDA
Map Verona Right 3. Closed 12–4.30.
This large church was begun in 1477 on the site of a 12th-century church, and was completed on a design by Michele Sanmicheli, who added the cupola and who also began the unfinished campanile. The façade dates from the 17th century. It contains numerous fine paintings (although some of the them are difficult to see). Above the west door is a very darkened *Baptism of Christ* **by Tintoretto**. The fourth altar on

the south side has the Madonna between the archangels by Felice Brusasorci. The organ doors are painted by Girolamo Romanino. In the sanctuary, the main apse has a fine altar by Sanmicheli which incorporates the *Martyrdom of St George*, a very crowded work by **Veronese**, probably painted around 1555 the year he left his native city for good to take up his brilliant career in Venice. The two huge paintings here are by Paolo Farinati (right) and Felice Brusasorci (left), both skilled local painters who certainly influenced the young Veronese.

On the north side, the painted doors high up on either side of the organ were also painted by Girolamo Romanino, and beneath the organ is a painting of *St Cecilia* between four other female saints by Il Moretto. The fourth chapel has a very beautiful painting of the *Madonna with Saints and Angel Musicians*, decorated with branches of lemons, by Girolamo dai Libri. In the third chapel, the polyptych in a fine gilded frame, includes Sts Roch and Sebastian, the Transfiguration, and a predella all by Giovan Francesco Caroto, who also painted the altarpiece of *St Ursula and the Virgins* in the first chapel.

Opposite the façade of the church is Sanmicheli's **Porta San Giorgio** (1525), in his town walls, beyond which is a little public garden on the riverfront.

TEATRO ROMANO AND THE MUSEO ARCHEOLOGICO
Map Verona Right 4. From Ponte della Pietra it is a short walk to the entrance at no. 2 Rigaste Ridentore through a little old house on the busy road on the riverfront; open Tues–Sun 8.30–7.30, Mon 1.30–7.30.

The Romans typically chose superb positions for their theatres, and Verona's is no exception, dug into a steep hillside on the bend of the river. It was founded under Augustus and later enlarged. During the Middle Ages, houses and churches were built on the ruins of the cavea (and to this day the little church of Santi Siro e Libera, dating from 920 but altered in the 14th century, survives here). After excavations begun in 1834, the two entrances, the arches that supported the cavea, and the scena itself (now a third of its original height) were all exposed. The seats have been restored and the theatre is still usually used for a summer drama season. The present entrance is through the remains of the scena, with its huge blocks of tufa, and a few statues found in the theatre are on display. Here can be seen also some lead pipes which were part of the aqueduct the Romans built to supply water to the city.

At the back of the theatre, steps lead up to the lift which gives access to the 15th-century convent building above, with its refectory, cloister and chapel (frescoed in 1508 by Giovan Francesco Caroto), which houses the **Museo Archeologico**, founded in 1857. The interesting little collection of Roman finds from Verona and its environs includes Hellenistic bronzes, well-preserved glass, sculpture, mosaic fragments, inscriptions and sepulchral monuments. From the windows are splendid views of the theatre and the city beyond.

On the hillside high above the theatre can be seen **Castel San Pietro**, where the Austrians built their barracks on the foundations of a Visconti castle destroyed by the French in 1801.

SANTA MARIA IN ORGANO

The church (*map Verona Right 4; usually closed 11.30–3*), well worth a visit, was built by Olivetan friars in the late 15th century, although it is thought to have been founded in the 7th century. The very unusual façade is part early Gothic and part Renaissance, and the graceful campanile, dating from 1533, is ascribed to Fra' Giovanni da Verona, who also made the beautiful choir stalls inside.

In the interior, the nave, with its wonderful old columns all with different capitals, is frescoed with Old Testament scenes by two contemporaries, Nicolò Giolfino and Giovan Francesco Caroto. The transept chapels have two altarpieces by important painters not elsewhere represented in Verona: Guercino (south side), born in 1591 near Ferrara, and Luca Giordano (north side), born in Naples in 1634. You are allowed to go behind the high altar to see the magnificent stalls by Fra' Giovanni, inlaid with street scenes and musical instruments, as well as the lectern and a candelabrum (now in front of the high altar). They are his masterpiece and were carried out from 1494 to 1500 while he was a friar in this monastery. The backs of the benches here have very pretty paintings by Domenico Brusasorci. In the apse of the north transept there is a delightful life-size Palm Sunday figure of Christ on an ass dating from the mid-13th century and frescoes by Brusasorci. Here is the entrance to the sacristy, with more exquisite inlaid intarsia work on the cupboards, again by Fra' Giovanni da Verona, made some years after the choir stalls (in 1519–23). The walls are frescoed with portraits of Benedictine monks by Francesco Morone and there is a 14th-century dossal here in local stone with a relief of the *Madonna and Saints*. The crypt preserves ancient columns and capitals.

GIARDINI GIUSTI

Map Verona Right 4. Entrance at no. 2 Via Giardino Giusto, a busy one-way road; open every day 9 to dusk.

As soon as you have passed through the open portico, with its wooden ceiling and huge lantern, and entered the garden gate, you are immersed in a lovely peaceful green garden. Behind the Giusti palace, it was laid out in the 16th century and has survived through the centuries, beautifully maintained. The ancient cypresses and formal box hedges surround fountains and statues. The maze, dating from 1786, is one of the oldest in Europe (it has been partly replanted in the last few years). At the end of the central cypress avenue, steps lead up to a grotto beneath the rockface, at the top of which a colossal grotesque masque dominates the view. Paths lead up left through a small wood to a tower (with a spiral staircase), which gives access to the upper terrace. There is a panoramic balcony above the mask and the little informal garden here has paths between the lawns and pines and cypresses. On the left, beyond a locked gate, can be seen an attractive old building with a loggia, and there is a view of the old town defences above the upper perimeter wall of the gardens.

Coryate, Evelyn and Goethe were among the famous travellers who came here and recorded their visits: in 1608 Thomas Coryate claimed that he found it 'a second paradise', and John Evelyn and Goethe were particularly struck by the venerable cypresses (Goethe even confessed that in September 1786, he actually picked some cypress branches here, as well as some caper blossom).

MUSEO DEGLI AFFRESCHI AND THE 'TOMBA DI GIULIETTA'

Map Verona Right 11–15. Entrance at no. 35 Via del Pontiere; open 8.30–7.30, Mon 1.30–7.30.

This museum, although in a not particularly attractive part of town, is visited because of its associations with Shakespeare's Juliet: unfortunately spurious, though the tradition goes back some centuries. In the 1930s an empty sarcophagus was placed in the very atmospheric crypt below the cloister of the former monastery here and declared to be that of Juliet. But even in Byron's day the tomb was shown to visitors. 'I have been over Verone,' he wrote to Augusta Leigh, 'Of the truth of Juliet's story they seem tenacious to a degree, insisting on the fact—giving a date (1303), and showing a tomb. It is a plain, open, and partly decayed sarcophagus, with withered leaves in it, in a wild and desolate conventual garden, once a cemetery, now ruined to the very graves. The situation struck me as being very appropriate to the legend, being blighted as their love. I have brought away a few pieces of the granite, to give to my daughter and my nieces.' Today the place is well worth visiting for its museum of frescoes and works of art.

CROWE AND CAVALCASELLE

This museum is named after Giovanni Battista Cavalcaselle, born in Verona in 1819, whose *History of Painting in Italy* (the first volume of which was published in 1864), which he wrote together with the Englishman Joseph Archer Crowe (1825–96), became a famous handbook and is still often quoted by art historians. Crowe simply stated that 'It was my ambition to distinguish one painter from another by studying his peculiarities of drawing, touch, finish, and general execution.' Cavalcaselle, who had been an active supporter of Manin's revolution in 1848, was sentenced to death by the Austrians but was saved at the last minute by Italian insurgents. He later joined Garibaldi's forces and was imprisoned by the French in 1849, but he ended up in London where he met Crowe, and was finally able to return to Italy in 1857. He died a year after Crowe, and was remembered by Langton Douglas in 1903 as 'the greatest connoisseur of the painting of Italy that ever lived.'

On the ground floor are small fresco fragments of the heads of saints, dating from 1330–40. Stairs lead down to an underground room with an impressive display of Roman amphorae found during excavations in the courtyard outside, which now has a lapidary collection. Upstairs there are extremely interesting frescoes from Santi Nazaro e Celso, dating from as early as the 10th century; 16th-century frescoes by Brusasorci and Bernardino India detached from a palace in Verona; and (in a room overlooking a garden) sinopie by Altichiero. A room with a fireplace with frescoes by Paolo Farinati has been reconstructed from a 16th-century house in Verona.

Stairs lead down to the **church of San Francesco**, rebuilt in the early 17th century when the chapel covered with stuccoes was decorated. It contains 18th-century paintings by Antonio Balestra and Louis Dorigny as well as early 16th-century works by Giovan Francesco Caroto, Francesco Morone (*Washing of the Feet*, in very good condition) and Girolamo Bonsignori (two panels of the *Annunciation*).

In the far walk of the lovely Romanesque cloister, steps lead down to an ancient **crypt**, once used as a cemetery (as described by Byron) and which, with its empty pink sarcophagus, provides a fitting setting for the legend of the tragic heroine Juliet.

OTHER CHURCHES IN VERONA

Since Verona has so many important monuments, churches and museums, widely spread out over a large area of the city, many visitors will not have the time to visit all of the minor ones: a selection is given here.

Santa Maria della Scala
(*map Verona Right 7; closed 12–3*)
The name comes from the Della Scala family, since Cangrande ordered its erection in 1324 and the apse survives from that time. On the right side the second altar has a votive fresco and in the chapel to the right of the sanctuary are numerous scenes from the life of St Jerome, frescoed by Giovanni Badile in the early 15th century. The very fine wall monument of a certain Guantieri of Florence, who died in 1430, is carved from pink Verona marble and includes a fresco of the *Crucifixion* and *Pietà* in the tympanum, also by Badile. In the sanctuary are more good fresco fragments by Badile and Altichiero, and in the chapel to the left of the sanctuary a delightful *Madonna and Saints* by Francesco Ubertini, showing the influence of Perugino, with an angel playing a lute.

San Nicolò all'Arena
(*map Verona Right 7*)
Built in the 17th century, this church was given an imposing Ionic facade completed on Neoclassical lines by Giuseppe Barbieri. It faces a little piazza recently redesigned with three olive trees, strangely out of place in this urban context. The interior is gloomy but interesting since nearly all the works date from the late 17th or early 18th century .

San Lorenzo
(map *Verona Left 6* and *Verona Right 7*)
On the busy Corso Cavour, but entered through a little courtyard, this church was erected around 1110 and preserves its beautiful tall, narrow Romanesque interior with bands of red and white brick. The two unusual cylindrical towers outside the west door served as approaches to the matroneum.

Santi Apostoli and Santi Tosca e Teuteria
(*map Verona Right 7*)
Dating from 1194, Santi Apostoli has a fine exterior including a Romanesque tower, apse and cloister. From the sacristy stairs lead down to Santi Tosca e Teuteria, a domed cruciform shrine of the 5th century, consecrated in 751 as a baptistery and reduced again to a burial chapel by the Bevilacqua (two tombs and a relief) in 1427.

Sant'Eufemia
(*map Verona Right 7*)
Founded in 1262, and rebuilt in 1375, there are fine tombs on the exterior. Inside are works by Domenico

Brusasorci. Also here are more works by Giovan Francesco Caroto, Martino da Verona and Moretto.

San Tomaso Cantuariense

(*map Verona Right 8*)

Dedicated to St Thomas Becket, this church has a fine west front and rose window dating from 1493. It contains a monument to Michele Sanmicheli erected in 1884, centuries after his death, and a painting by Girolamo dai Libri.

San Paolo

(*map Verona Right 12*)

Reconstructed in 1763, this church had to be rebuilt after 1944. It contains a good altarpiece of the *Madonna and Saints*, painted in 1526 by Girolamo dai Libri. The painting of the *Madonna and Child*, with saints and donors, was commissioned from Veronese by the Marogna family for their chapel here around 1562. Giovan Francesco Caroto painted the high altarpiece.

Santi Nazaro e Celso

(*map Verona Right 8*)

Built in 1463–84 near the site of a 10th-century shrine. The chapel of San Biagio has a pretty vault over the apse, an altarpiece by Girolamo dai Libri, and interesting frescoes by Bartolomeo Montagna. In the sacristy is a triptych by Francesco dai Libri (Girolamo's father), and part of a polyptych by Montagna. On the second north altar is the best known work by Antonio Badile, who was Veronese's first master.

San Giovanni in Valle

(*map Verona Right 4*)

This church stands on the hillside above the left bank of the Adige, approached from Vicolo Borgo Tascherio, and has a charming interior, rebuilt in the 12th century with a raised presbytery, and two good early Christian sarcophagi in the crypt. In the garden, part of a small cloister survives.

PALACES & FORTIFICATIONS BY SANMICHELI

The architect and sculptor Michele Sanmicheli, born just outside Verona in 1486, carried out numerous buildings in the city, and also designed the splendid gates in her defensive walls. He became very well known also outside Verona: he was called to Rome to work for the Papacy and in Venice he was put in charge of the defences not only in the city itself but also throughout her Empire. Among the best classically-inspired palaces he built for the distinguished citizens of Verona are Palazzo Pompei overlooking the river on the left bank, dating from around 1530. It houses the excellent **Museo di Storia Naturale** (*map Verona Right 12; open Mon–Thur 9–5; Sat, Sun and holidays 2–6; closed Fri*), one of the most interesting museums of its kind in Italy.

Sanmicheli's **Palazzo Canossa** on Corso Cavour (*map Verona Left 6*) dates from around the same time. **Palazzo Bevilacqua**, on the other side of the Corso (*map Verona Right 7*), is an unusually ornate work by this architect. Sanmicheli also worked on chapels and altar screens in the churches of San Bernardino, Sant'Anastasia, San Giorgio in Braida and the Duomo.

In the early 16th century he erected the town walls on the lines of the older ramparts erected by the Della Scala. They are the earliest example of a new type of military engineering that was later developed by Vauban. The **Porta del Palio** (*map Verona Left 9*) shows Sanmicheli's skill in combining structural beauty with military strength, and his **Porta Nuova** (*map Verona Left 14*) also survives intact.

ROMAN MONUMENTS

Apart from the famous Arena and the Roman Theatre, a number of ancient gates survive from Roman Verona. The main entrance to the city was the splendid **Porta dei Borsari** (*map Verona Right 7*), the outer front of which is now in the centre of the city. It was built in the mid-1st century AD with a double archway surmounted by two stages of windows and niches. It was here that the Via Postumia arrived and the decumanus maximus began. As the inscription states, it was restored by Gallienus in AD 265. Roman masonry can be seen in some of the adjoining houses. At the other end of Corso Cavour is the Roman arch called the **Arco di Gavi** (*map Verona Left 6*), also dating from the 1st century AD, erected astride the Via Postumia in honour of the Gavii family. Although it was demolished in 1805, it was reconstructed in 1932 and was being restored at the time of writing. Via Leoni (*map Verona Right 7–8*) is named after the Roman Porta dei Leoni, dating from the same century, which survives in a damaged state.

VERONA PRACTICAL TIPS

INFORMATION OFFICE

Via degli Alpini 9 (Piazza Brà; *map Verona Right 11*), *T: 045 806 8680, www.tourism.verona.it.*
The **Verona Card** gives free admission to museums, churches and monuments (and free transport on the AMT city bus services); it can be purchased valid for 2 or 5 days at the tourist office or the museums. See *veronacard.it.*

GETTING AROUND

By air: Villafranca (12km southwest). Shuttle bus service every twenty minutes from the railway station (Porta Nuova).
By train: The main railway station is at Porta Nuova (*map Verona Left 14*). It has a left luggage office.
By bus: Buses from elsewhere in the Veneto (and the Lake Garda) run by ATV (*T: 045 8871111, www.atv.verona. it*). Bus terminal in front of Porta Nuova railway station. Town buses are also run by ATV. The most useful are the following: from the Station to Piazza Bra (nos 11, 12); from the station to Castelvecchio (nos. 21, 22, 23); and from Castelvecchio to San Zeno (no. 31 to Piazza Corrubio).

By car: A Verona Park ticket, available at tobacconists or bars, allows parking for up to 2hrs on the street (marked blue). Free car parks at the Stadium, Porta Palio and Piazzale Guardini. Information from *www.comune.verona. it*, under '*muoversi in città*'.

By bicycle: Bike.sharing, *T: 800896948, www.bikeverona.it.*

WHERE TO STAY

€€€ **Due Torri.** Luxury-class with splendidly furnished rooms. Part of a group of exclusive hotels. The l'Aquila restaurant is also very grand. *Piazza Sant'Anastasia 4, T: 045 595 044, duetorrihotels.com. Map Verona Right 3.*

€€€ **Gabbia d'Oro.** A small luxury-class hotel (27 rooms) beautifully furnished with a pleasant atmosphere, situated in the very centre of the old town. *Corso Porta Borsari 4a, T: 045 800 3060, hotelgabbiadoro.it. Map Verona Right 7.*

€€ **Bologna.** A very comfortable hotel with 32 rooms renovated in 2012, in a quiet corner a few steps away from the Arena. *Piazzetta Scalette Rubiani 3 Via A. Mario), T: 045 8006830, hotelbologna.vr.it. Map Verona Right 7.*

€ **Torcolo.** A very basic, old-fashioned hotel in a small square near the Arena, in a peaceful position. Closed Jan. *Vicolo Listone 3, off Via Cattaneo, T: 045 800 7512, www.hoteltorcolo.it. Map Verona Left 6.*

WHERE TO EAT

€€€ **Dodici Apostoli.** An elegant restaurant located in a historic building in the heart of the city centre, serving traditional Veronese dishes since 1750. Closed Sun evening, and all day Mon.

Corticella San Marco 3, between Via Pelliciai and Corso Porta Borsari. T: 045 596999, 12apostoli.com. Map Verona Right 7.

€€€ **Antico Café Dante.** Verona's most famous café founded in the early 20th century, in her most beautiful square, which has tables outside in summer. In winter it operates only as a restaurant. Closed Sun evening and all day Monday. *Piazza dei Signori 2. T: 045 800 0083, caffedante.it. Map Verona Right 7 and Verona Left 2, Inset.*

€€ **Antica Bottega del Vino.** 🍷 An historic wine bar first opened in 1890 with a very atmospheric cosy old interior: the first room has tables mostly occupied by locals, who often come in just for a drink, and the room beyond is a restaurant, serving Veronese dishes (including horse) . In a quiet lane off Via Mazzini, very close to Piazza delle Erbe. Closed Tues and Sun 11–2. *Vicolo Scudo di Francia 3 (off Via Mazzini), T: 045 800 4535, www. bottegavini.it. Map Verona Right 7.*

€€ **Maffei.** With tables outside, in Verona's most colourful square in summer. Closed Sun in winter. *Piazza delle Erbe 38, T: 045 801 0015. Map Verona Right 7 and Verona Left 2, Inset.*

€ **San Matteo Church.** Very large self-service restaurant and pizzeria in a former church. Quick efficient service with good food and very reasonable prices. Frequented by the Veronese. No closing day. *Vicolo del Guasto 4, off Corso Porta Borsari. T: 045 800 4538. Map Verona Right 7.*

PASTICCERIE

Cordioli, Via Cappello 39 (*map Verona Right 7*) and Flego, Via Stella (*map Verona Right 7*).

MARKETS

A daily market (mostly now for tourists) is held in Piazza delle Erbe. There is a large general market on Tues and Friday in Piazza San Zeno (*map Verona Left 5*).

FESTIVALS AND EVENTS

The **opera season** is held from mid-June–early Sept at the Arena (*T: 045 800 5151, www.arena.it*). Box office in Via Dietro Anfiteatro 6/b, opposite an entrance to the Arena. The cheapest (unreserved) tickets are for the highest stone steps. Summer events in the Roman Theatre, *estateteatraleveronese. it.*

The **Festa di Santa Lucia**, with a street market in Piazz Brà and Via Roma, is celebrated from 10–13 Dec. **Carnival celebrations**, which have been held in the town since the 16th century, culminate on the Friday before Shrove Tuesday (*Venerdì gnocolar*). **Festival of St Zeno**, the patron saint, on 12 April.

Soave & Valpolicella: the Monti Lessini

THE WINES OF SOAVE AND VALPOLICELLA

Soave is one of the best known of all Italian wines. It is grown on the fertile hillsides east of Verona, around the village that bears its name (*map Veneto West C3*). Though a great deal of wine is produced, quality fluctuates wildly from the barely drinkable to the exquisite. The soil here is volcanic, perfect for the Garganega grape that makes up 70 percent of all Soave. One of the best producers in Leonildo Pieropan, who has vineyards on some of the best sites in the Soave Classico zone, including Calvarino and La Rocca, where the vines cluster around the old Della Scala castle. Monteforte d'Alpone, famous for its cherries, is also known for its Soave Classico. Though Roberto Anselmi's wines are labelled in the IGT category—it was Anselmi's own decision to leave the DOC system—they are distinctly characterful, subtly crafted vintages, with all the soft, lemony intensity that Soave is famous for.

The DOC of Valpolicella (*map Veneto West B2*) embraces 19 villages stretching from Lake Garda to just north of Verona. The most valuable grape grown here is Corvina, yielding wines of impressive power and density. DOC regulations permit only 70 or 80 percent Corvina in the wine, leaving lesser varieties to make up the rest. This has led to some of the most talented and adventurous producers opting out of the DOC system—a story now familiar in Italy—and producing 100 percent Corvina wines, some of them true classics, though not labelled Valpolicella.

There are three styles of Valpolicella. Straight Valpolicella is a youthful, easy-drinking wine, often slightly rustic. 'Valpolicella Superiore' on the label means that the alcohol content is slightly higher, and that the wine has been at least a year in the bottle. Recioto and Amarone are made from selected bunches, picked two weeks before the harvest and dried on wooden slats under a straw roof. If the wine ferments to dryness, it is Amarone. If there is residual sugar, it is Recioto. It is probable that *retico*, to which—according to Suetonius—Augustus Caesar was particularly partial, was precisely the same wine, with all its smoky, fruity, marzipan flavours. The third type of Valpolicella is Ripasso, made by a second fermentation of ordinary Valpolicella on used Recioto skins. The result is a full bodied, powerful, alcoholic wine. The best producers include Allegrini in Fumane (key wines are La Poja and La Grola); the Tedeschi family near Pedemonte; and Giuseppe Quintarelli (key wines are his Monte Ca' Paletta Recioto and his Valpolicella Classico Superiore) and the Galli family (Le Ragose estate), both in Negrar.

BETWEEN VERONA & SOAVE

The road from Verona to Soave passes the sanctuary of the **Madonna di Campagna**, at San Michele Extra (*map Veneto West B3*), a very unusual round church with a peristyle, designed at the end of his life by Michele Sanmicheli, who was born in the village in 1484. **Caldiero** (*map Veneto West C3*) has a spa with hot springs.

Soave (*map Veneto West C3*) is a pleasant little town which gives its name to the famous white wine (*see above*), celebrated in a festival here in Sept. The impressive battlemented walls, extremely well preserved, were built by the Della Scala (Scaligeri) before 1375. In the central Piazza Antenna (named after a mast from which the flag of St Mark was flown in 1405 when Verona voted to join the Venetian Republic) are Palazzo Cavalli, a Venetian Gothic palace of 1411, and Palazzo di Giustizia (1375). A paved path leads up from the piazza to the medieval castle (also reached by road), enlarged by the Scaligeri in 1369. The keep is defended by three courtyards, each on a different level. Privately owned (*open summer Tues–Sun 9–12 & 3–6.30; winter 9–12 & 2–4*), it was restored and partly reconstructed in 1892. The residence has an armoury on the ground floor, and above are rooms with Gothic Revival painted decorations and imitation furniture. There is a fine view from the battlements.

THE MONTI LESSINI

To the north of Verona are the volcanic Monti Lessini (*map Veneto West B2*), with the valleys of the *tredici comuni*, a high-lying district occupied by the descendants of Germanic settlers who migrated here in the 13th century, and who retained a marked dialect up until a few decades ago. This pleasant, remote area, protected as a regional park since 1990, has cherry trees and chestnut and beechwoods. The flint outcrops in the limestone hills were used in the Palaeolithic era for making tools, and a shelter used by Palaeolithic hunters has been found. There are remarkable fossils in the volcanic and sedimentary rocks, and small museums in various localities preserve these, including **Roncà** and **Bolca** (*map Veneto West C2*), famous for its fossilised tropical fish. Some of the houses still have characteristic roofs made out of slabs of local stone. This stone is also sometimes used for drystone walls around fields.

Bosco Chiesanuova, the main resort (*map Veneto West B2*), has a museum illustrating the history of Lessinia—as the region as a whole is known. The Val d'Illasi is known for its wrought-iron craftsmen: the most famous workshop is at **Cogollo** (*map Veneto West C2*), responsible for the town's pretty, locally-made street lights. At the head of the valley is **Giazza** (*map Veneto West B2–C2*), where a German dialect is still spoken, and with another local ethnographic museum.

THE VALPOLICELLA REGION

The Valpolicella, in the westernmost part of Lessinia (*map Veneto West B2*), is a hilly district near a bend in the Adige. **Sant'Ambrogio** has quarries of *rosso di Verona* marble, used for the pavements of Verona, in some of the floors of Venetian churches and often for well-heads. In a valley of cherry trees at **Volargne**, the 15th-century Villa del Bene (*open Tues–Sun 9-12 & 3-6*) has frescoes by Brusasorci, Gian Francesco Caroto and Bernardino India. For the wines of Valpolicella, see above.

VILLAFRANCA DI VERONA

South of Verona, Villafranca di Verona (*map Veneto West B3*) preserves a castle of the Della Scala (1202), now home to a Risorgimento museum (*open Sat 4–6, Sun 3–7; second Sun of every month 10–12*). The armistice of Villafranca was concluded here on 11 July 1859 between Napoleon III and Austrian emperor Franz Joseph. Through the secret deals he negotiated with Cavour, Napoleon III had done much to set the independence ball rolling in Italy. When that ball began to reach full momentum after the bloody battle of Solferino, the French leader began to be wary and concluded an armistice with Austria, in effect halting Italian expansion into Austrian territory. It wasn't until the 1860s, when Prussia defeated Austria at Königgratz, that Italy's dreams of independence came nearer to fulfilment.

SOAVE & VALPOLICELLA PRACTICAL TIPS

INFORMATION OFFICE

For the Monti Lessini: At Bosco Chiesanuova (*map Veneto West B2*), Piazza della Chiesa 34, T: 045 705 0088.

GETTING AROUND

The nearest airport and railway station serve Verona (*see previous chapter*). An excellent service of country buses run by www.atv.verona.it links Verona with Soave in 30mins (via Caldiero); to Villafranca di Verona (in 50mins), and to Bosco Chiesanuova and Volargne, both in little over 1hr.

WHERE TO STAY

VALPOLICELLA

€€€ **Villa del Quar.** Just 18 rooms, in a splendid villa. Closed Jan–Feb. *Via Quar 12, Località Pedemonte (map*

Veneto West B2), San Pietro in Cariano, T: 045 800681, hotelvilladelquar.it.
€€ **Villa Quaranta.** An 18th-century villa in a lovely old park, with a fitness centre and open-air pool. *Via Brennero 65, Località Ospedaletto, Pescantina (map Veneto West B2), T: 045 676 7300, villaquaranta.com.*
€ **Locanda dalla Rosa Alda**, *see restaurant below.*

WHERE TO EAT

SOAVE
€€ **Alpone.** Restaurant offering delicious local food and home-grown wine. Closed Sun evening, Tues, Jan and Aug. *Via Pergola 17, Costalunga, Montecchia di Crosara (9km north; map Veneto West C2), T: 045 617 5387.*
VALPOLICELLA
€€ **Dalla Rosa Alda.** A simple, genuine *trattoria* with a good wine list. Closed Sun evening (except in summer), Mon. *Strada Garibaldi 4, Frazione San Giorgio di Valpolicella, Sant'Ambrogio di Valpolicella (map Veneto West B2), T: 045 770 1018.* It also runs a simple but pleasant little *locanda* (closed Jan and Feb), with 10 rooms. dallarosalda.it.
€€ **Enoteca della Valpolicella.** Not merely a wine bar, but a renowned country restaurant in a 15th-century farm complex. Closed Mon and midday Sat. *Via Osan 45, Fumane (map Veneto West B2), T: 045 683 9146, enotecadellavalpolicella.it.*
€ **Trattoria alla Ruota.** Carefully prepared local specialities, served on a large scenic terrace in summer. Closed Mon and Tues (except in summer). *Via Proale 6, Località Mazzano di Negrar (map Veneto West B2), T: 045 752 5605, trattoriaallaruota.it.*

Treviso

This pleasant town (*map Veneto East C1*) has numerous canals, branches of the Sile and Cagnan rivers, and in parts resembles Venice, though the narrow arcaded streets are also reminiscent of Padua. Although the historic centre, still within its walls, is relatively small, it is oddly enough a rather difficult place to orientate yourself.

HISTORY OF TREVISO

Finds have proved that there was a Bronze Age settlement on the site of Treviso, and traces of a Roman town dating from the 1st century ad have also been found here. In the Middle Ages, Treviso was capital of a defensive outpost of the Carolingian empire, and later became known for its hospitality to poets and artists, especially under the Da Camino family (1283–1312). A Venetian governor took control of the city as early as 1389, and Treviso remained faithful to Venice until the fall of the Republic. During both world wars it suffered severely from air raids, notably on Good Friday 1944, when half the city was destroyed in a few minutes. One thousand six hundred civilians were killed in bombings which destroyed 3,783 houses, and 10,261 citizens were either imprisoned for political reasons or deported. In recent years, partly because of the development of its airport (used also as an alternative to Venice airport), Treviso has justly begun to receive an increasing number of visitors.

ARTISTS CONNECTED WITH TREVISO

The best works of **Tommaso da Modena**, a brilliant follower of Giotto who was at work in Treviso in the early 14th century, can be seen in all four of the town's most important churches as well as in its two excellent museums. During his lifetime Tommaso was one of the best-known artists in northern Italy and his fame was such that even the emperor Charles IV commissioned works from him. Paris Bordone, who is known to have belonged to the workshop of Titian, was born in Treviso in 1500 and his works can also be seen in the town. Lodewijk Toeput, always known as **Pozzoserrato**, was born around 1550 in Antwerp, where he worked in the studio of Marten de Vos. Both men visited Rome and Venice but Vos returned to become one of the most famous Flemish artists of his day, whereas Pozzoserrato settled in Treviso, where he died around 1605. He combines a Flemish style with the influence of Tintoretto, with whom it is thought he worked for a period. He is known particularly for his landscapes and scenes of country fairs and markets. **Luigi Serena** is a little-known artist whose works can be seen

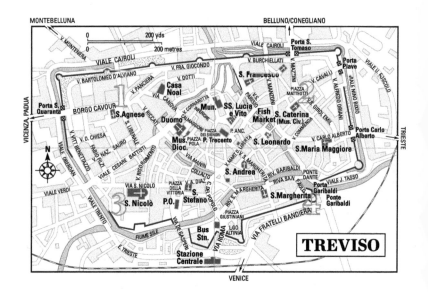

almost exclusively in Treviso, where he died in 1911. After having studied at
the Accademia in Venice together with the better-known Giacomo Favretto,
he came to live for the rest of his life here and his works are particularly
charming documents of life in the countryside around the town at that time.
The light effects in some of his paintings can even be compared to those of the
Tuscan Macchiaioli school. He also painted some good portraits.

PIAZZA DEI SIGNORI & THE CALMAGGIORE

Piazza dei Signori (*map Treviso 1–2*), now really little more than a road junction, is
in the geographical centre of the old town, and was once where the governors lived.
Palazzo del Podestà was rebuilt in antique style in 1877 and the adjoining Palazzo
del Trecento, first built in the 14th century, has also been much restored. Behind
them in a little cobbled piazza is the former Monte di Pietà pawnshop (now owned
by a bank). On the façade is a relief of Christ as the Man of Sorrows; the quaint
brick campanile of San Vito (*see below*) rises above the roof. The oldest part of the
building incorporates a charming 16th-century chapel (entrance at no. 3, but not
normally open) with paintings by Ludovico Fiumicelli and Ludovico Pozzoserrato.

To the right, an arched passageway leads to steps down to the two
intercommunicating medieval churches of **Santa Lucia** and **San Vito** (*map Treviso
2; usually open 8–12*), preceded by a portico. A hospice for pilgrims is documented
as attached to San Vito as early as 981, and the building was enlarged in the 13th

century. It contains Veneto-Byzantine frescoes of the 12th–13th century, a carved tabernacle dated 1363, and an oval ceiling painting of the *Coronation of the Virgin* by Antonio Zanchi (17th century). Santa Lucia, consecrated in 1389, has good frescoes by Tommaso da Modena and pupils, including a *Crucifixion* scene, and a charming balustrade around the altar with half-figures of saints, probably dating from the late 14th century.

The attractive **Calmaggiore** is the main shopping street of the town, with arcades on both sides. To the right (south side of the street) a modern shopping arcade has an inscription in the pavement recording that in 1973 part of the main street of the Roman town dating from the 1st century AD was discovered here some 3m below ground level. Calmaggiore passes the extraordinary exterior of the duomo.

THE DUOMO & MUSEO DIOCESANO

With its seven green domes and massive squat campanile next to another bell-tower, that of San Giovanni beside it (now the baptistery), the **duomo** (*map Treviso 1*), founded in the 12th century, has one of the most eccentric exteriors in Italy, with one flank on Calmaggiore and an oversize, ugly Neoclassical façade added in 1836. (*The entrance is usually by the side door close to the baptistery.*)

Interior of the duomo

On two pilasters in front of the second south chapel are *St John the Baptist* by Alessandro Vittoria and a bas relief of the *Visitation* attributed to Lorenzo Bregno, with the Virgin embracing St Elizabeth. Steps at the end of this aisle lead up to the **Cappella Malchiostro**, added in 1519 by Canon Broccardo, who commissioned the frescoes and altarpiece from two of the best artists at work in the Veneto at the time, Pordenone and Titian. Pordenone's frescoes include a very crowded *Adoration of the Magi*, dominated by the huge figure of one of the Kings, and Mary and Joseph depicted as an unusually young couple. Titian's altarpiece of the *Annunciation* includes the kneeling figure of the canon in the background (but it was subsequently repainted by another artist). On either side are shadowy niches frescoed by Pordenone with the figures of two saints. In the vestibule of the chapel are the jambs of the 12th-century west portal, a lovely *Adoration of the Shepherds* painted by Paris Bordone around 1557, and the *Madonna del Fiore* by Girolamo da Treviso il Vecchio dating from the previous century. Also here is the tomb of Bishop Castellano, who died in the 14th century.

In the **retro-choir** (unfortunately usually cordoned off) are frescoes by Lodovico Seitz (1880) and two very fine tombs, one of them Baroque and the other Renaissance: that of Pope Alexander VIII, who died in 1691 (and had been a canon in Treviso) includes a remarkable portrait-statue by Giovanni Bonazza. The superb monument to Bishop Zanetto, who died in 1485, is by Antonio and Tullio Lombardo with the help of their father Pietro. (Tullio Lombardo also probably sculpted the supposed portraits of the three delightfully named martyrs Teonisto, Tabra and Tabrasta on their urn on the high altar.) The **Chapel of the Sacrament** is also usually cordoned off so it is difficult to see its good sculptures (all dating from the very first years of the 16th century) by Giovanni Battista and Lorenzo Bregno, and the very fine tomb of Bishop Franco in the vestibule.

In the **north transept** is a lovely painting of St Justina with saints and the kneeling donor, painted by Francesco Bissolo around 1530, and a sculpted *St Sebastian* in the outer niche of the first nave pillar.

On the right of the sanctuary, steps lead down to the lovely 11th-century **crypt** with its 68 columns. It has fragments of early frescoes and part of its original mosaic pavement (as well as 16th-century majolica tiles in the apse). A door here (not always open) leads into the Museo Diocesano, but this is usually entered from a door outside (as described below).

Next to the Duomo is the little rectangular church of San Giovanni, dating from the 12th century, which used to serve as the **baptistery** (*now only open for exhibitions*). It contains 13th-century fresco fragments and a Roman funerary stele of the 3rd century AD.

MUSEO DIOCESANO D'ARTE SACRA
Map Treviso 1. Open 9–1, Sat 3.30 or 4–6.30 or 7; closed Sun and Mon.

On the right of the huge portico of the duomo is the Bishop's Palace, and here, beneath an arch, is a passageway where (if it is not protected by sand) you can usually see a circular **palaeochristian polychrome mosaic pavement** dating from the early 4th century AD, which probably once belonged to a baptistery. Round the corner, in the picturesque Vicolo del Duomo and Via Canoniche, is the entrance to the ancient Gothic Canoniche Vecchie, which house the Diocesan Museum.

This interesting large collection is excellently displayed. Room 1 has architectural fragments including a circular altar. The Sacello di San Prosdocimo, with its barrel vault, probably dates from the 4th century. Upstairs is a portrait of the Venetian ambassador Francesco Benaglio by Pompeo Batoni. Reached by another flight of steps are Rooms V–XIII, with the most interesting works. These include a painting by Pietro de Saliba (nephew and pupil of the more famous Antonello da Messina) of Christ crowned with thorns; and a 17th-century German silver statue of St Liberale, patron saint of Treviso; and a very interesting early 13th-century silk funerary winding cloth with pairs of parrots, of Persian origin. The room with detached frescoes includes very early (probably mid-13th-century) scenes of *Christ in Limbo* and the *Martyrdom of St Thomas Becket* (which includes a representation of Canterbury cathedral complete with domes, looking like St Mark's in Venice; Henry II is shown enthroned on the right). It is thought that this (unknown) artist also worked on some of the mosaics in St Mark's. More steps lead up to Room VIII, which has a detached fresco of *Christ in Pietà* by Tommaso da Modena and *St Sebastian* by the school of Gentile da Fabriano. There is also a display of 16th-century antiphonals. Ecclesiastical treasures include a 13th-century bronze ewer in the shape of an animal; an altar frontal in gilded wood with a relief of the *Last Judgment*; a very beautiful 15th-century processional Cross and two exquisite croziers; and a 14th-century sarcophagus which belonged to a Bishop of Treviso. Some remains of the frescoes which once decorated the walls of this building are also preserved. The display ends with English alabaster reliefs and a 16th-century Flemish tapestry.

THE MUSEI CIVICI AT SANTA CATERINA

Map Treviso 2. Open 9–12.30 & 2.30–6 except Mon. At the end of Via Santa Caterina, the entrance is in Piazzetta Mario Botter. The courtyard in front, with a little portico, was restored in 2007 and the wall has a very original silhouette in steel netting of a house painter up a ladder.

Reopened in 2008 in the former 14th-century convent of the Servi di Maria, the town museum is divided into three sections: the archaeological collection, the ex-church of Santa Caterina, and the Galleria d'Arte Medievale, Rinascimentale e Moderna, all with excellent displays.

THE ARCHAEOLOGICAL COLLECTION
The material is arranged in strictly chronological order. In the basement there are palaeolithic and mesolithic artefacts, a unique collection of bronze sword-blades dredged from the Sile and its tributaries (Hallstatt period: 7th–6th centuries BC), and five remarkable bronze ritual discs (5th century BC) from Montebelluna. The display continues upstairs, with finds from Treviso itself from the Bronze and Iron Ages (including a reconstruction of the various levels identified during excavations); artefacts from Roman period, notably mosaic pavements, glass, inscriptions (all of them transcribed for the visitor), a small head of Venus, a fine group of busts (1st–2nd centuries AD), a relief of the Dioscuri (Castor and Pollux), large sarcophagi and small Roman bronzes. The last section has material owned by wealthy private citizens who left their collections to the city.

EX-CHURCH OF SANTA CATERINA
From the cloister, with pleasant places to sit, is the entrance to the deconsecrated church of Santa Caterina, which was begun in 1346 and completed at the beginning of the 15th century. It has numerous very interesting frescoes and is also used to display detached frescoes from other churches in Treviso.

At the west end, the Cappella degli Innocenti was built onto the south wall of the church in 1430 and the very interesting frescoes survive in a damaged state. The *Crucifixion* and *Massacre of the Innocents* (a fragment with the onlookers at windows) are attributed to an unknown master named the 'Maestro degli Innocenti' from these frescoes, though some scholars identify him with Nicolò di Pietro. The frescoes in the vaults, with the Evangelists and their symbols, are much better preserved.

On the south wall of the church (by the door) is a remarkable damaged fresco (attributed to Gentile da Fabriano) of the *Miracle of St Eligius*, an interior scene showing the saint as a farrier in his smithy (Eligius is the patron saint of goldsmiths and metalworkers) with his horse and instruments of his trade. Very unusually, the

Devil is represented by the figure of a woman (with her tail issuing from her skirts). A fresco on this wall of the Madonna in lovely flowing red robes with saints and angels and St Catherine interceding for Treviso (a model of the city is shown in her hand) is also attributed to him: these may have been painted by Gentile on his first trip to the Veneto when he was called to work in the Doge's Palace in Venice. The last (earlier) scene here of the *Annunciation* shows the angel in billowing white robes with daisies in his hair.

In the chapel to the right of the sanctuary are two very damaged detached frescoes on easels from the sanctuary itself, both by Tommaso da Modena (dating from 1358 or earlier): of Christ (from a *Noli me Tangere*) and *Christ at Emmaus*.

In the centre of the nave and in the sanctuary there is a splendid display (also on easels) of a superb fresco cycle (arranged in groups of four) by Tommaso da Modena of the *Story of St Ursula*, dating from 1355–58, from the church of Santa Margherita degli Eremitani. The frescoes were detached by Luigi Bailo in 1883 (his annotations can be seen on the backs) and have survived remarkably well, even though the colours have faded. A touch screen explains the scenes in detail: they include the Ambassadors being despatched by the King of England, as well as St Ursula on her way to Rome with all her companions tucked into a boat, and (in the sanctuary) the largest scene of all showing the saint's martyrdom.

GALLERIA D'ARTE MEDIEVALE, RINASCIMENTALE E MODERNA

The collection is displayed on the upper floor of the former convent. One room is dedicated to the great Italian sculptor Arturo Martini, born in Treviso in 1889. His bronze *La Pisana,* cast in 1930, is considered his masterpiece. Besides his sculptures here, there is also a collection of his ceramics and drawings.

Two of the masterpieces of the collection of paintings are displayed side by side: two *Madonnas*, one by Giovanni Bellini and the other by Cima da Conegliano. They are both wonderful paintings, even though scholars are agreed that both were painted with the assistance of collaborators in the artists' workshops. Other fine works include a *Madonna and Saints* by Pier Maria Pennacchi (he was at work in Treviso in the late 15th century), a damaged frieze of putti by the workshop of Donatello, and two *Adoration of the Magi* by Girolamo da Santacroce and Girolamo da Treviso the Younger. There are also bronze plaquettes attributed to Maderno and small bronzes by Girolamo Campagna. Works by Paris Bordone include a *Holy Family*, a *Resurrection* and a scene of Paradise, and they give a good idea of the production of this Treviso-born painter. There is a very fine large *Crucifixion* by Jacopo Bassano.

The two most famous portraits in the collection are by Lorenzo Lotto (a Dominican friar, the guardian of Santi Giovanni e Paolo in Venice, dating from 1526) and Titian (the Humanist Sperone Speroni, with his hands resting on a golden casket, dating from 1544). The interesting scene of a concert in a villa (with its garden), dating from around 1585, is attributed to Ludovico Pozzoserrato. A miniature Crucifix in box wood is by the great woodcarver Andrea Brustolon. The small *Preaching of St John the Baptist* by Gian Domenico Tiepolo is a lovely spontaneous work, lightly 'sketched' in oil. There are portraits by Pietro Longhi (a Venetian gentleman in a splendid waistcoat) and his son Alessandro, and (in pastel) by Rosalba Carriera.

Nineteenth-century artists well represented include Pietro Zandomeneghi, Francesco Hayez (a curious portrait of the artist himself as a young child with his family), Thomas Lawrence (an excellent portrait of Canova) and a collection of good works by the little-known painter Luigi Serena (1855–1911).

SAN NICOLÒ

From Piazza della Vittoria (*map Treviso 3*), with its huge war memorial by Arturo Stagliano inaugurated in 1931, walk west along the arcaded Via San Nicolò to reach the church of the same name (*closed 12–3.30*). This huge Dominican foundation is particularly remarkable for its extraordinary height. It was built in brick in the 13th–14th century (but only completed in the 19th century). Inside, the splendid triple polygonal apse has tall lancet windows which are continued all round the church. The great ship's keel roof in the nave is almost too high up to see. The massive columns have very well preserved frescoes: the one by the stoup at the entrance has a continuous series of scenes by Tommaso da Modena, right round it, including the delightful St Jerome in his study surrounded by piles of books, St Romuald, St Agnes, and St John the Baptist.

Interior of San Nicolò

In the **south aisle** there is a lovely carved altar with statues of the *Risen Christ* and two saints and the *Madonna and Child*, all by Lorenzo Bregno. The aisle is dominated by the huge fresco of 1410, reaching almost up to the vault, of *St Christopher*, with fish in the river at his feet. It is attributed to the local artist Antonio da Treviso. Here by the door into the sacristy is the 16th-century organ by Gaetano Callido, beautifully decorated with paintings by Antonio Palma.

In the **chapel to the right of the sanctuary** is an altarpiece of the *Risen Christ*, and beneath it eight portraits (six gentlemen and two ladies), which include Bernardo de' Rossi, Bishop of Treviso who became Lorenzo Lotto's patron when the artist was living in Treviso from 1503–06, and whom he painted in a famous portrait now in the Capodimonte Museum in Naples. Through a little door in this chapel you can see the **sanctuary**, with the splendid tomb of Agostino d'Onigo (c. 1500), which has sculptures by Antonio Rizzo and, on either side, frescoes of pages, attributed by some scholars to Lotto. The splendid high altarpiece in the apse, in a very fine carved marble frame, is by Marco Pensaben and Savoldo. The monument on the right wall was set up in 1693 to record the great Dominican pope St Benedict XI (Nicolò Boccasini, 1240–1304), born in Treviso and the founder of this church.

Outside on the right of the church is the Seminario Vescovile, from which you can enter the **cloister**, which has a well in the middle of its little garden, and the **Chapter House** (*open 8–5.30 or 6*), a charming room which contains a delightful frieze around the top of the walls, one of the best known works by Tommaso da Modena, signed and dated 1352. It depicts 40 learned Dominicans including bishops, cardinals and two popes (St Benedict XI and Innocent V), as well as simple friars, all at their desks intent on their studies, surrounded by their books. The two 13th-century popes are shown next to each other on the right of the right window, and are easily distinguished because of their headgear. Cardinal Hugh of Provence is shown wearing spectacles, the first dated example known in painting. On the walls below are remains of a *Crucifixion* dating from around 1250.

SANTA MARIA MAGGIORE

Map Treviso 2–4. Closed 11.45–3. Approached along the arcaded Via Carlo Alberto.
This church was built in 1474 and has a tall plain brick campanile with a clock, still working. The interior has a lovely little Renaissance chapel decorated with polychrome marble inlay attributed to Pietro Lombardo, which frames a charming fresco of the *Madonna and Child* enthroned, shown in a typically Byzantine pose. Known as the '*Madonna Grande*', it is much venerated, as the numerous ex votos here attest. There are two kneeling warriors on either side and the Child, dressed in red and yellow and tucked into the Madonna's lap, has a golden halo and his arms open in an embrace, while the Madonna in a white robe wears a jewelled gold crown. Tommaso da Modena was called in to restore this ancient fresco in 1349, and it has since been retouched. There are also two curious little reliquary caskets here, with a pair of spurs and chains.

At the end of this aisle is a recomposed tomb with three very intricate beautiful high reliefs and five statues, all made in the 16th century by Bambaia, and in the opposite aisle is a wood Crucifix dating from the same century.

SAN FRANCESCO

This large brick church (*map Treviso 2*) dates from the 13th century. In the floor near the south door is the modest pavement tomb of Petrarch's daughter Francesca, who died in Treviso in childbirth in 1384. In the north transept is the hanging sarcophagus of Pietro Alighieri, the eldest of Dante's six sons, with his effigy. Pietro died in Treviso in 1364, over 40 years after the death of his father the great poet, who, however, almost certainly visited the town at the time of Gherardo Da Camino, who invited poets and men of learning to his court. It is a strange coincidence indeed that the children of the two greatest Italian poets, both from Tuscany, should be buried in the same church here in the Veneto. But both poets had connections to the Veneto. Petrarch was the son of a Florentine friend of Dante's but he lived the last years of his life near Padua (*see Arquà Petrarca, p. 93*). Dante himself lived for many years in exile in Verona.

In the chapel to the left of the high altar is a fresco by Tommaso da Modena (1360) of the *Madonna and Child with seven Saints*.

THE RIVERS & CANALS

The waterfront on the Sile river, especially along **Riviera Garibaldi** (*map Treviso 4*), is particularly attractive and reminscent of Amsterdam. Ponte Dante here crosses the Cagnan canal at the point where it runs into the Sile. Nearby the **Ca' dei Carraresi**, dating from the 14th century, is used for exhibitions. The picturesque **fish market** has been on an island in the Cagnan canal since 1856 (and there is a market square nearby).

From Piazza San Vito by the church of San Vito (*map Treviso 2*), Via Campana leads across two canals. By the first one is an ancient house with a brick exterior and a projecting upper storey on wooden brackets and a portico along the canal. It was carefully restored by Mario Botter in 1974 and is still in excellent condition with some faded frescoes. At the second bridge, Ponte San Francesco (very well rebuilt in 2002), there is an old mill and two wooden water wheels still working.

The Calmaggiore is prolonged by Via Canova downhill, passing several cloisters before it crosses the Siletto canal. A short way further on is the 15th-century **Ca' da Noal** (no. 38; *map Treviso 1*) in Venetian Gothic style. Having been restored in 1938, it had to be reconstructed after being hit by a bomb in 1944. Next to it is the Casa Robegan (used for exhibitions), which has almost nothing left of the frescoes by Domenico Capriolo (dating from the year of his death in Treviso, 1528) on its façade. Just beyond on the right, behind a gate in a garden of palm trees, is a little domed Neoclassical Tempietto dating from the 19th century. The road curves round into Borgo Canova, with groups of ilexes and the church of Sant'Agnese, opposite which is a large former museum (its contents are now in the ex-church of Santa Caterina). Outside the old museum building are two cement statues by the Treviso-born sculptor Arturo Martini. At the end of the street is **Porta dei Santi Quaranta**, a town gate, with Venice's Lion of St Mark guarding it on the outer face, by the bridge over another canal. You can see a stretch of the low **walls** erected in 1509–18 by Fra' Giocondo here and walk clockwise along the pleasant path on top of them, as far as Porta San Tomaso, another fine gateway (*map Treviso 2*), near where the river Botteniga reaches the town from the north.

TREVISO PRACTICAL TIPS

INFORMATION OFFICE

Piazzale Duca d'Aosta (at the bus station by the railway station; *map Treviso 3*), *trevisoinfo.it, turismo. provincia.treviso.it*.

GETTING AROUND

By air: Airport Sant'Angelo (Antonio Canova), only about 3km outside the town. Linked by bus no. 6 to Treviso railway station (in c. 15mins). Buses run by ATVO from the airport to

Mestre and Piazzale Roma in Venice and by Barzi to Venice Tronchetto.

By rail: Treviso is very well linked by train to other places in the Veneto. Frequent services to Venice 30mins. Other lines to Belluno and Vicenza.

By bicycle: Cycles can be hired through ACCT, Piazzale Duca d'Aosta (*bicincitta.com*). The GiraSile bicycle route begins at Ponte della Gobba and follows bicycle lanes and secondary roads for some 40km as far as the park of the river Sile. Information from *visittreviso.it* and *parcosile.it*.

By boat: You can hire an electric boat to visit the river Sile, for information, visit barchiamo.eu.

WHERE TO STAY

There are very few hotels in the historic centre of Treviso; nearly all of them are a few kilometres outside.

€ **Campeol.** A small (14 rooms), family-run establishment with a good restaurant, a stone's throw from Piazza dei Signori. *Piazza Ancilotto 11, T: 0422 56601, albergocampeol.it. Map Treviso 2.*

€ **Scala.** A small hotel (20 rooms) in a patrician home next to the gardens of Villa Manfrin, along the road to Conegliano. *Viale Felissent 1, T: 0422 307 600, hotelscala.com. Beyond map Treviso 2.*

€ **Relais San Nicolò.** Opposite the church of San Nicolò, this very simple little hotel above a modern café was opened in 2013 by a friendly young proprietor and is a very clean, simple place to stay. *Via Risorgimento 54, T: 0422 590114, relais-sannicolo.com. Map Treviso 3.*

WHERE TO EAT

€€ **Alfredo-el Toulà.** An elegant restaurant in a historic building, serving regional specialities and classic Italian dishes with a wide selection of wines. Closed Sun evening and Mon. *Via Collalto 26, T: 0422 540 275. Map Treviso 3.*

€€ **Antico Ristorante Beccherie.** In a historic building, locally renowned for its good food using local products. Closed Sun evening and Mon. *Piazza Ancilotto 10, T: 0422 540 871. map Treviso 2.*

€€ **L'Incontro.** Good food in the shadow of the old town gate. Closed Wed and Thur morning. *Largo Porta Altinia 13, T: 0422 547 717. Map Treviso 4.*

€€ **Toni del Spin.** Typical *trattoria* much loved by the *trevigiani*. Closed Sun, Mon morning. *Via Inferiore 7, T: 0422 543 829. Map Treviso 1.*

LOCAL SPECIALITIES

Treviso is famous for its *radicchio rosso* (red chicory), which has a slightly bitter taste. It is particularly good when grilled, but is also served raw as a salad.

FESTIVALS AND EVENTS

Treviso in Fior, flower show, May–Sept; *Concorso Internazionale Cantanti Lirici*, opera competition, June; *Autunno Musicale Trevigiano*, Classical music, autumn.

Castelfranco Veneto, Asolo, Maser & Environs

CASTELFRANCO VENETO

According to a medieval chronicle, anyone who settled in this *castello* (*map Veneto East B1*) was freed (*affrancato*) of all fiscal obligations, hence the town's name. It was built by Treviso in 1199 to defend its western frontier, and a rectangular fortification with five towers and brick walls and doorways, encircled by a moat (the *castello* proper), still encloses its centre. You enter the old walled enclosure up across the moat from the old market square, Piazza Giorgione (north), or through the arch under the bell-tower in the walls (east). The main street, Via Francesco Maria Preti, is named after the architect of the brick Teatro Accademico and of the duomo. Throughout the town are small porticoed palaces, some of them frescoed.

The sky, the clouds, and green fields of the environs are those of Giorgione (c. 1476–1510) who was born and began to paint here. His famous altarpiece of the *Madonna and Child with St Francis and a Saint in Armour* (c. 1505) is in the Palladian-style **duomo** (San Liberale, on Via Preti; *open 8–12 & 3 or 3.30–6 or 7*), in the south apsidal chapel. It is his largest painting known and his only altarpiece. It was commissioned by the Costanzo family, whose coat of arms is prominent on the lowest step of the Virgin's podium. The superb bright colours of her dress and the fabrics protecting her throne are in contrast to the dark tunic of St Francis and the magnificently painted shining suit of armour of his fellow saint. The chequered pavement is painted in perfect perspective and shows the shadows of the figures and in the background there is a wonderful landscape. Also in the cathedral, in the sacristy, are works by Palma Giovane and Jacopo Bassano and early frescoes by Paolo Veronese (*Allegorical Figures*, 1551) brought from the destroyed Villa Soranza. The cathedral's campanile is one of the towers of the defensive walls.

Opening off the same piazza, left of the duomo, is the 15th-century **Museo Casa di Giorgione** (*open Tues–Sat 9.30–12.30 & 3–6, Sun 10–7, museocasagiorgione.it*), where Giorgione lived and worked. The main room has a fascinating chiaroscuro frieze, with symbols of the liberal and mechanical arts, generally attributed to him.

Outside the walls, the old market square (Piazza Giorgione) is lined with 16th–18th-century townhouses, some with frescoed façades. To the east along Borgo Treviso, Villa Revedin, on the site of a villa by Vincenzo Scamozzi dating from 1607, is the work of Giambattista Meduna (1852–65) and is now used by the University of

Padua. It is surrounded by the large **Parco Bolasco** (*open at weekends*), also laid out in the 19th century with a rustic amphitheatre for equestrian events decorated with over 50 statues, many by Orazio Marinali, which were recuperated from the original 17th-century garden.

VILLAS AROUND CASTELFRANCO

There are some particularly interesting villas in the environs of Castelfranco, two of them by Palladio.

ISTRANA (*map Veneto East B1*)
Villa Lattes. Built in 1715 on a design by Giorgio Massari. Furnished as a house museum it is especially known for its musical boxes and dolls collected by the Lattes family in the 19th and early 20th centuries. *For opening times see marcadoc.com, or T: 0422 831810.*

SANT'ANDREA (*map Veneto East B1*)
Villa Corner (now Chiminelli). Built in 1578 for the Soranzo, it was frescoed by Veronese's brother Benedetto Caliari. *Now used for events, it is open by appointment, T: 0423 482072, villacornerchiminelli.it.*

FANZOLO (DI VEDELAGO) (*map Veneto East B1*)
Villa Emo. This is often considered Palladio's masterpiece, and survives intact in what must have been a wonderful site: the main approach is now flanked by a small railway station (on the branch line between Castelfranco Veneto and Montebelluna). The villa was commissioned from Palladio around 1558 from Leonardo Emo as his country residence in the middle of the family's large farming estate. The central building, preceded by a wide, stepped ramp, has a monumental porch with Doric columns surmounted by a triangular pediment. At the sides,

provided for the agricultural activity, are two long, symmetrical *barchesse*, terminating in the little towers of the dovecotes. The lovely interior is frescoed with delightful mythological and allegorical rustic scenes by Giovanni Battista Zelotti, possibly with the help of Paolo Veronese. *Open May–Oct Mon–Sat 3–7, Sun and holidays 9.30–12.30 & 3–7;Nov–April 10–12.30 & 2–30–5.30, Sun and holidays 9–12.30 & 2–6. www.villaemo.org.*

PIOMBINO DESE (*map Veneto East B1*)
Villa Cornaro. This villa (*open May–Sept on Sat, 3.30–6*) beside the river Dese, was begun by Palladio for Giorgio Cornaro in 1553, and building continued in the following decade (and it was finished in 1588 by Vincenzo Scamozzi). Although not closely related to the surrounding countryside and in a less attractive site than many villas, it has two storeys and the impressive façade has a double loggia with open arcades.

LEVADA (*map Veneto East B1*)
Ca' Marcello was built in 1550, but altered in the 18th century by Francesco Maria Preti, when it was frescoed by Crosato and the park (*open April–Oct Sun–Fri 9.30–7*) was laid out.

CITTADELLA

Cittadella (*map Veneto East A1–B1*), in the northern part of the province of Padua, was built by the Paduans in 1220 as a reply to Castelfranco (*see above*), which had been fortified by Treviso some 20 years earlier. The old centre is enclosed in medieval walls and a moat, elliptical in shape and extremely well preserved (but you can only really appreciate the design from the air). Within the walls the town is symmetrically planned, with the main north–south and east–west streets meeting in the centre. The streets probably follow the lines of the old Roman thoroughfares. The **gates**, Porta Padova (south) Porta Bassano (north), Porta Vicenza (west) and Porta Treviso (east) are named after the towns to which they lead and all four are frescoed. The Padua and Bassano gates have the stylised cartwheels of the Carraresi, who were lords of Padua in the 14th century. Porta Treviso has remains of an *Annunciation* and *Coronation of the Virgin*, while the *Crucifixion* adorns Porta Vicenza. The Torre di Malta by the Padua gate, built in 1251 by Ezzelino III da Romano, now houses the **Archaeological Museum**, with local finds (*closed Tues and for an hour at lunchtime*).

In the central piazza where the four roads meet is the Neoclassical **duomo** (completed 1826; *open 9–12 & 3.30–6.30*). There is an art gallery in the sacristy which has a *Supper at Emmaus* by Jacopo Bassano.

ASOLO

Asolo (*map Veneto East B1*) is a quaint little town, somewhat forgotten by the modern world. Once it was known as the 'Pearl of the Veneto' and the 'City of a Hundred Horizons' for its matchless views onto glistening snow-capped peaks. 'I assure you,' wrote Robert Browning, 'that, even though I have knowledge of and have seen with my own eyes the most beautiful panoramas in Italy and elsewhere, I have found nothing quite like the view one can enjoy from the tower of the Queen's palace.' It was largely thanks to Browning that Asolo became so famous. Today it is surrounded by numerous private villas, some with luxuriant gardens where programmed 'mow-bots' silently and incessantly trim the grass. Motorised traffic is strictly regulated in the old centre and the old arcaded central streets are peaceful and picturesque. Many of the buildings still retain traces of fresco on the façades. There are plenty of things to see in the surroundings, and good walks are to be had in the hills.

HISTORY OF ASOLO

Roman Asolo (Acetum) is mentioned by Pliny the Elder in his *Natural History*. It seems to have been a place of considerable prosperity, with a theatre and baths. In the late Middle Ages, the town was presented by Venice to Queen Caterina Cornaro in exchange for her dominions of Cyprus, and she lived in the castle here from

1489 to 1509. From the name of this town Cardinal Bembo (who frequented Queen Catherine's court) coined the term *'asolare'* (to spend time in amiable aimlessness), from which is derived *Asolando*, the name chosen by Robert Browning 'for love of the place' for his last volume of poems (1899). Browning's first visit to Asolo was in 1836, and it is the scene of *Pippa Passes*, published five years later. The actress Eleonora Duse (1850–1924) also had a house in Asolo, and the traveller and writer Dame Freya Stark (1893–1993) lived here for most of her life. Both are buried in the cemetery of Sant'Anna, just outside the town to the west. Other past visitors to Asolo include Henry James, Ernest Hemingway, Arnold Schoenberg and the architect Carlo Scarpa.

PIAZZA GARIBALDI AND THE CATTEDRALE
The centre of the town is the sloping **Piazza Garibaldi**, with a fountain and cafés and, overlooking its higher end (officially Piazza Brugnoli), the grandiose Villa Scotti, with an impressive terraced garden (the remains of the Roman baths lie under it). On the bottom corner of the piazza, where Via Regina Caterina leads off to the right (west), is the 15th-century **Loggia del Capitano**, with a fine portico and frescoed façade of 1560. Once the seat of municipal government, today it and the adjoining palace host the **Museo Civico** (*open Sat and Sun 10–12 & 3–7*), with archaeological collections from the Asolo area dating from prehistoric to Roman times, a picture gallery, Browning and Duse memorabilia and a room dedicated to Caterina Cornaro. Down steps from here is the **cattedrale** (*closed 12–3.30*), of very early foundation (Christianity is said to have been brought to these hills by Prosdocimus, Bishop of Padua) though most of the building that stands today dates from 1747. It is dedicated to the Assumption of the Virgin and contains some fine paintings including, over the high altar, a copy of Titian's *Assumption* (in the Frari in Venice). On either side of the altar are two angels by Torretti (to whose nephew Canova was apprenticed). A copy by Leandro Bassano of Titian's *Martyrdom of St Lawrence* (original in the Gesuiti, Venice) is on the south side, as is the baptistery, with a font by Francesco Graziolo, the favourite architect of Caterina Cornaro. The font was donated to the church by her and it features her coat of arms. On the south side of the church (*coin-operated light*) are two paintings of the *Assumption*, one by Jacopo Bassano (1549) and the other, very lovely indeed and worth the trip to Asolo to see, by Lorenzo Lotto (1506; with an interesting predella). There is also a *St Jerome* by Sebastiano Bastiani (1488) with very Asolo-like hills on the skyline.

THE CASTLES
Via Regina Caterina leads to the remains of the **castle** where Caterina Cornaro lived (before she moved down to the Barco at Altivole). In the late 18th century, the castle's audience chamber was turned into a theatre, with stalls and boxes modelled on La Fenice in Venice. Eleonora Duse often performed here but the fittings were sold to Sarasota, Florida and reassembled there after the Second World War. Today there is not a great deal to see at Asolo castle, though the battlements may be visited and a pleasant café operates here in fine weather. Part of the large garden that surrounded the castle was purchased by Browning (despite local opposition) so that he could construct the Villa La Torricella (in Via Sottocastello) for his son Pen (1849–1912).

From the top end of Piazza Garibaldi, past the Al Sole hotel, a road winds uphill past the site of a Roman aqueduct (which still feeds the fountain on Piazza Garibaldi) to the empty **Rocca**, which looms above the town (*open Sun 9–dusk; closed in bad weather*). There are fine views from the ramparts. It can be reached by car from Via Rocca. Beyond this, a very pretty walk can be taken through woodland where there are picnic tables, marked trails and a spring-fed pool (**Sorgente del Tritone**) inhabited by spotted salamanders.

CATERINA CORNARO

Caterina Cornaro was betrothed, at the age of 14, to James II Lusignan, King of Cyprus. The Cornaro family had always been influential in Cyprus, and this match was brokered by Caterina's father and uncle. The wedding was celebrated in 1472, but James died only a year later, in 1473, leaving the kingdom to Caterina and her unborn child. When the infant James III died the following year Caterina found herself ruler of Cyprus—but not for long. A number of conspiracies weakened her hold on the kingdom until, in 1489, she ceded her dominions to the Republic of Venice. In return she was granted a large estate at Asolo, which she turned into a famous resort of artists and poets. The Renaissance cardinal and scholar Pietro Bembo wrote extensively of his life at her court, and the 19th-century composer Gaetano Donizetti has written an opera about her.

VIA BROWNING

Via Browning, with an arcade down one side and remains of frescoes on the housefronts, leads down past the house where Browning stayed (plaque on the left as you go down from Piazza Garibaldi) to Villa Freya, where Freya Stark lived (the house is now owned by the province). Beyond it is the site of the Roman theatre and the car park. The restored 'Parco Archeologico Giardino di Villa Freya' is open for guided tours (45mins) on the 1st Sat of the month, by appointment (*see bellasolo.it*).

CONTRADA CANOVA

Off the top end of Piazza Garibaldi, to the left, Via Dante leads into Contrada Canova. Eleonora Duse's former home is on the left, just before Porta Santa Caterina (marked with a plaque, whose wording was composed by the great actress's sometime lover Gabriele d'Annunzio). Beyond this the road leads past the Hotel Villa Cipriani and the **church of Santa Caterina** (remains of 14th-century frescoes) past grand villas to the **Casa Lombarda**, built by Francesco Graziolo, Caterina Cornaro's Lombard architect, as his residence. The façade is very fancifully carved. Above it on a hill to the left is the harmonious 16th-century Villa Contarini, known as **Villa degli Armeni** since it was bought by the Armenian fathers of San Lazzaro in the Venetian lagoon. Beyond the road leads to the lovely **cemetery of Sant'Anna**, with the graves of Eleonora Duse and Freya Stark, and, on clear days, wonderful views of the mountains beyond.

AROUND ASOLO

The countryside around Asolo, once a harmonious ensemble of handsome farms and vineyards, is today very densely populated and home to much light industry and new-build housing, which mars the ancient beauty. The countryside is still dotted with fine old villas: at **Maser** (*map Veneto East B1*), in a lovely setting at the foot of the vine-clad hills to the east of Asolo, is one of Palladio's most famous works, the **Villa Barbaro**, built in the late 1550s for Daniele Barbaro, patriarch of Aquileia, and his brother Marcantonio (*open March, July and Aug Tues, Thur and Sat 10.30–6, Sun 11–6; April, June, Sept and Oct Tues–Sat 10–6, Sun 11–6; Nov, Feb, Sat–Sun and holidays 11–5; times are subject to change, see villadimaser.it*). It is one of the architect's finest achievements: following the traditional plan of the Venetian Renaissance farm, it has a central manor house with engaged Ionic columns and carved tympanum, and symmetrical porticoed *barchesse*. The interior contains famous and beautiful frescoes (1560–62) by Veronese, cleverly incorporating real architectural elements of the building into witty *trompe l'oeil* scenes (Palladio is said not to have approved of what Veronese did to the purity of his building). The cross-shaped hall is decorated with idealised landscapes with Classical ruins. A manservant and a chubby blonde girl famously appear from behind *trompe l'oeil* doors. In the central room, Giustina Barbaro, wife of Marcantonio, is depicted on a *trompe l'oeil* balcony with her three children, their nurse and pet dog. The **Tempietto**, a private chapel built on a centralised plan (on the main approach road in the village), was one of Palladio's last works (1580).

The 18th-century **Villa Falier**, below Asolo on the valley floor in the village of Ca' Falier, is where, according to popular legend, the young Canova came to the attention of Giovanni Falier, the Venetian noble who became his first patron. Preparations for a banquet were in the final stages when news reached the kitchens that the pastrychef had spoiled the centrepiece. There was consternation all round until the 12-year-old grandson of a stone-carver, who was employed as a kitchen-boy, shyly offered to carve something from butter. The result—a figure of a lion—so impressed Falier and his guests that Falier took the boy under his wing and arranged for him to be apprenticed to a master sculptor.

In the cemetery of **San Vito di Altivole**, 5km southeast of Asolo, is Carlo Scarpa's Brion tomb, a cult piece among modern architects. **Altivole** itself is home to Caterina Cornaro's 'Barco', built by her favourite architect Graziolo. During the heyday of her court, many dinners, banquets, jousts and masques were held here, with performances by the famed Padua-born actor and playwright Ruzante.

POSSAGNO

Possagno (*map Veneto East B1*) was the birthplace in 1757 of the famous sculptor Antonio Canova. His patrons were many, and included the Habsburg court in Vienna and Napoleon Bonaparte. In 1802, at Napoleon's express request, he went to Paris to model a nude statue of the emperor as Mars, holding a Victory in his hand. That statue is now in Apsley House, London (former home of Napoleon's nemesis the

Duke of Wellington), while a bronze replica survives in the courtyard of the Brera in Milan and a clay model for it is preserved in the Museo Revoltella in Trieste. Even more famous is Canova's sculpture of Napoleon's sister Pauline, who married Camillo Borghese: he portrayed her, half nude, as *Venus Victrix* (the statue is in the Galleria Borghese in Rome). But it is perhaps his supremely elegant marble groups of mythological figures such as the *Three Graces* and *Eros and Psyche* for which he is justly best remembered. The style he invented for sepulchral monuments, with the effigies often accompanied by mourning figures (and his use of the pyramid form derived from ancient classical tombs), greatly influenced later funerary sculpture. In 1815 Canova went back to Paris on a papal mission: to retrieve the treasures which Napoleon had seized from Italy. He succeeded in large measure and his fundamental role in this operation, and also as a sensitive protector of Italian art in general, has always been recognised. However, soon after his death in Possagno in 1822, his fame as a sculptor quickly waned, and his works were less appreciated in the Romantic era. With a revival of interest in the Neoclassical period in the 20th century, Canova was once again acclaimed as one of Italy's greatest sculptors (his works are to be found in many of the most important museums of the world). He was also an extraordinarily skilled draftsman and some very fine painted portraits by him (one of which is in the Museo Correr in Venice) also survive.

Surrounded by a little garden, his house in Possagno can be visited (*open Tues–Sun 9.30–6, museocanova.it*), next to a Museum (a Gipsoteca) which preserves all the plaster casts which were in Canova's studio in Rome at the time of his death, and which his brother had transported here (although some of them were irreparably damaged in the First World War). In 1957 Carlo Scarpa was called in to redesign the exhibition space, which also displays some of the sculptor's models in clay, terracotta and wax which illustrate his working method.

He is buried here in the Tempio, a memorial chapel of his own design (and for which he sculpted the metopes), and which he built to serve as the parish church (his heart is in Venice, in his famous mausoleum in the Frari). The Tempio contains two of Canova's works: a bronze *Pietà* and a painting, The *Descent from the Cross*.

CONEGLIANO VENETO & VITTORIO VENETO

The wine-growing town of **Conegliano Veneto** (*map Veneto North B3*) has many attractive 16th–18th-century houses, especially in the central Via XX Settembre. It was the birthplace of Giovanni Battista Cima (c. 1459–1518), always known as Cima da Conegliano, and the cathedral has a fine altarpiece by him dating from 1492. The Casa di Cima at Via Cima 24 has an archive dedicated to the painter. The front of the guildhall (Scuola dei Battuti) is covered with 16th-century frescoes attributed to Pozzoserrato, and inside (*open Sun and holidays 3–6.30*) are 15th-century frescoes by Andrea Previtali, Jacopo da Montagnana and Girolamo da Treviso.

The hills to the west of Conegliano, particularly around **Valdobbiadene**, are famous for their vineyards: this is the heartland of Prosecco production.

Vittorio Veneto (*map Veneto North B3*) was created in 1866 by merging the lower (now industrial) district of Ceneda (where the cathedral, rebuilt in 1776, has an altarpiece of 1547 by Titian) with the old walled town of Serravalle. But it was renamed 'Victory of the Veneto' after the final victory here of the Italians over the Austrians in October 1918 (*for more, see the section on the Great War in the Veneto*).

CASTELFRANCO, ASOLO & MASER PRACTICAL TIPS

GETTING AROUND

By car: There is nowhere to park in Asolo. You will need to leave your car in the car park outside the old centre to the south (follow Via Browning). In Castelfranco there is parking in Piazza Giorgione, the old market square outside the walls to the north.

By train: Castelfranco Veneto is served by direct trains from Padua (30mins), Vicenza (40mins; less frequent) and Treviso (25mins). Direct services to Cittadella take 45mins from Padua, 30mins from Vicenza and 40mins from Treviso. Fanzolo (for Villa Emo) can be reached by train from Castelfranco in under 10mins or from Padua in 45mins. Istrana is served by trains from Castelfranco and Treviso (both in c. 10mins). Piombino Dese is reached from Castelfranco in c. 10mins and from Venice in c. 50mins. Frequent services from Treviso (in 30mins) to Conegliano and (10mins more) Vittorio Veneto.

The nearest train station to Possagno (with a bus connection) is at Bassano del Grappa (but there are also buses from the rail stations of Castelfranco Veneto and Montebelluna).

By bus: Local buses run by CTM (*ctmspa.com*) have services linking Castelfranco, Fanzolo and Altivole (no. 201); Castelfranco and Possagno (no. 224); Castelfranco, San Vito di Altivole, Asolo and Possagno (no. 204) and Bassano and Possagno. La Marca (*www.lamarcabus.it*) runs buses from Bassano del Grappa to Asolo and Maser, and from Montebelluna to Possagno. NB: The bus stops for Asolo are on the main road on the valley floor. Shuttle buses from the car park serve the old town.

WHERE TO STAY

ASOLO (*map Veneto East B1*)
€€€ **Villa Cipriani.** ▬ A 16th-century villa beautifully appointed and well run. Elegant yet homely. Bar and restaurant and a pretty flower garden. Many of the rooms have stunning views, some have sun terraces. *Via Canova 298, T: 0423 523411, villaciprianiasolo.com.*
€€ **Al Sole.** Overlooking the central Piazza Garibaldi, a historic old hotel fully renovated and now one of the Small Luxury Hotels of the World group. *T: 0423 951332, albergoalsoleasolo.com.*
€ **Duse.** Small (12 rooms), comfortable, and centrally located. *Via Robert Browning 190, T: 0423 55241, www. hotelduse.com.*

CASTELFRANCO VENETO (*map Veneto East B1*)

€€ Alla Torre. A pleasant hotel very conveniently located in the heart of the historic city. *Piazzetta Trento e Trieste 7, T: 0423 498 707, www.hotelallatorre. it.*

€€ Fior. A comfortable place with garden and swimming pool, and good restaurant. *Via dei Carpani 18 (just northeast of Parco Bolasco), T: 0423 721 212, hotelfior.com.*

€ Al Moretto. In a building dating from the 17th century, this simple hotel has been managed by the same family for three generations. Excellent location. *Via San Pio X 10, T: 0423 721313, albergoalmoretto.it.*

WHERE TO EAT

ASOLO (*map Veneto East B1*)

€€€ Locanda Baggio. ▰ A short drive out of town to the north (Via Foresto Casonetto). Two generations of the Baggio family have dedicated themselves to fine cuisine for over 30 years, carefully sourcing ingredients and combining traditional recipes with experimentation. Closed Mon. *Via Bassane 1, T: 0423 529648, www. locandabaggio.it.*

   There are also plenty of places in central Asolo itself: on Piazza Garibaldi there is the **Caffè Central** (closed Tues) and on Via Browning either the simple (but reliable) chain restaurant **Pane e Vino** or the very local and atmospheric **Al Bàcaro** (closed Wed). **€€ Tappobar** (*Via Roma 55, T: 0423 952201*) is friendly and welcoming, a bar in the front opening off Piazza Garibaldi, and a restaurant through to the right. For fish there is **€€€ Bistrot** on Via Pietro Bembo (evenings only,

closed Sun, *T: 0423 529592, www. ristorantebistrotasolo.com*), and on the corner of Piazza Garibaldi/Via Roma and Via Dante, two simple places: **Epoca** (snacks and pasta, open all day) and **Ostaria Corte del Re**.

CASTELFRANCO VENETO (*map Veneto East B1*)

€€ Alle Mura. An elegant place set against the medieval town walls and specialising in seafood. Closed Thur, Jan and Aug. *Via Preti 69, T: 0423 498098, ristoranteallemura.com.*

€€ Rino Fior. Old-established restaurant with sound Venetian cooking, a favourite with locals. A short way northeast of the walled centre. Closed Mon evening and Tues, in Jan and July–Aug. *Via Montebelluna di Salvarosa 27, T: 0423 490 462, www. rinofior.com.*

CONEGLIANO (*map Veneto North B3*)

€€ Al Salisà. A good restaurant with a pleasant (enclosed) terrace overlooking the garden. Closed Tues evening, Wed and Aug. *Via XX Settembre 2, T: 0438 24288, ristorantealsalisa.com.*

€€ Tre Panoce. Impeccably prepared regional dishes in an 18th-century villa with gardens. Closed Sun evening, Mon, Jan and Aug. *Via Vecchia Trevigiana 50, T: 0438 60071, www. trepanocekiri.com.*

FESTIVALS AND EVENTS

On the 3rd Sun in Oct the fair known as the *Fiera Franca* has been held since 1608 in Cittadella.

The Great War in the Veneto

At the outbreak of the First World War, Italy, as a member of the Triple Alliance which had been signed in 1882 with Germany and Austria, at first remained neutral. But in May 1915 the country entered the War as an ally of France, Britain and Russia against Austria, having been given the guarantee that the Trentino, South Tyrol, Trieste and part of Dalmatia would all become part of Italy at the end of the hostilities. However, Italy was totally unprepared for war and many Italians were opposed to the abandonment of her neutrality. Despite the general conviction that the War would be rapidly concluded, bitter fighting on Italian territory against Austria ensued for three years and, after 1916, for two more years against Germany. Up until 1917 the front line remained substantially the same, with the Austrians holding the Adige valley and the plateau of Asiago and the Italians defending the Isonzo (although Italy had managed to cross the river and win Gorizia in 1916).

But after the Russian front collapsed in October 1917 the combined forces of Austria and Germany won an important battle at Caporetto, now Kobarid in Slovenia (northeast of Cividale del Friuli). The name of Caporetto has entered the Italian language as a synonym for 'devastating defeat'. The enemy quickly invaded the Veneto and Monte Grappa (*map Veneto West D1*), and their advance was only arrested by the Italians along the Piave river, which they defended bravely, and won a famous victory at (the later renamed) Vittorio Veneto in late October 1918. The following month the Austro-Hungarian empire collapsed.

At the end of the War, Italy had its northern boundaries redrawn along the natural mountainous frontier to include the Trentino and South Tyrol, and most important of all gained the port of Trieste. But Fiume, today's Rijeka, and much of Dalmatia was not included in Italy's gains which left many Italians critical of the 'mutilated peace' terms and questioning whether the terrible loss of life had been justified, with Pope Benedict XV's famous phrase that it had been an '*inutile strage*' (a 'useless massacre') often repeated.

WAR MEMORIALS AND MUSEUMS

The First World War is recorded in many places in the Veneto. There is a museum dedicated to the battles along the Piave river at San Donà di Piave (which had to be totally rebuilt after the War; *map Veneto East C1*). As a volunteer with the US Red

Cross, Ernest Hemingway was wounded in 1918 at the age of 19 at **Fossalta di Piave** (see *A Farewall to Arms*), and a memorial stele was set up there in 1979 (*map Veneto East C1*). At **Ponte della Priula** (**Susegana**), due north of Treviso (*map Veneto East C1*), there is a votive temple commemorating the War.

The heavy fighting in the mountainous districts is recorded on **Monte Pasubio** (2235m; *map Veneto West C1*) where a ring of boundary-stones defines the 'Zona Sacra', dedicated to those who died here. On the **Pian delle Fugazze** (1159m) is the Sacello del Pasubio, another war memorial with a battle museum. On **Monte Cimone** (*map Veneto West C1*) there is a war memorial and cemetery. **Schio** has an ossuary-cloister on the Asiago road, with 5,000 graves of soldiers who fell in 1915–18.

In **Vittorio Veneto** (*map Veneto North B3*) the lower district of Ceneda has a museum relating to the famous Italian victory.

THE WAR CEMETERIES

Monte Grappa (1775m; *map Veneto West D1*) north of Bassano was the scene of heavy fighting between Austrians and Italians in 1917–18, in three historic battles which ended in the loss of 12,615 Italian soldiers (only 2,283 of whom could be identified). On the summit is a monumental cemetery built in 1935 by Giovanni Greppi, with a votive chapel dedicated to the Madonnina del Grappa. Nearby is the Austro-Hungarian cemetery, with the remains of 10,295 soliders (only 295 of whom were identified).

At **Asiago** (*map Veneto West C1–D1*) there were also terrible losses on both sides: a monumental war cemetery (1932–38) has the remains of 33,086 Italian and 18,505 Austro-Hungarian dead. Nearby is a museum illustrating the history of the battles.

At **Caporetto**, now in Slovenia, there is the Sacrario Militare Italiano (with 7,002 graves).

THE INVOLVEMENT OF BRITISH TROOPS

For the last year of the War, British troops were sent south from the trenches in Flanders to reinforce the Italian fronts at Asiago and along the Piave. There are five Commonwealth cemeteries in the woods on the Asiago plateau (*map Veneto West C1–D1*): at Barenthal, Cavelletto, Boscon, Granezza, and Magnaboschi (where 712 British soliders lie buried), and two near the Piave in the province of Treviso at Tezze (*map Veneto North B3*) and Giavera (*map Veneto North A3–A4*) with 773 graves. In the cemetery of Giavera there is also a memorial to 150 fallen in Italy in the Great War whose places of burial are unknown. There is another Commonwealth cemetery at Padua. All of these are described in detail on the website of the Commonwealth War Graves Commission (*www.cwgc.org*). The museum in Padua in the Stabilimento Pedrocchi also includes a graphic account of the First World War.

Feltre & Belluno

FELTRE

Feltre (*map Veneto North A3*) was a Roman centre, probably a *municipium*, and before that it may have been a Raetian community on the Via Opitergium–Tridentum (Roman Opitergium is the modern-day village of Oderzo). In the Middle Ages Feltre was a free *comune* and a seigniory of various families before coming under Venice in 1404. The Venetian heads of state dated their dispatches *ex cineribus Feltri*, 'from the ashes of Feltre', after forces of the Holy Roman Empire sacked the city twice (in 1509 and 1510) during the War of the League of Cambrai. The architectural uniformity of the city centre, Feltre's most distinctive asset, is a direct consequence of this double debacle and of the ambitious programme of reconstruction that followed it.

ALONG VIA MEZZATERRA

The old walled city has numerous 16th-century buildings with projecting roofs and façades bearing frescoes or graffiti. Almost all the city gates date from the Renaissance. The porticoed Via Mezzaterra begins at the 16th-century Porta Imperiale, or Castaldi, and runs eastwards uphill through the old city to the Renaissance **Piazza Maggiore**. This is laid out on several levels. On the north side stands the church of San Rocco (1599); the fine fountain is attributed to Tullio Lombardo (1520). On the west is the 19th-century Gothic-revival Palazzo Guarnieri; and on the south, the unusual Palazzo della Ragione or Palazzo del Municipio, actually two buildings meeting at the corner—the one with the rusticated arcade (1558) is the former Palazzo dei Rettori Veneti, attributed to Palladio. Inside is a small wooden theatre of 1802. Above the square rises the *castello* with its square keep, a Roman watchtower rebuilt in the Middle Ages.

The continuation of Via Mezzaterra, named Via Luzzo after the painter Lorenzo Luzzo, born in Feltre around 1485 (and whose works can best be appreciated in this town), is lined with interesting houses. The Venetian-Gothic-revival building at no. 23 is home to the **Museo Civico** (*open at weekends, 10-30–12.30 & 3–6 or 4–7*), containing a small portrait by Gentile Bellini, a triptych by Cima da Conegliano, a *Resurrection of Lazarus* by Palma Giovane and four views by Marco Ricci. There are also works by the native artists Pietro Mariscalchi and Lorenzo Luzzo (sometimes but not unanimously identified with the lugubrious name of Morto da Feltre).

Outside the walls at the northeast end of the town (Via Borgo Ruga) is the 15th-century **church of the Ognissanti**, with a 9th- or 10th-century campanile and fragmentary frescoes on the outside. Inside there is a painting of the Resurrection and a fresco, both by Luzzo, as well as a *Madonna with Sts Victor and Nicholas of Bari* by Tintoretto.

GALLERIA D'ARTE MODERNA
From Piazza Maggiore, Via del Paradiso leads past the elaborately decorated Monte di Pietà to the Galleria d'Arte Moderna Carlo Rizzarda (*Via del Paradiso 8; open Tues–Sun 10.30–12.30 & 3–6, morning only on Fri*) in the 16th-century Palazzo Cumano. The building was acquired by Carlo Rizzarda (a local sculptor especially skilled in wrought-iron work) in 1926, five years before his death. It contains his art collection, which includes 19th- and 20th-century Italian paintings and sculpture by Giovanni Fattori, Francesco Paolo Michetti, Carlo Carrà and Arturo Tosi, as well as furniture, decorative arts and the ironwork produced by Rizzarda himself.

SAN PIETRO
Just outside the walls to the south, Via Roma leads to the cathedral of **San Pietro**. Its present appearance dates from the 16th century, notwithstanding the 14th-century Gothic apse and campanile. The three-aisled interior, with its 9th-century crypt, conserves paintings of the *Adoration of the Shepherds* and *St John the Baptist* by Pietro Mariscalchi, the tomb of Andrea Bellati by Tullio Lombardo (in the sanctuary), the 13th-century throne of Bishop Vilata (at the end of the north aisle), a fine Byzantine crucifix of 542 (in the Archivio Capitolare), and other interesting artworks. Steps behind the cathedral ascend to the **baptistery of San Lorenzo**, with a 15th-century apse, a 17th-century doorway on the façade and a Renaissance doorway on the side. Inside are a baptismal font of 1399 with a Baroque wooden cover, and paintings by Leandro Bassano and other artists of the 16th and 17th centuries. Beneath the piazza is an **archaeological area** (*open March–Oct weekends 10–1 & 3.30–6.30 or 4–7*) with excavations of part of the Roman city and an early Christian baptistery.

AROUND FELTRE

The **sanctuary of Santi Vittore e Corona** (*map Veneto North A3*) is a Byzantine-Romanesque church of 1096–1101 with a narrow façade adorned with chiaroscuro frescoes. The three-aisled interior has 13th–15th-century frescoes (some of which are thought to be by the school of Giotto) and 11th-century sculptures. The adjoining convent of 1494 has more frescoes in the cloister.

The 15th-century church of Santa Maria Assunta at **Lentiai** (*map Veneto North A3*) has a coffered ceiling and paintings by Palma Vecchio; and at **Soranzen** (*map Veneto North A3*) the villas Facino-Pasole and Martini date from the 17th and 18th centuries respectively.

BELLUNO

The old town of Belluno (*map Veneto North A2–B2*) stands on a rocky eminence at the point where the River Ardo flows into the Piave—a position which protected it over the centuries both from foreign incursions and from seasonal flood waters. Here you immediately feel the nearness of the Alps (the Dolomiti Bellunesi, the most southerly of the Dolomite ranges, rise just to the west) and of the forests that have long been the city's principal asset. From Belluno, in fact, came the piles on which Venice is built; and something of the deep greens and browns of the Alpine woodlands can be seen in the paintings of Sebastiano Ricci (*see below*) and his nephew Marco, who were born here in 1659 and 1679, respectively. The Baroque wood-sculptor Andrea Brustolon (1660–1732) was also a native.

SEBASTIANO RICCI

Ricci (1659–1734) is famous as much for the scandals in his private life as for his painting. He had a marked appetite for other men's wives, and often found himself having to leave town in a hurry when his liaisons were discovered. Nor was he above resorting to desperate measures to cover his traces. When he made one of his lovers pregnant in Venice, he hatched a plot to poison her. The lady in question had Ricci imprisoned instead. He escaped to Bologna, where he continued to receive commissions from enthusiastic noblemen and prelates. All this tends to obscure his value as an artist. And because he often finished his paintings in a hurry, his style is sometimes too dashing, and he has been accused of superficiality. But Ricci was a virtuoso talent. And the helter-skelter energy which compelled him to rush his works to completion translates into nervous brushwork which give them an amazing lightness of touch. Ricci has been compared to Veronese. He certainly studied Veronese, and reinterpreted him in a dazzling, colourful style which was to lift early 18th-century Venetian painting out of its doldrums and steer it on a new course, towards the later brilliance of Tiepolo. Ricci was highly sought-after in his own lifetime, and travelled widely to commissions both in and outside Italy, including Vienna (Karlskirche, Schönbrunn) and London, where he narrowly lost a competition to fresco the dome of St Paul's. Ricci's intemperate eating, drinking and womanising took its toll on his health: he suffered acutely from gallstones, and died on the operating table.

ON AND AROUND PIAZZA DUOMO

The **duomo** of Santa Maria delle Grazie is a 16th-century edifice designed by Tullio Lombardo, with an unfinished façade and a detached campanile (1743) by Filippo Juvarra. The luminous interior has paintings by Jacopo Bassano (third south altar) and Palma Giovane (fourth south altar). The two small marble statuettes in the first north chapel are attributed to Tullio Lombardo. The baptistery dates from the 16th century.

On the north side of Piazza del Duomo is the 19th-century Town Hall and its historic predecessor, the **Palazzo dei Rettori** (now the prefecture), a Venetian Renaissance building of 1491 with porticoed façade, mullioned windows, central loggias and an imposing clock-tower (1549) over the eastern corner. Opposite, the former palace of the bishop-counts (1190) has been completely rebuilt, the Torre Civica being the only vestige of the original structure.

The **Museo Civico** (Via Duomo 16; *open Tues and Fri 9–12 & 3–6, otherwise only in the mornings; closed Mon*) is arranged in the 17th-century Palazzo dei Giuristi. It has works by Bartolomeo Montagna, Palma Giovane and Sebastiano and Marco Ricci.

The street continues to **Piazza Erbe** or Piazza del Mercato, on the site of the Roman forum, and surrounded by porticoed Renaissance buildings, the finest of which is the former pawnbroker, the Monte di Pietà (1531), adorned with coats of arms and inscriptions. The fountain in the centre dates from 1410.

SANTO STEFANO

From Piazza Erbe, continue north along Via Rialto and then, beyond the ancient Porta Doiona, go up Via Roma until you come to the late Gothic church of **Santo Stefano** (1468), with a large 15th-century doorway on the side. The Cappella Cesa, within, has frescoes by Jacopo da Montagnana (c. 1487) and painted wood statues of Matteo, Antonio, and Francesco Cesa, by Andrea Brustolon, over the altar.

SAN PIETRO

South of Piazza Erbe is Via Mezzaterra, lined with Venetian-style townhouses. Turn left into Vicolo San Pietro for the Gregorian church of **San Pietro**, a 14th-century edifice rebuilt in 1750, with a bare façade and, inside, paintings by Sebastiano Ricci (over the high altar) and two wooden altar panels carved by Andrea Brustolon.

FELTRE & BELLUNO PRACTICAL TIPS

INFORMATION OFFICE

Belluno. Piazza Duomo 2, T: 0437 940083, *www.infodolomiti.it*.

GETTING AROUND

By train: For Feltre, there are direct trains from Padua in 1hr 40mins and from Castelfranco Veneto in c. 1hr. Other routes involve a change at Montebelluna. The same is true for Belluno: direct trains from Castelfranco Veneto make the journey in 1hr 40mins and from Padua in c. 2hrs. Other services almost always involve changing at Montebelluna.

By bus: There are buses run by DolomitiBus (*www.dolomitibus. it*) between Feltre and Belluno via Soranzen (no. 17) and via Lentiai (no. 20). For Santi Vittore e Corona at Anzù (4km away), buses from Feltre are operated by La Marca (*www. lamarcabus.it*).

WHERE TO STAY

BELLUNO (*map Veneto North A2–B2*)
€€ **Delle Alpi.** An old-established comfortable hotel with a restaurant, midway between the train station and the duomo. *Via Jacopo Tasso 13, T: 0437 940545, dellealpi.it.*
€€ **Park Hotel Villa Carpenada.** A pleasant hotel in an 18th-century villa with park, 2km west of the town centre. *Via Mier 158, T: 0437 948343, hotelvillacarpenada.it.*
FELTRE (*map Veneto North A3*)
€€ **Doriguzzi.** A pleasant central hotel which claims to be the oldest in town. Modern bedrooms. Favoured by cyclists. *2 Viale del Piave, T: 0439 2003, hoteldoriguzzi.it.*
€ **Nuova de Cesero.** A very old hotel, still family run and with comfortable rooms and a friendly atmosphere. *Vicolo Fornere Pazze 5, T: 0439 2110, hotelnuovo.it.*

WHERE TO EAT

BELLUNO (*map Veneto North A2–B2*)
€ **Al Borgo.** Traditional fare and regional, Italian and imported wines in an 18th-century villa with gardens. Closed Mon evening, Tues, Jan and July. It is also a small hotel. *Via Anconetta 8, T: 0437 926755, alborgo.to.*

€ **Taverna.** A simple *trattoria* with good local dishes, behind the Teatro Comunale. Closed Sun and July. *Via Cipro 7, T: 0437 25192, tavernabelluno. wordpress.com.*
€ **Terracotta.** A good restaurant in the old centre, with a wisteria-covered terrace in summer. Very reasonable lunchtime all-inclusive menu. Closed Tues and Wed at lunch. *Via Giuseppe Garibaldi 61, T: 0437 291692, ristoranteterracotta.it.*

LOCAL SPECIALITIES

Skilled artisans produce excellent woodcarving and wrought-iron work.

FESTIVALS AND EVENTS

Belluno Music festivals and concerts are held frequently. In Feltre, the *Palio della Città*, a historic pageant, is held the first weekend in Aug.

The Dolomites

he northern Veneto, where the Dolomites merge with the white limestone
peaks of the eastern Alps, is renowned above all for its ski resorts, the most
famous of which is Cortina d'Ampezzo (*map Veneto North A1*). But there are
also a number of places you can visit out of season, where natural beauty goes hand-
in-hand with historical heritage.

PARCO NAZIONALE DELLE DOLOMITI BELLUNESI

For all information see dolomitipark.it.
This protected area covers the southernmost ramifications of the Dolomites,
including the great limestone massifs of the Talvena (2542m), the Schiara (2565m),
the Monti del Sole (2240m) and the Alpi Feltrine (Sass de Mura, 2550m). These
mountains join typically alpine landscapes, characterised by bold peaks and powerful
vertical walls, with the grassy meadows and shady forests and valleys of the Prealpi.
The park's flora is one of its prime assets, and includes numerous native species and
rarities. Magnificent beechwoods yield at higher altitudes to fir and larch.

THE CADORE
The Cadore is the mountainous district surrounding the upper valley of the Piave
and its western tributaries. Until 1918 only the southeastern half of the district was
Italian territory, and there was heavy mountain fighting during the First World
War on the old frontier line. The *Cadorini* still speak Ladino, a Romance language,
with Ladino-Venetian dialects in the lower valleys; but German is understood
everywhere from Cortina northwards.

Pieve di Cadore (878m; *map Veneto North B1*), the chief town of the region, is a
summer and winter resort beneath the southern foothills of the Marmarole. The
Palazzo della Magnifica Comunità Cadorina (*open at weekends 10–12.30 & 3.30–
6.30*), rebuilt in 1525, contains a small archaeological museum. Outside is a statue
of Titian, who was born here c. 1488. His modest birthplace has a small museum
(*open in summer 10–12.30 & 3.30–6.30*). The parish church has a *Madonna with
Saints* by him. The Casa di Babbo Natale, on the hillside of Montericco, receives mail
addressed to Father Christmas.

Cortina d'Ampezzo (1210m at the church; *map Veneto North A1*) is a summer
and winter resort once frequented by the best society, though now nowhere near as

fashionable as it was. It lies in a sunny upland basin, and the view of the mountains on all sides is magnificent. The church has a wooden tabernacle by Andrea Brustolon and an altarpiece by Antonio Zanchi. The pinacoteca contains works by Filippo de Pisis (1896–1956), who often stayed in Cortina, and other modern Italian painters. Aldous Huxley wrote much of *Point Counter Point* here in 1926–27. A spectacular road across the Dolomites, built by the Austrians in 1901–09, leads west from here to Canazei and Bolzano. The Lago di Misurina (1737m), northeast of Cortina, is one of the most beautifully situated lakes in the Dolomites.

VENETO DOLOMITES PRACTICAL TIPS

INFORMATION OFFICES

Cortina d'Ampezzo. Ufficio Informazioni Turistiche, Piazza Roma, T: 0436 869086, *dolomiti.org*; Cortina Turismo, 15/b Via Marconi, T: 0436 866252, *cortina.dolomiti.org*.

GETTING AROUND

By bus: Buses to Cortina (bus station in Via Marconi) run by Cortina Express from Treviso and Venezia (*cortinaexpress.it*). Other services all over the Dolomites run by DolomitiBus (*dolomitibus.it*). Local buses and ski buses run by SE.AM Servizi Ampezzo (*serviziampezzo.it*).
By train: The nearest station is at Calalzo di Cadore (35km from Cortina; *map Veneto North B1*) where there are connecting buses run by DolomitiBus.

WHERE TO STAY

NB: Some hotels are closed in May and Oct and Nov.

CORTINA D'AMPEZZO (*map Veneto North A1*)
€€€ Park Hotel Faloria. A luxury establishment in two immense chalets, with 30 suites. Fitness centre and swimming pool. Restaurant. *Località Zuel 46, T: 0436 2959, parkhotelfaloria. it.*
€€ De la Poste. The classic place to stay in Cortina, in the very heart of the town. With a celebrated restaurant. Closed May and Oct–Nov. *Piazza Roma 14, T: 0436 4271, www.delaposte.it.*
€ Oasi. A small place with pleasant rooms and lovely atmosphere, near the centre of Cortina. Closed Oct. *Via Cantore 2, T: 0436 862019, hoteloasi.it.*

Although Cortina d'Ampezzo has by far the most hotels of all categories in the Dolomites, other resorts well supplied with them include **San Vito di Cadore** (*map Veneto North B1*), **Pieve di Cadore** (*map Veneto North B1*), **Santo Stefano di Cadore** (*map Veneto North B1*), **Sappada** (*map Veneto North C1*) and **Auronzo** (*map Veneto North B1*).

WHERE TO EAT

CORTINA D'AMPEZZO (*map Veneto North A1*)
€€€ De La Poste. Closed Wed. See hotel listing above.

€€ **Baita Piè Tofana** (with rooms). A lodge, popular with hikers and climbers, with good traditional food and fabulous views. Ten mins from the centre of Cortina. Closed Wed, June and Oct. *Località Rumerlo, T: 0436 4258, baitapietofana.it.*

Lake Garda

Lake Garda (Lago di Garda; *map Veneto West B1–A2*) is the largest and perhaps the most beautiful of the northern Italian lakes. Its mild climate permits the cultivation of olives and lemon trees, and the vegetation of its shores is characterised by numerous cypresses in thick woods. Most of its resorts were developed in the 1920s and 1930s, although some grand hotels had already been built at the end of the 19th century for Austrian and German visitors who came to the mild western shore, many of them to cure respiratory disorders. Sirmione, in a spectacular position on a narrow peninsula on the south shore, was known in Roman times as a resort on Lacus Benacus (the name derived from a Celtic word meaning 'horned').

The inspiring beauty of the lake has made it traditionally popular with writers. Goethe visited Garda at the start of his Italian journey in 1786 and saw his first olive trees here. Byron stayed at Desenzano in 1816, and Tennyson visited the lake in 1880. D.H. Lawrence lived on its shores in 1912 and 1913, and he describes the lemon gardens in *Twilight in Italy*.

Citrus cultivation around the lake dates from at least the 16th century and reached a height in commercial production in the early 19th century. It was the northernmost locality in the world where citrus fruits could be grown commercially. A few of the characteristic hothouses (*limonaie*), built of tall stone struts roofed over with wooden slats in winter, and protected by glass panes in front, where lemons and citrons were cultivated in the 19th century, still survive at Gargnano, San Vigilio and Torri del Benaco. These shelters, unique to Garda, were designed for maximum protection from the cold.

Duck and swans flourish on the lake, and fishing is still practised in a few localities. The *carpione* (*Salmo carpio*), a kind of large trout, is found only in Garda; other fish include pike, trout and eel. Menus often feature *lavarello* (*Coregonus lavaretus*), freshwater whitefish (also known as *coregone*).

The best time to visit Lake Garda is in May and June: in August it is very crowded and can be extremely hot. The breezier upper part of the lake, where the water is deepest, is much used for sailing and windsurfing (boats can be hired), and there are regattas in summer. The predominant winds (which can swell into violent storms) are the *sover* (or *soar* or *sora*), from the north, in the morning, and the *ora*, from the south, in the afternoon. The waters are considered the cleanest of the big Italian lakes, and swimming is permitted (the best places include the peninsula of Sirmione, the Isola dei Conigli off Moniga, the Baia del Vento between Salò and Desenzano, and the Isola San Biagio).

SIRMIONE

Sirmione (*map Veneto West A2*) stands at the tip of a narrow promontory 3.5km long and in places only 119m wide, in the centre of the southern shore of the lake. It was a Roman station on the Via Gallica, halfway between Brescia and Verona. Now it is a famous resort with numerous hotels and is very popular with tour groups in season (though deserted in winter). There are many enjoyable walks on the peninsula, and you can swim in the lake on the east side. The peninsula tip is covered with the remains of a vast Roman villa, thought to have belonged to the poet Catullus.

The picturesque 13th-century **Rocca Scaligera** (*open Tues–Sun 8.30–7.30*), where Dante is said to have stayed, marks the entrance to the town. Completely surrounded by water (copper-headed Pochard ducks inhabit its moat), it was a stronghold of the Della Scala family, lords of Verona. The massive central tower, 29m high, has a good view.

Via Vittorio Emanuele (closed to cars) leads north from the castle through the scenic little town towards the ruins of Catullus' vast villa at the end of the peninsula. A road on the right leads to the 15th-century church of **Santa Maria Maggiore** (or Santa Maria della Neve), which preserves some antique columns in its porch, one of the outermost ones being a Roman milestone. There are traces of frescoes in the interior, including a lion of St Mark with drawn sword. At the end of Via Vittorio Emanuele is a spa with a hotel that uses warm sulphur springs rising in the lake. Via Catullo continues, passing close to **San Pietro in Mavino**, a Romanesque church of 8th-century foundation with early frescoes. At the end of the road is the entrance to the so-called **Grotte di Catullo** (*open March–Oct Tues–Sat 8.30–7, until 6 on Sun and holidays; Nov–Feb 8.30–5, until 2 on Sun and holidays*). These are the sprawling ruins of a large Roman villa, called '*grotte*' because before excavation, the vaulted substructures seemed like natural caverns. This is the most important example of Roman imperial domestic architecture in northern Italy. It is set amid olive groves on the end of the headland, with splendid views out over the lake and of the rocks beneath the clear shallow water. The extensive ruins belong to a succession of country houses dating from of the 1st century BC to the late 3rd century AD, when the building was abandoned. It is conceivable that the villa may have belonged to the family of the Valerii Catulli. Many wealthy Romans came to Sirmione for the summer, and Catullus—who is known to have had a villa here—speaks of '*Paene peninsularum, Sirmio, insularumque ocelle*' ('Sirmione, gem of all peninsulas and islands'). The site was only properly investigated in the 19th and beginning of the 20th centuries. Near the entrance is a small antiquarium, with pottery and exquisite fragments of frescoes dating from the 1st century BC. Of the villa itself, little that is readily comprehensible remains, as it was plundered for building material over the centuries and its site is now covered by an olive grove. The most conspicuous survivals are the vast substructures and vaults (the eponymous *grotte*), built to sustain the main upper floor, which occupied an area over 160m long and 100m wide. There are also a number of huge cisterns, as well as a baths complex and the ruins of what would once have been long, graceful seaview terraces with a covered walkway (cryptoporticus) below the western colonnade.

The low moraine hills south of the lake, formed by the ancient glacier of the Adige, have been the theatre of many battles: during Prince Eugene's campaign in the War of the Spanish Succession (1701–06); during Napoleon's enterprises (1796–1814); and during the Wars of Italian Independence (1848–49, 1859 and 1866). From Rivoltella, halfway between Sirmione and Desenzano, a by-road leads away from the lake up to the tower (74m high) of **San Martino della Battaglia** (*map Veneto West A3*), which commemorates Vittorio Emanuele II's victory over the right flank of the Austrian army on 24th June 1859. The interior (*open March–Sept Mon–Sat 9–12.30 & 2.30–7, Sun and holidays 9–7; Oct–Feb Tues–Sun 9–12.30 & 2–5.30; www.solferinoesanmartino.it*) contains sculptures and paintings relating to the campaign.

THE BATTLEFIELD OF SOLFERINO

At nearby **Solferino**, Napoleon III, in alliance with Vittorio Emanuele, defeated the rest of the Austrian army on the same day. The Austrians were under the personal command of the 29-year-old emperor Franz Joseph, the last time he ever led his troops into battle. An ossuary chapel in the little town (follow Via Ossario) displays the skulls of the 7,000 dead, collected from the battlefield and placed in grisly formation here, completely covering the sanctuary walls of the chapel. The Swiss businessman Henry Dunant was an eyewitness of the conflict and was so appalled by the suffering he witnessed of wounded soldiers abandoned and left to die uncomforted that he personally organised aid and relief work to tend them, regardless of which side they were on (the altarcloth in the chapel is embroidered with the words 'Omnes Fratres; Tutti Fratelli; Alle Brüder; Tous Frères'). Dunant's *A Memory of Solferino* was the inspiration for the foundation of the International Red Cross. The museum on the square in front of the ossuary chapel has mementoes of the battle (*open March–Sept Tues–Sun 9–12.30 & 2.30–7; Oct–Feb by appointment, T: 338 750 1396; www.solferinoesanmartino.it*). The little Albergo 'Alla Vittoria' offers coffee. It is also possible to climb the square Rocca, known as the 'Conning Tower of Italy' (*La Spia d'Italia*), from where there are fine views of the lovely countryside that hosted these two most sanguinary encounters.

DESENZANO

Desenzano del Garda (*map Veneto West A2*) is a pleasant little resort. From the quay, a bridge crosses the entrance to a picturesque harbour for small boats, with cafés, restaurants and the Galleria Civica around it. Behind is the main piazza, with pretty arcades and a monument to St Angela Merici (1474–1540), foundress of the Ursuline order, who was born here. Just out of the piazza is the duomo with a *Last Supper* by Giambattista Tiepolo.

Nearby to the northwest, on Via Crocefisso, is the entrance to the excavations of a **Roman villa** (*open Tues–Sun 8.30–dusk*), mostly dating from the 4th century AD but on the site of an earlier edifice of the 1st century AD. It is the most important late Roman villa in northern Italy, of great interest for its colourful 4th-century mosaics. The grandiose design of the reception rooms of the main villa includes an octagonal hall, a peristyle, an atrium with two apses, and a triclinium with three apses, all with mosaics. Other, less grand rooms to the south may have been baths. An antiquarium (beneath which the Roman edifice of the 1st century AD, with an underfloor heating system, was discovered) has finds from the site, including remains of wall paintings. Separate excavations to the north have revealed a residential area, with part of an apsidal hall and baths, to the east. The villa was discovered in 1921, and excavations have continued, even though the site is in the centre of the town.

SALÒ

Salò (*map Veneto West A2*), the Roman *Salodium*, is perhaps the most appealing town on the western lakeshore, with a slightly old-fashioned atmosphere. It has two gates, one surmounted by a lion, the other by a clock. It was the birthplace of Gaspare Bertolotti (also known as Gaspare da Salò, 1540–1609), generally considered to be the first maker of violins. But his fame is eclipsed by its notoriety in recent Italian history for it was Salò that gave its name to Mussolini's short-lived puppet republic (*see below*).

Near the waterfront is the **cathedral**, a fine building in a late-Gothic style built at the end of the 15th century, with a good Renaissance portal (1509). It contains an altarpiece of St Anthony and a donor dated 1529 by the prolific painter from Brescia called Girolamo Romani, known as Romanino, who often produced particularly colourful and original works. Palazzo Fantoni is the seat of the Biblioteca Ateneo, which has its origins in the Accademia degli Unanimi, founded by Giuseppe Milio in 1564. The Unanimi were a group of around 20 well-born young men of Salò who got together to discuss ethics and other questions: probably much like the Academy of the Olympians in Vicenza, whom Goethe describes as convening to argue about whether invention or imitation had contributed more to the fine arts. Milio was a poet and a writer on horitcultural subjects, and was apparently keen on bee-keeping. The emblem of the Unanimi was a beehive. Today the library has over 25,000 volumes, many of great historical interest.

THE REPUBLIC OF SALÒ

The Republic of Salò or Italian Socialist Republic (*Repubblica Sociale Italiana* or RSI) was formed in September 1943 as a puppet state of Nazi Germany, set up by Hitler in a last attempt to re-establish the Fascist government of Italy. In 1943, four days after the Armistice, the Germans brought Mussolini here having released him from prison. It was an ideal place to govern from, as the borders of the German Reich had reached Limone, only 20km north, with the annexation of the Trentino-Alto Adige. Germany and Japan were the only countries to recognise the Republic, which carried out brutal policing activities throughout Italy. It ended with the Liberation of Italy by the Allies in 1945 and Mussolini's execution by partisans a few days later as he fled northwards towards the Alps. For the brief months of its existence, the Republic commandeered numerous grand villas on the shores of Lake Garda, for use as ministries, hospitals and residences, including for Mussolini himself (at Gargnano) and for his mistress Clara Petacci (at Gardone Riviera). Many of those buildings are now hotels. Signboards have been placed outside the buildings today, with a map showing the extent of the Republic, the number of properties taken under its control, and detailing who and what they were used for. The huge Villa Alba at Gardone, for example, built in 1910 for a wealthy businessman from Magdeburg, served as a military communications and radio control centre. The Hotel Bellariva at Fasano housed officials from the German Embassy and was linked to the embassy building itself by an underground tunnel. At Maderno, the Hotel Golfo was the seat of the Fascist Party of the Republic and headquarters of the Black Brigades.

GARDONE RIVIERA

Gardone Riviera (*map Veneto West A2*) was once famous as a winter resort. It has a sheltered position and its parks and gardens are planted with rare trees. On the lakefront and in the hills behind rise grand villas, many of them built by German and Austrian industrialists who came here for the mild winters, but now used as hotels in summer (most of them are closed between late October and Easter). On the waterfront, by the boat landing, is a short *lungolago* with hotels, bars and pizzerias. Villa Fiordaliso was the home of Claretta Petacci, Mussolini's mistress, during the Republic of Salò (*see above*). It is now a hotel and restaurant. The huge, Neoclassical Villa Alba (1904–10), on the landward side of the main road, is now a conference centre and a popular venue for weddings. It was built for a German businessman, Richard Langensiepen, who had large holdings of land on the lake which he used for the commercial cultivation of flowers.

Above the main road, at Via Roma 1, is a **botanical garden** belonging to the André Heller Foundation (*open March–Oct daily 9–7, www.hellergarden.com*). The gardens were originally laid out by the doctor, dentist and botanist Arturo Hruska over a long period between 1910 and 1971. Since their acquisition by Heller they have been planted with works of contemporary sculpture and turned into a 'garden of ecological awareness', filled with Tibetan prayer flags, palm trees with their trunks painted to resemble peace flags, Buddha statues, a Torii gate rising above smoking undergrowth (the smoke being produced by nozzles which emit water vapour), pools overstocked with large koi carp and staff in tie-dye shirts. Hruska's botany is somewhat overwhelmed. The statuary includes works by Heller himself (spitting heads), Miró, Keith Haring, Roy Lichtenstein and Mimmo Paladino. When you buy your ticket you will be given a handlist and map.

Via Roma continues to wind uphill to **Gardone Sopra**, a very pretty little enclave of narrow streets and clustering houses with a few cafés and restaurants. At the Accadueocafé on Via Carera you can sit out under a vine trellis with a glass of good house white wine and a sandwich or bruschetta, looking out at the lake below, which shimmers through the trees. Also in Gardone Sopra is the famous Vittoriale, last home of Gabriele d'Annunzio (*see below*). Pleasant walks along marked trails can be taken in the hills behind Gardone and Salò.

VITTORIALE DEGLI ITALIANI

The Vittoriale degli Italiani (*open 8.30–7, Oct-March 9–4; museum closed Mon*), the famous last residence of Gabriele d'Annunzio (*see below*), was created for him by a local and otherwise unknown architect called Giancarlo Maroni, who lived here from 1922 until his death in 1952. Evidently the eccentric martial poet worked in close collaboration with his architect and together they created its elaborate and gloomy décor as well as the garden surrounding it (with an amphitheatre).

Near the entrance (you will be given a map of the complex with your ticket) is the **Museo d'Annunzio Segreto**, highly recommended, with film and stills documenting d'Annunzio's life (unfortunately there is nowhere to sit while you watch) and exhibits including his huge collection of shoes. Beyond this stretch the gardens and villa itself, the **Prioria** (shown on a 30-min tour), which has been preserved as a museum. The interior, including an Art Deco dining room, is crammed with a jumble of Art Nouveau *objets d'art*, chinoiserie, mementoes, sacred objects, Indian works of art, and even an organ. Off the dark hallway is a reception room with an inscription that D'Annunzio made Mussolini read on his visit here: 'Remember that you are made of glass and I of steel.' The garden in front of the villa harbours odd statuary and columns surmounted by projectiles. A path descends through the pretty woods of the Acquapazza valley towards the main road. The gardens also include a **dog cemetery** (D'Annunzio was famously fond of dogs).

Opposite the villa an **auditorium** houses the biplane from which D'Annunzio dropped leaflets on Vienna announcing Italian victory in 1918. Viale di Aligi leads past a fountain filled with small dogfish to a building that houses the motorboat in which D'Annunzio took part in the assault on Fiume. The boat is named *MAS 96*, 'MAS' standing for *Memento Audere Semper*: Remember Always to Dare. Beyond lies D'Annunzio's grand **mausoleum** at the top of the hill, where he and his architect are buried. The mausoleum is circular, in imitation of the imperial mausolea of Hadrian and Augustus in Rome or of Theodoric in Ravenna. At the top are ten sarcophagi containing the remains of ten heroes of Fiume, which D'Annunzio claimed for Italy and was unwilling to relinquish when it was declared a free buffer state at the end of the First World War. Concrete sculptures of dogs loll on the mausoleum roof. In the interior is a huge bronze Crucifix by Leonardo Bistolfi (1926). From here, a path leads through woods to the prow of the ship *Puglia*, donated to D'Annunzio by the Italian Navy and reconstructed here as a monument.

GABRIELE D'ANNUNZIO

Gabriele d'Annunzio (1863–1938) was born Francesco Rapagnetta, the son of a well-to-do and politically prominent landowner. He married the daughter of a duke but was not a model husband—among his mistresses was Eleonora Duse, for whom he wrote a number of plays (no longer performed today). He also wrote a play set to music by Debussy; Marcel Proust was at the opening night and said the best thing about it were the lead actress's legs.

D'Annunzio began his career as a poet: his first verses, *In Early Spring*, were published when the author was just 16; they were closely followed by *New Song* (1882), which established his fame. His best-known poetic work is the anthology *In Praise of Sky, Sea, Earth and Heroes* (1899). His novels raised eyebrows because of their self-seeking, amoral Nietzschean-superman heroes, but stylistically they were dull and academic.

Outside Italy D'Annunzio is much better known for his military exploits. In 1914–16 he called for Italy to enter the First World War on the side of Britain and France, rather than honour the Triple Alliance, the secret agreement between Germany, Austria-Hungary and Italy formed in 1882. He volunteered for dangerous duty in several branches of service, notably the air corps, and lost an eye in action. When Italy lost Istria at the Treaty of Versailles, he and a few hundred supporters occupied the port city of Fiume and held it for 18 months, until forced to withdraw by the Italian navy. He made peace with Mussolini, but never held an important government position (his legions were the first to wear the black shirt that became emblematic of the Fascists). He spent his last years writing here on Lake Garda. When he died in 1938 he was given a state funeral.

TOSCOLANO-MADERNO

Toscolano-Maderno (*map Veneto West A2*) is a lively resort, formed of two small settlements, each with its own port at the two sides of a peninsula formed by deposits brought down by the Gaino stream. Up until recently the peninsula was covered in olive plantations. Today it has holiday villas and bungalows and a large working paper mill.

As you approach from Gardone, you come into **Maderno**, with a bustling main square on the waterfront and very narrow streets behind (driving along them not recommended). On the waterfront square is the 12th-century church of **Sant'Andrea**, which shows remains of Roman and Byzantine architecture, especially in the decoration of the pillar capitals, doors and windows: an older church seems to have been incorporated in the building. The interior has remnants of frescoes and, in the sanctuary (on the left), a painting of the *Virgin and Child* by Veronese. Another painting by Veronese, of the bishop Herculanus (Ercolano), is in the 18th-century parish church which stands across the square from Sant'Andrea.

To reach **Toscolano**, you cross the Gaino. Signed from the old hump-backed bridge is the **Museo della Carta**, arranged in a pretty old paper mill, one of many that operated in this valley from the 15th century until the mid-20th (*open mid-April–Sept daily 10–6, Oct at weekends 10–5, valledellecartiere.it; café*). The short, easy walk to the museum, up the narrow, gorge-like valley, is interesting, lined with information boards about the paper mills and hydroelectric station.

On the north side of the promontory, in Toscolano, where Isabella Gonzaga of Mantua came to spend time in the summer, is the church of **Santi Pietro e Paolo**, with paintings by Andrea Celesti, a Venetian artist who was much in favour in the Serenissima until, for reasons unclear, he fell foul of Doge Alvise Contarini (legend has it that he painted a likeness of the doge with ass's ears). By 1688 he was at work in Toscolano. The **Santuario della Madonna di Benaco**, behind Santi Pietro e Paolo on the lake, has a barrel vault and numerous 15th-century frescoes. Four Roman columns stand in front of the church. Nearby, entered from the car park in front of the modern paper mill, is an enclosure with scant remains of a **Roman villa**, occupied from the the 1st–5th centuries AD, with remnants of mosaic, a baths complex and nymphaeum. Only a small part of the villa survives. In its heyday it must have been magnificent indeed, opening out directly onto the water. Toscolano, called Benacum, was the chief Roman settlement on the west shore of the lake. The villa has been identified as belonging to the family of the Nonii Arrii, specifically to a certain Marcus Nonius Macrinus, a 2nd-century consul from a patrician family of Brescia. At the time of writing, opening times were subject to change (*for information and to book, T: 0365 546023 or ask at the information office in Toscolano-Maderno*).

GARGNANO AND LIMONE

Beyond Toscolano the landscape becomes prettier. At **Bogliaco**, overlooking the lake, is the huge 18th-century Villa Bettoni (*not open*), with a superb garden.

Gargnano (*map Veneto West A2*) is a very attractive little port. Several large stone pavilions where lemon trees were once cultivated can be seen on the terraced hillside. San Francesco is a 13th-century church with a cloister. An inland road from Gargnano to Limone has spectacular views: it passes the hill sanctuary of Madonna di Monte Castello, which has the finest view of the whole lake. Mussolini lived here, at Villa Feltrinelli, from 1943 until three days before his death.

Limone sul Garda (*map Veneto West B1*) takes its name from its lemon groves, said to be the first in Europe. Up until the beginning of the 20th century it was surrounded by terraced lemon and citron gardens. Limone was accessible only by boat before the road along the shore from Gargnano was built in 1931, and its unattractive buildings and numerous hotels date from its development as a resort in the 1950s and 1960s. In previous centuries it was a very romantic spot, possibly the inspiration for one of Goethe's best-known lyrics: *Kennst du das Land, wo die Zitronen blühn* ('Do you know the land where the lemon trees blossom; where golden oranges gleam amidst dark foliage...?'). Goethe had sailed down from Torbole past Limone, where he admired the lemon gardens.

RIVA DEL GARDA &
THE NORTH END OF THE LAKE

The northern end of the lake is in the region of Trentino-Alto Adige and has a distinctly more alpine feel. **Riva del Garda** (*map Veneto West B1*), the Roman *Ripa*, a lively, somewhat overgrown little town, is the most important place on the lake. Sheltered by Monte Rochetta to the west, it became a fashionable winter resort at the turn of the 20th century—Thomas Mann and Franz Kafka both came to take the waters here—and remained in Austrian territory until 1918. The centre of the old town is Piazza III Novembre, overlooking the little port. Here are the 13th-century Torre Apponale, the 14th-century Palazzo Pretorio, the 15th-century Palazzo Comunale and some medieval porticoes. The Rocca, a 14th-century castle encircled by water, has been heavily restored over the centuries and now houses the Museo Civico (*open Easter–Oct Tues–Sun 10–12.30 & 1.30–6; July–Sept daily same times*) It has two main sections: a Pinacoteca with local painting and sculpture from the 14th–19th centuries, including works by the Neoclassical painter Giuseppe Craffonara (born in Riva in 1790) and the *Last Supper* of Pietro Ricchi, a pupil of Guido Reni known for his candlelit night scenes. The *Last Supper* was painted for the refectory of the Inviolata (*see below*) c. 1645. The second section has archaeological finds from the north Garda region, including a display of extraordinary stone stelae from Arco (4th–3rd millennia BC), of suggestively human form and decorated with incised daggers, spears and talismanic objects. North of the waterfront, on Largo Marconi (between Via Negrelli and Viale dei Tigli) is the church of the Inviolata, with a fine Baroque interior and paintings by Pietro Ricchi (*see above*).

At the mouth of the Vale di Ledro, a valley of great botanical interest, is the **Lago di Ledro** (*map Veneto West A1–B1*), nearly 3km long, with the little resort of Pieve di Ledro. When the water is low, on the east side of the lake near Molina, you can see some of the c. 15,000 larchwood stakes from lake dwellings of the early Bronze Age, discovered in 1929. There is a fascinating museum here (Museo delle Palafitte; *open March–June and Sept–Nov Tues–Sun 9–5; July and August daily 10–6, palafitteledro. it*), and a clutch of Bronze Age huts has been reconstructed on a wooden platform above the water.

Torbole sul Garda (*map Veneto West B1*), a summer resort on the lake's northeastern tip, played a part in the war of 1439 between the Visconti and the Venetians, when fleets of warships were dragged overland by teams of oxen and launched into the lake here. Goethe stayed at Torbole in 1786.

THE EASTERN SHORE

The east side of Lake Garda is bounded by the cliff of Monte Altissimo di Nago (2078m). This is the northern peak of Monte Baldo, the high ridge which lines the shore as far as Torri del Benaco. A region of great interest for its flora and fauna, part of it is a protected area once known as *Hortus europae* from its remarkable vegetation, which varies from lemon trees and olives on its lower slopes to beech woods and Alpine flowers on the summit. The highest peaks are Cima Valdritta (2218m) and Monte Maggiore (2200m). There are numerous marked hiking trails on the slopes (*maps and walking guides are available from bookshops locally*).

Malcesine (*map Veneto West B1*) is a likeable resort with a little port. It was the seat of the Veronese Captains of the Lake in the 16th–17th centuries, and their old palace is now used as the Town Hall. The little garden on the lake is open to the public. Narrow roads lead up to the castle of the Scaligeri, of Lombard origin but in the hands of the Della Scala from 1277. It was restored by Venice in the 17th century and later was used as an Austrian defence post. It is open to the public (*April–Oct daily 9.30–7, Nov–March Sun and holidays 11–4*) and contains a museum of Natural History, illustrating the flora and fauna of the lake and of Monte Baldo. There is also a room dedicated to Goethe, who had been forced by unfavourable winds to land for a night at Malcesine, and while sketching the castle was almost arrested as an Austrian spy. The next day he docked at Bardolino, where he mounted a mule to cross into the Adige Valley for Verona. There is a fine view from the top of the tower. Concerts are often held in the castle. A cableway runs to the top of Monte Baldo, and there are pleasant walks in the area.

To the south, the coast becomes less wild. At **Cassone** (a suburb of Malcesine) there is a small Museo del Lago (*open Tues–Sun 10–12 & 3–6*) in a building on the waterfront that was once a fish incubating plant. Further on, the road passes a cemetery and the early-12th-century church of San Zeno, and at Pai there is a magnificent view of the opposite shore of the lake. The coast here is known as the Riviera degli Olivi, from its many olive trees.

Torri del Benaco (*map Veneto West A2*), the Roman Castrum Turrium, was the chief town of the Gardesana during the years of Venetian rule. The Gardesana federation comprised ten towns between Malcesine and Lazise, headed by a Capitano del Lago. Today Torri has a pretty horseshoe-shaped port and the town itself is lively and attractive. In places you can still see stretches of its fortifying walls. At one end of the terrace of the waterfront Gardesana hotel (once the headquarters of the Gardesana council) is a monument to Domizio Calderini, a Humanist scholar born in Torri in 1444. The Latin epitaph is by his friend, the great Tuscan poet Poliziano. Behind it, the oratory of the Holy Trinity, now a war memorial chapel, has 15th-century frescoes, including a *Last Supper* with fine fish. Looming above the port are the swallowtail battlements of the impressive Castello Scaligero, a castle of the Della Scala dating from 1383 (*open April–mid-June 9.30–12 & 2.30–6, mid-June–mid-Sept 9.30–1 & 4.30–7.30, mid-Sept–Oct 9.30–12.30 & 2.30–6*). It contains a small museum illustrating the history of fishing on the lake and the production of olive oil. There is a also a section dedicated to the rock carvings found in the district, the oldest supposedly dating from 1500 BC. A splendid *limonaia* of 1760, which protects a plantation of huge old lemon trees—as well as citrons, mandarins and oranges—against its south wall, can also be visited: the scent of blossom is delicious in spring. This is one of very few such structures to survive on the lake where once lemons were cultivated in abundance. Unfortunately it backs onto a field where boys play football, and most of the glass panes have fallen victim to their over-enthusiastic kicks.

The headland of **Punta di San Vigilio** (parking on the main road) is a romantic and secluded place, now occupied by a hotel with a fine restaurant. The hotel complex includes a walled lemon garden and a café-bar on the waterfront, with tables out on the harbour mole. From here it is possible to walk all the way along the foreshore to the town of Garda (about 30mins).

In the hills behind San Vigilio, a path leads to the **rock carvings** of the Roccia de la Griselle. A short way towards Garda, on the left, you will see the path (marked 'Graffiti') It leads uphill and then forks right into woodland. Follow the 'Graffiti' signs. A narrow path takes you to a flat rock (the second one you come to) covered with incised images of ships and weapons.

The resort of **Garda** (*map Veneto West A2*) was developed after the Second World War at the head of a deep bay. It was famous in the Roman and Lombard periods, and was later a fortified town; it still retains some fine old houses and a string of agreeable cafés. A very simple market is held on the waterfront.

BARDOLINO

The hills become lower and the landscape duller as the broad basin at the foot of the lake opens out. Bardolino (*map Veneto West A2*), another ancient place retaining some commercial importance, is well known for its wine: not great wine, it is true, but fresh and fruity and easy to drink. In 2013 the Cantina Guerrieri Rizzanti opened a new cellar here. A tower and two gates remain from an old castle of the Scaligeri. In a little courtyard, is the tiny Carolingian church of San Zeno, which retains its 9th-century form with a tower above the crossing and ancient paving stones. It has four old capitals and fragments of frescoes. The 12th-century church of San Severo has contemporary frescoes.

Lazise (*map Veneto West A2*), with a very pretty waterfront, retains part of its medieval wall and a castle of the Scaligeri, with Venetian additions. The 16th-century double-arched Venetian customs house on the lakefront attests to its former importance. San Nicolò is a 12th-century church with 16th-century additions and 14th-century frescoes.

Peschiera del Garda (*map Veneto West A2–A3*), an ancient fortress and one of the four corners of the Austrian 'quadrilateral' (the other three are Verona, Mantua and Legnago), stands at the outflow of the Mincio from Lago di Garda. The impressive fortifications, begun by the Venetians in 1553, were strengthened by Napoleon and again by the Austrians. Close by is Italy's most famous theme park for young children, called **Gardaland**, which was based on Disneyland when it opened in 1975. Today it receives around 3 million visitors a year (and is especially popular with children under ten).

LAKE GARDA PRACTICAL TIPS

INFORMATION OFFICES

General websites about the Lake include: *visitgarda.com*, and *lagodigarda.it*. Local tourist offices include the following (and more are open during the summer):
Desenzano del Garda. Via Porto Vecchio 34, T: 030 914 1510.
Garda. Piazza Donatori di Sangue 1, T: 045 627 0384.
Bardolino. Piazza Aldo Moro, T: 045 721 0078.
Lazise. Via Francesco Fontana 14, T: 045 758 0114.
Sirmione. Viale Marconi 2, T: 030 916114.
Toscolano-Maderno. Via Garibaldi 24, T: 0365 644298, *prolocotoscolanomaderno.com*.

GETTING AROUND

By train: The Venice–Milan line serves Peschiera del Garda, Desenzano del Garda–Sirmione and Lonato, from which there are frequent country bus services to outlying points. Regional trains connect the lake stations to Verona or Brescia in less than 30mins; fast trains stop at Desenzano–Sirmione only, making the run in c. 20mins.
By bus: Bus services run several times daily by the roads on the west and east banks from Peschiera and Desenzano to Riva. Frequent service from Verona via Lazise and Garda to Riva, and from Brescia to Desenzano, Sirmione, Peschiera and Verona, and between Salò and Desenzano, and Desenzano, Salò and Riva. Run by ATV, see *www. atv.verona.it*.

By boat: Boat services (including two modernised paddle-steamers built in 1902 and 1903) are run by Navigazione Laghi (head office Piazza Matteotti 1, Desenzano, T: 800 551801, *www. navigazionelaghi.it*). These operate from around mid-March–early Nov (the timetable changes three times a year). Printed timetables are available from tickets offices, information offices and hotel lobbies. A daily boat service runs between Desenzano and Riva in 4hrs, calling at various ports en route—but not all services follow the same route. Check the website for details. Hydrofoils run twice daily in 2hrs 40mins (with fewer stops). All year round a car ferry operates between Maderno and Torri di Benaco in 30mins (every 30mins, but less frequently in winter) and there is a summer ferry from Limone to Malcesine in 20mins (hourly). Tickets are available allowing free travel on the lake services for a day. Tours of the lake in the afternoons in summer are also organised.

Motor boats and sailing boats for rent are available from Garda Yachting Charter on Lungolago Zanardelli in Maderno (*www.gyc.it, T: 0365 548347 or 329 424 5000*). The northern tip of the lake around Riva is reserved for sailing boats only.

Boat trips can also be made at certain times from April to October to the privately-owned **Isola del Garda** (Garda Island), where guided tours of the grounds and neo-Venetian mansion of the Borghese Cavazza family are given. Booking is required. For information, times, departure ports and prices, see *www.isoladelgarda.com*, or T: 328 384 9226.

By cablecar: For details of the cablecar (*funivia*) service from Malcesine to Monte Baldo, see *funiviedelbaldo.it*.

WHERE TO STAY

NB: Most of the places on Lake Garda are open during the summer season only, April/May–Oct.

GARDA (*map Veneto West A2*)
€€–€€€ **Hotel La Vittoria.** Plainly elegant, comfortable rooms in a renovated harbourfront villa. Restaurant and coffee terrace. *Lungolago Regina Adelaide 57, T: 045 627 0473, hotellavittoria.it.*

GARDONE RIVIERA (*map Veneto West A2*)
€€–€€€ **Bella Riva.** Family-friendly hotel right on the lake at Fasano, between Gardone and Maderno. In an old villa used for German embassy staff during the Republic of Salò, renovated with modern décor. Pleasant gardens right on the lakefront, with swimming pool. *Via Podini Mario 1/2, T: 0365 540773, www.bellarivagardone.it.*
€€€ **Grand Hotel Fasano e Villa Principe.** A former hunting lodge of the emperors of Austria set in a lovely park with garden terrace overlooking the lake. *Corso Zanardelli 190, Località Fasano del Garda, T: 0365 290220, ghf. it.*
€€€ **Villa del Sogno.** The former villa of a German industrialist, used as a convalescence home by German officers during the Republic of Salò. Set in a beautiful garden with swimming pool and tennis court, the hotel is gracious and old-fashioned, impeccably run, with a vast and ample terrace

overlooking the water, divided into a variety of sitting areas, for breakfast, pre-dinner cocktails, or dinner in the candlelit gazebo. *Via Zanardelli 107, T: 0365 290181, villadelsogno.it.*

GARGNANO (*map Veneto West A2*)
€€€ **Villa Feltrinelli.** A magnificent villa with frescoed rooms, set in a lakeside park. The only thing against it is that it was Mussolini's home during the Republic of Salò. *Via Rimembranza 38/40, T: 0365 798 000, villafeltrinelli. com.*
€€ **Villa Giulia.** A lakeside villa with lovely garden, which has long been a favourite place to stay for those who would like to economise. *Viale Rimembranza 20, T: 0365 71022, villagiulia.it.*

LIMONE SUL GARDA (*map Veneto West B1*)
€ **Capo Reamol.** Park, pool, and everything from Oriental medicine to windsurfing. *Via IV Novembre 92, T: 0365 954040, hotelcaporeamol.it.*
€€ **Park Hotel Imperial.** An elegant establishment, in a shady park with pool. Extensive health facilities. *Via Tamas 10b, T: 0365 954 591, parkhotelimperial.it.*

MALCESINE (*map Veneto West B1*)
€–€€ **Hotel Castello Lake Front.** An excellent summer hotel. Modern and airy, no clutter, large windows with lake views, and its own beach. Right in the heart of the old town. *Via Paina 21, T: 045 740 0233, h-c.it.*
€ **Meridiana.** Modern design, good value. On the landward side of the main lakeside road, but close to the centre. *Via Navene Vecchia 39, T: 045 740 0342, hotelmeridiana.it.*

RIVA DEL GARDA (*map Veneto West B1*)
€€ **Du Lac et du Parc.** A luxurious

establishment in a large park, offering peace and quiet, elegance, and refinement. *Viale Rovereto 44, T: 0464 551500, www.hoteldulac-riva.it.*

€€ Grand Hotel di Riva. A classic hotel with a quiet park, frequented also for its roof-garden restaurant. *Piazza Garibaldi 10, T: 0464 521800, gardaresort.it.*

SALÒ (*map Veneto West A2*)
€€ Duomo. On the lakefront, with tastily furnished rooms and pleasant views. *Lungolago Zanardelli 91, T: 0365 21026, hotelduomosalo.it.*

€ Vigna. Historic *locanda* with quiet rooms and panoramic breakfast room. *Lungolago Zanardelli 62, T: 0365 520144, hotelvignasalo.it.*

SAN VIGILIO (*map Veneto West A2*)
€€€ Locanda San Vigilio. Well-appointed rooms in the 15th-century house and its outbuildings right on the lake. Rooms vary a great deal; the nicest ones are in the house itself. Excellent restaurant attached. *T: 045 725 6688, locanda-sanvigilio.it.*

SIRMIONE (*map Veneto West A2*)
€€€ Palace Hotel Villa Cortine. Luxury accommodation in a 19th-century villa with large park, on the lakeshore. *Via Grotte 6, T: 030 990 5890, hotelvillacortine.com.*

€€ Ideal. One of the finest settings on the peninsula, a tranquil olive grove overlooking the lake and the Grotte di Catullo. *Via Catullo 31, T: 030 990 4245, www.hotelidealsirmione.it.*

TORBOLE SUL GARDA (*map Veneto West B1*)
€€ Piccolo Mondo. A modern establishment in a quiet park, with a good restaurant and well-equipped wellness centre. *Via Matteotti 7, T: 0464 505271, hotelpiccolomondotorbole.it.*

TORRI DEL BENACO (*map Veneto West A2*)
€–€€ Albergo Gardesana. ▬ Comfortable, friendly hotel overlooking the harbour and the castle. Very good value. Restaurant. Parking. *Piazza Calderini 5, T: 045 722 5411, gardesana.eu.*

WHERE TO EAT

DESENZANO DEL GARDA (*map Veneto West A2*)
€€€ Esplanade. Fresh seasonal cuisine with a garden overlooking the lake. This has been a good place to eat for many years. Closed Wed. *Via Lario 10, T: 030 9143361. ristorante-esplanade.com.*

€ Cavallino. An well established restaurant with good seasonal dishes made with the freshest ingredients. Closed Mon. Via Murachette 29, T: 030 912 0217, ristorantecavallino.it.

€ Ristorante-Pizzeria Garda. Safe, unpretentious, reliable place. Friendly service. A good lunch spot—it is very close to the Roman villa, on the waterfront. *Lungolago Cesare Battisti 21, T: 030 914 1714.*

GARDONE RIVIERA (*map Veneto West A2*)
€€ Villa Fiordaliso (with rooms). In business since 1890, in an old villa in a small park with summer seating on a terrace above the lake. Closed Mon, midday Tues. *T: 0365 20158, villafiordaliso.it.*

€ Wimmer. Cheerful pizzeria on the waterfront, named after Luigi Wimmer, an entrepreneur of Austrian descent who built the first lodging house in Gardone and who rose to beome its mayor. Closed Mon. *Piazza Wimmer 5, T: 0365 20631.*

GARGNANO (*map Veneto West A2*)
€€€ **La Tortuga.** A gourmet's delight, known for fine food and excellent selection of regional, Italian, and imported wines. Closed Tues. By the harbour. *Via XXIV Maggio, T: 0365 71251.*

LAZISE (*map Veneto West A2*)
€€ **Porticciolo.** Traditional cuisine of the lake area, especially fish. Closed Tues. *Lungolago Marconi 22, T: 045 758 0254.*

MALCESINE (*map Veneto West B1*)
€€ **Vecchia Malcesine.** Lake fish, quail, white chocolate 'soup': a high-quality offering just south of the harbour. *Via Pisort 6, T: 045 740 0469, vecchiamalcesine.com.*

€ **Osteria Santo Cielo.** Very close to the park that surrounds the Town Hall, south of the port, a snug vaulted tavern serving salads, platters of cold meat and cheese and other snacks, to be washed down with a beaker of house wine. *Piazza Turazza 11, T: 045 740 0469, osteriasantocielo.com.*

PESCHIERA DEL GARDA (*map Veneto West A2–A3*)
€ **Papa** (with rooms). Good local food and wine. Closed Wed. *Via Bell'Italia 40, T: 045 755 0476, albergo-papa.com.*
€ **Pescatore** (with rooms). Friendly family-run *trattoria* specialising in fish. Closed Tues evening. *Località Fornaci, T: 045 640 0316.*

RIVA DEL GARDA (*map Veneto West B1*)
€€ **Villa Negri.** Good traditional cuisine and an exceptional position on high ground overlooking the entire lake, with summer seating outside. *Via Bastioni 31–35, T: 046 455 5061.*

SALÒ (*map Veneto West A2*)
€€ **Gallo Rosso.** Excellent small restaurant in the historic town centre.

Closed Wed. *Vicolo Tomacelli 4, T: 0365 520757, ristorantegallorosso.it.*
€ **Osteria dell'Orologio.** Wine bar with good selection of snacks and light meals downstairs and full restaurant service upstairs. Closed Wed. *Via Butturini 26, T: 0365 290158, osteriadellorologiosalo.com.*

SAN VIGILIO (*map Veneto West A2*)
€€€ **Locanda San Vigilio.** ◼ Superb restaurant with an excellent wine list. In a lovely secluded spot. Eat either in the narrow loggia overlooking the water or in the old living room (with an open fire in chilly weather). *T: 045 725 6688, locanda-sanvigilio.it.*

SERNIGA (SALÒ) (*map Veneto West A2*)
€ **Il Bagnolo.** An *agriturismo* (with rooms) in a splendid location overlooking the lake, serving its own meats and other fresh products. Open May–Sept daily; Oct–April Fri evening–Sun. *Località Bagnolo Ovest, T: 0365 20290, ilbagnolo.it.*

SIRMIONE (*map Veneto West A2*)
€€€ **La Rucola.** Acclaimed restaurant very close to the castle. Open at midday upon reservation only; advisable also to book evenings. *Via Strentelle 3, T: 030 916326, ristorantelarucola.it.*
€€€ **Osteria del Vecchio Fossato.** Inventive menu featuring local specialities and influences from further afield. A restaurant with a contented following. *Via Antiche Mura 16, T: 030 919331, osteriadelvecchiofossato.it.*
€ **Pizzeria Scaligeri's.** Simple, unfussy, reliable pizza place right by the castle. Ideal as a no-frills lunch stop. *Via Dante 5, T: 030 916581, scaligeri.info.*

TORRI DEL BENACO (*map Veneto West A2*)
€€ **Agli Olivi.** *Trattoria* with a wide

terrace commanding lovely views of the lake. In the olive groves of Albisano, just above Torri (can be reached on foot, a pleasant half-hour walk; or by car). Fillets of lake perch, fish ravioli, delicious desserts (the chocolate salami is particularly good). *Via Valmagra 7, T: 045 722 5483, agliolivi.com.*

€€ **Bell'Arrivo.** Cosy *trattoria* with inner garden. Right on the harbour. *Piazza Calderini 10, T: 0456 299028, galvanihotels.com.*

FESTIVALS AND EVENTS

Riva del Garda *Intervela,* international sailing week, July; *Flicorno d'Oro,* international band competition, Aug. *Mostra Internazionale di Musica Leggera Vela d'Oro,* pop festival, Sept.

Salò Music festival, July.

Torri del Benaco *Festa dell'Olio,* with food fair, market of local products and folk music, Jan.

Practical Information

PLANNING YOUR TRIP

WHEN TO GO
The best time to visit northern Italy is May–June or September–October. The earlier spring and later autumn months are often wet and chilly, with strong northerly winds. The height of the summer is unpleasantly hot, especially in the Po Valley and the larger towns. The upper Alpine valleys are cool in summer, while in the high Alps the winter sports season can extend to midsummer. Seaside resorts are crowded from mid-June to early September; before and after this season many hotels are closed and the beaches are practically deserted.

DISABLED TRAVELLERS
All new public buildings are obliged to provide facilities for the disabled. Historic buildings are more difficult to convert, and access difficulties still exist. Hotels that cater for the disabled are indicated in tourist board lists. Airports and railway stations provide assistance, and certain trains are equipped to transport wheelchairs. Access to town centres is allowed for cars with disabled drivers or passengers, and special parking places are reserved for them. For further information, contact the tourist board in the city of interest.

GETTING AROUND

BY CAR
The easiest way to tour northern Italy is by car. Regardless of whether you are driving your own car or a hired vehicle, Italian law requires you to carry a valid driving licence. You must also keep a red triangle in the car (you can hire one from ACI for a minimal charge and returned it at the border).

As 80 per cent of goods transported travel by road, lorries pose a constant hazard on, and the degree of congestion in even the smallest towns defies imagination.

Certain customs differ radically from those of Britain or America. Pedestrians have the right of way at zebra crossings, although you're taking your life in your hands if you step into the street without looking. Unless otherwise indicated, cars entering a road from the right are given precedence. Trams and trains always have right of way. If an oncoming driver flashes his headlights, it means he is proceeding and not giving you precedence. In towns, Italian drivers frequently change lanes without warning. They also tend to ignore pedestrian crossings.

ROADS IN ITALY

Italy's motorways (*autostrade*) are indicated by green signs or, near the entrance ramps, by large boards of overhead lights. All are toll-roads. At the entrance to motorways, the two directions are indicated by the name of the most important town (and not by the nearest town), which can be momentarily confusing. Dual-carriageways are called *superstrade* (also indicated by green signs). Italy has an excellent network of secondary highways (*strade statali, regionali* or *provinciali*, indicated by blue signs marked SS, SR or SP; on maps simply by a number).

PARKING

Many cities have closed their centres to traffic (except for residents). Access is allowed to hotels and for the disabled. It is always advisable to leave your car in a guarded car park, though with a bit of effort it is almost always possible to find a place to park free of charge, away from the town centre. However, to do so overnight is not advisable. Always lock your car when parked, and never leave anything of value inside it. Many car parks operate the '*disco orario*' system, which allows you to park free for 2hrs. You indicate the time that you parked on the adjustable disc. Hire cars are usually fitted with a disc in their windscreens. They are also available at petrol stations and tobacconists.

BY TRAIN

Information on rail links is given in individual chapters. The Italian Railways (Trenitalia) have good, cheap services and an excellent website: *trenitalia.com*.

BY BUS

Information on regional bus services is given in each individual section.

TAXIS

These are hired from ranks or by telephone; there are no cruising cabs. Before engaging a taxi, it is advisable to make sure it has a meter in working order. Fares vary from city to city but are generally cheaper than London taxis, though considerably more expensive than New York taxis. No tip is expected. Supplements are charged for late-night journeys and for luggage. There is a heavy surcharge when the destination is outside the town limits (ask roughly how much the fare is likely to be).

LANGUAGE

Even a few words of Italian are a great advantage in Italy, where any attempt to speak the language is appreciated. Local dialects vary greatly, but even where dialect is universally used, nearly everybody can speak and understand standard Italian. Double consonants call for special care as each must be sounded. Consonants are pronounced roughly as in English with the following exceptions:

c and **cc**	before e and i have the sound of **ch** in chess
ch	before e and i has the sound of **k**
g and **gg**	before e and i are always soft, like **j** in jelly
gh	always hard, like **g** in get
gl	nearly always like **lli** in million (there are a few exceptions, for example, *negligere*, where it is pronounced as in English)
gn	like **ny** in lanyard
gu and **qu**	always like **gw** and **kw**
j	like **y** in you
s	voiceless like **s** in six, except when it occurs between two vowels, when it is pronounced like the English **z** or the **s** in rose
sc	before e and i is pronounced like **sh** in ship
ss	always voiceless
z and **zz**	usually pronounced like **ts**, but occasionally have the sound of **dz** before a long vowel

OPENING TIMES

The opening times of museums and monuments are given in the text, though they often change without warning. National museums and monuments are usually closed on Mondays. Archaeological sites generally open at 9 and close at dusk.

Some museums are closed on the main public holidays: 1 January, Easter, 1 May, 15 August and 25 December. Smaller museums have have suspended regular hours altogether and are now open by appointment only. Their telephone numbers are included in the text. Entrance fees vary. EU citizens under 18 and over 65 are entitled to free admission to national museums and monuments but you need to provide ID.

Churches open early in the morning (often for 6 o'clock Mass), and most are closed during the middle of the day (12–3, 4 or 5), although cathedrals and larger churches may be open throughout daylight hours. Smaller churches and oratories are often open only in the early morning, but the key can usually be found by inquiring locally. The sacristan will also show closed chapels and crypts, and a small tip should be given. Some churches now ask that sightseers do not enter during a service, but normally visitors may do so, provided they are silent and do not approach the altar in use. At all times they are expected to cover their legs and arms, and generally dress with decorum. An entrance fee is often charged for admission to treasuries, cloisters, bell-towers and so on. Lights (operated by coins) have been installed in many churches to illuminate frescoes and altarpieces. In Holy Week most of the images are covered and are on no account shown.

Shops generally open Mon–Sat 8.30/9–1 and 3.30/4–7.30/8, although larger stores and shops is bigger towns do not close for lunch.

ADDITIONAL INFORMATION

CRIME AND PERSONAL SECURITY

Pickpocketing is a widespread problem in towns all over Italy: it is always advisable not to carry valuables, and be particularly careful on public transport. Crime should be reported at once to the police or the local *carabinieri* office (found in every town and small village). A statement has to be given in order to get a document confirming loss or damage (essential for insurance claims). Interpreters are provided. For all emergencies, T: 113. The switchboard will co-ordinate the help you need. For medical assistance: T: 118.

PHARMACIES

Pharmacies (*farmacie*) are usually open Mon–Fri 9–1 & 4–7.30 or 8. A few are open also on Saturdays, Sundays and holidays (listed on the door of every pharmacy). In all towns there is also at least one pharmacy open at night (also shown on the door of every pharmacy).

PUBLIC HOLIDAYS

Italian national holidays are as follows:

1 January	15 August (Assumption)
Easter Sunday and Easter Monday	1 November (All Saints' Day)
25 April (Liberation Day)	8 December (Immaculate Conception)
1 May (Labour Day)	25 December (Christmas Day)
2 June (Festa della Repubblica)	26 December (St Stephen)

Each town keeps its patron saint's day as a holiday.

TELEPHONE AND POSTAL SERVICES

Stamps are sold at tobacconists (*tabacchi*, marked with a large white 'T') and post offices. For all calls in Italy, dial the city code (for instance, 041 for Venice), then the telephone number. For international and intercontinental calls, dial 00 before the telephone number. The country code for Italy is +39.

TIPPING

Service charges are normally included and tipping in Italy is not routinely expected. It is normal to round up the bill and leave a few coins in appreciation.

ACCOMMODATION

HOTELS

A selection of hotels, chosen on the basis of character or location, is given at the end of each chapter. They are classified as follows: €€€€ (€900 or over), €€€ (€350–900), €€ (€150–300) or € (€150 or under). It is advisable to book well in advance, especially between May and October; if you cancel the booking with at least 72 hours' notice you can claim back part or all of your deposit. Service charges are included in the rates. By law breakfast is an optional extra, although a lot of hotels will include it in the room price. When booking, always specify if you want breakfast or not. If you are staying in a hotel in a town, it is often more fun to go round the corner to the nearest café for breakfast.

FARM STAYS—*AGRITURISMO*

The short-term rental of space in villas and farmhouses (*agriturismo*) is an alternative form of accommodation. Terms vary greatly, from bed-and-breakfast to self-contained flats. For travellers with their own transport, or for families, this as an excellent (and usually cheap) way of visiting the Italian countryside. Some farms require a minimum stay. Cultural or recreational activities, such as horse-riding, are sometimes also provided. For more details, see veneto-agriturismo.it.

BLUE GUIDES RECOMMENDED

Hotels, restaurants and *osterie* that are particularly good choices in their category—in terms of excellence, location, charm, value for money or the quality of the experience they provide—carry the Blue Guides Recommended sign: ▬. All these establishments have been visited and selected by our authors, editors or contributors as places they have particularly enjoyed and would be happy to recommend to others. To keep our entries up-to-date, reader feedback is essential: please do not hesitate to contact us (*blueguides. com*) with any views, corrections or suggestions, or join our online discussion forum.

FOOD & DRINK

RESTAURANTS

Italian food is usually good and inexpensive. Generally speaking, the least pretentious *ristorante* (restaurant), *trattoria* (small restaurant) or *osteria* (inn or tavern) provides the best value. A selection of restaurants is given at the end of each chapter. Prices are categorised as follows: €€€€ (€80 or more per head), €€€ (€60–80), €€ (€40–50) and € (€30 or under). Many places are considerably cheaper at midday. It is always a good idea to reserve.

Prices on the menu do not include a cover charge (shown separately, usually at the bottom of the page), which is added to the bill. The service charge (*servizio*) is now almost always automatically added at the end of the bill; tipping is therefore not strictly necessary, but a few euro are appreciated. Note that many simpler establishments do not offer a written menu.

BARS AND CAFÉS

Bars and cafés are open from early morning to late at night and serve numerous varieties of excellent refreshments that are usually taken standing up. As a rule, you must pay the cashier first, then present your receipt to the barman in order to get served. It is customary to leave a small tip for the barman. If you sit at a table the charge is usually higher, and you will be given waiter service (so don't pay first). However, some simple bars have a few tables that can be used with no extra charge, and it is always best to ask, before ordering, whether there is waiter service or not.

COFFEE

Italy is considered to have the best coffee in Europe. *Caffè* or *espresso* (black coffee) can be ordered *alto* or *lungo* (diluted), *corretto* (with a liquor), or *macchiato* (with a dash of hot milk). A *cappuccino* is an *espresso* with more hot milk than a *caffè macchiato* and is generally considered a breakfast drink. A glass of hot milk with a dash of coffee in it, called *latte macchiato* is another early-morning favourite. In summer, many drink *caffè freddo* (iced coffee).

SNACKS

Gelato (ice cream) is always best from a *gelateria* where it is made on the spot. *Panini* (sandwiches) are made with a variety of cold meats, fish, cheeses, or vegetables, particularly *melanzane* (aubergines) or *zucchine* (courgettes) fried in vegetable oil; vegetarians may also ask for a simple sandwich of *insalata e pomodoro* (lettuce and tomato). *Pizze* (a popular and cheap food throughout Italy), *arancini* (rice croquettes with cheese or meat inside), and other snacks are served in a *pizzeria*, *rosticceria* and *tavola calda*. A *vinaio* often sells wine by the glass and simple food for very reasonable prices. Sandwiches are made up on request at *pizzicherie* and *alimentari* (grocery shops), and *fornai* (bakeries) often sell individual pizzas, focaccias, *schiacciate* (bread with oil and salt) and cakes.

PASTA

Pasta is an essential part of most meals throughout Italy. A distinction is drawn between *pasta comune* (spaghetti, rigatoni and so on) produced industrially and made of a simple flour and water paste, and *pasta all'uovo* (tortellini, ravioli and so on), made with egg.

Pasta comes in countless forms. An ordinary Italian supermarket usually stocks about 50 different varieties, but some experts estimate that there are more than 600 shapes in all. The differences of shape translate into differences of flavour, even when the pasta is made from the same dough, or by the same manufacturer. The reason for this is that the relation between the surface area and the weight of the pasta varies from one shape to another, causing the sauce to adhere in different ways and to different degrees. Even without a sauce, experts claim to perceive considerable differences in flavour, because the different shapes cook in different ways. Northern Italy is home to *pasta fresca*, usually home-made, from a dough composed of flour, eggs, and just a little water.

A SHORT HISTORY OF PASTA

Whereas the invention of egg pasta is generally credited to the Chinese, the origin of *pastasciutta* (flour-and-water pasta) may well be Italian. The Etruscan Tomb of the Reliefs at Cerveteri, near Rome, has stucco decorations representing pasta-making tools: a board and a rolling-pin for rolling out the dough, knives and even a toothed cutting-wheel for making decorative borders. References to lasagne may be found in Cicero and other Roman writers; the name itself is probably derived from the Latin *lagana* or *lasana*, a cooking pot.

By the end of the Middle Ages pasta was known throughout Italy. The 14th-century *Codice del l'Anonimo Toscano*, preserved in the library of Bologna University, contains several serving suggestions; and in the *Decameron*, Boccaccio describes an imaginary land of grated parmesan cheese inhabited by people whose only pastime is the making of '*maccheroni e raviuoli*'. Of course, tomato sauce was unheard of until the discovery of America: Boccaccio's contemporaries cooked their macaroni and ravioli in chicken broth and dressed it with fresh butter. An early American appreciator of *pastasciutta* was Thomas Jefferson, who in 1787 brought a spaghetti-making machine from Italy to the United States.

REGIONAL CUISINE

In the area around Venice rice is served in a variety of ways, especially with seafood and vegetables. Classic specialities are *risi e bisi* (risotto with peas) and *risotto nero* (coloured and flavoured with cuttlefish ink). Thick soups are also popular. The best of these is *pasta e fasioi* (pasta and beans), which is eaten lukewarm, having been left to 'set up' for an hour or so before being served—generally in deep plates or, better yet, clay bowls.

Fish and seafood form the basis of Venice's best main courses. Local specialities include *granseola* (lagoon crabs), *sarde in saor* (marinated sardines) and *seppioline nere* (cuttlefish cooked in their own ink). An outstanding seafood dish is the *brodetto di pesce* or *boreto di Grado*—rigorously in *bianco* (without tomatoes), which testifies to its origins in an age before the discovery of America. Cornmeal polenta is another staple, often served with the famous *fegato alla venziana* (calves' liver and onions).

Paduan cuisine is basically Venetian with local variations. Distinctive first courses are rice and tagliatelli in *brodo d'anatra* (duck broth), and *risotto con rovinasassi* (chicken giblets).

Rice is a basic ingredient of the cuisine of Vicenza, too. It was once grown extensively on the low, wet plains at the foot of the Alps. Here you'll find a wide range of *risotti*—with squash, asparagus, hops and quail, flanked by *bigoli* (a local variant of spaghetti) in duck sauce. The best-known local speciality is *baccalà alla vicentina* (salt cod stewed with milk and onions and grilled polenta), followed closely by *bovoloni*, *bovoletti* or *bogoni* (snails in butter, garlic, and parsley), *piccioni torresani allo spiedo* (pigeon on the spit) and *cappone alla canavera* (capon cooked inside an ox bladder).

Many Veronese specialities are also common in other cities of the Veneto. A

Veronese speciality is gnocchi in butter or tomato sauce, or topped with the famous *pastizzada de caval* (horsemeat stewed with aromatic herbs). Distinctive main courses include fish from Lago di Garda, including a rare variety of carp, and *boliti misti* with *pearà* (a sauce of breadcrumbs, butter, ox marrow, parmesan cheese, salt and pepper). Among Veronese sweets, the most delectable are certainly the great fluffy cake *pandoro* and the less well-known *natalini* and Easter *brasadella*.

The leading role in Trevisan cuisine is played by *radicchio trevigiano* (the long, narrow heads of Treviso's red lettuce), which is eaten in salads, grilled, fried or in risotto. Other specialities are *risotto al tajo* (made with shrimp and eel) and *risotto alla sbiraglia* (with chicken and chicken stock). Trevisans claim to have invented the rich dessert *tiramisù*.

In the hills and woodlands to the north, around Belluno, Feltre and Asolo, local dishes present a singular combination of alpine and Venetian influences. Characteristic first courses include *casunzei* (ravioli with pumpkin or spinach, ham and cinnamon) and *lasagne da formel* (dressed with a sauce of nuts, raisins, dried figs and poppy seeds). Favourite main courses feature game stewed in a rich sauce (*salmì*).

WINE

Most Italian wines take their names from the geographical area in which they are produced, the blend of grapes of which they are made, and the estate on which the grapes were grown. The best come in numbered bottles and are marked DOC (*di origine controllata*). This is Italy's *appellation controlée*, which specifies maximum yields per vine, geographical boundaries within which grapes must be grown, permitted grape varieties and production techniques. Superior even to DOC is the DOCG (*di origine controllata e garantita*), where the denomination is also guaranteed. This is not to say that DOCG wines are automatically superior to any other. The plethora of regulation inevitably runs the risk of sclerosis, and winemakers wanting to experiment with alternative grape varieties or vinification techniques found themselves barred from the DOC or DOCG classifications, and had to label their vintages IGT (*vino da tavola con indicazione geografica tipica*). IGT denotes a *vin de pays*, a wine of special regional character. This does not necessarily mean that an IGT wine is of lesser quality than a DOC. Indeed, in some cases it may be particularly interesting and many producers, frustrated by the inflexibility of the rules, have chosen to exit the DOC system. Simple *vino da tavola* is table wine. It can be excellent, but the quality is not guaranteed.

ORDERING WINES

Red wines are *vini rossi* on the wine list; white wines, *vini bianchi*; rosés, *chiaretti* or *rosati*. Dry wines are *secchi*; sweet wines, *amabili* or *dolci*. *Vino novello* is new wine. *Moscato* and *passito* is wine made from grapes that have been left on the vine or dried before pressing.

When ordering, remember also that many DOC wines come in versions labelled *spumante, liquoroso, recioto* and *amarone*. Spumante is the Italian equivalent of champagne and uses some of the same methods to obtain its foamy (*spumante*) effervescence. It is much bubblier than sparkling whites such as Prosecco, which is popular both before meals and as a light dinner wine. *Liquoroso* means 'liqueur-like' and usually refers to dessert wines. The term *recioto* is applied to wines made from grapes that have been dried like raisins; *amarone* is the dry, mellow version of *recioto*.

Wines of the Veneto

The shores of Lake Garda, the Soave district, the Valpolicella and a corner of the Valdadige produce Veronese DOC wines. From Garda come the red Bardolino, Bardolino Chiaretto and Bardolino Classico, and the Bianco di Custoza and Lugana whites. Soave makes an excellent dry white, while the Valpolicella region makes Valpolicella and Valpantena reds. Bardolino, Soave and Valpolicella Classico are made from grapes grown in the oldest vineyards.

The DOC wines of Vicenza come from Gambellara, from the Colli Berici and from the Breganzese. Gambellara is always white, whereas the Colli Berici and Breganzese areas produce both whites and reds.

Three different regional denominations precede the names of Trevisan DOC wines: Conegliano Valdobbiadene, Montello e Colli Asolani and Piave. The first is limited to Prosecco white (Prosecco di Valdobbiadene and Prosecco di Conegliano). Montello e Colli Asolani makes Cabernet and Merlot reds as well as Prosecco white. The Piave growing area, shared with the province of Venice, produces Cabernet, Merlot, Pinot Nero and Raboso reds, in addition to Pinot Bianco, Pinot Grigio, Tocai and Verduzzo whites.

The best Paduan wines are the Colli Euganei Bianco and Rosso, the Cabernet and Merlot reds and the Moscato, Pinot Bianco and Tocai Italico whites.

Glossary

Aedicule, originally a shrine; used to describe the frame of a door, window or other aperture, usually with columns or pilasters bearing a lintel

Ambo (pl. *ambones*), pulpit in a Christian basilica; two pulpits on opposite sides of a church from which the gospel and epistle were read

Amphora, antique vase, usually of large dimensions, for oil and other liquids

Ancona, retable or large altarpiece (painted or sculpted) in an architectural frame

Arca, wooden chest with a lid, for sacred or secular use. Also, monumental sarcophagus in stone, used by Christians and pagans

Architrave, lowest part of the entablature, resting on the columns

Archivolt, moulded frame carried round an arch

Atlantes (or Telamones), male figures used as supporting columns

Atrium, forecourt, usually of a Byzantine church or a classical Roman house

Attic, topmost storey of a Classical building, hiding the spring of the roof

Badia, *abbazia*, abbey

Baldacchino, canopy supported by columns, usually over an altar

Basilica originally a Roman building used for public administration; in Christian architecture, an aisled church with a clerestory and apse, and no transepts

Borgo, a suburb; street leading away from the centre of a town

Bottega, the studio of an artist; the pupils who worked under his direction

Bozzetto, sketch, often used to describe a small model for a piece of sculpture

Broletto, name often given to the town halls of northern Italy

Bucchero, Etruscan black terracotta ware

Campanile, bell-tower, often detached from the building to which it belongs

Camposanto, cemetery

Canopic vase, Egyptian or Etruscan vase enclosing the entrails of the dead

Cantoria, singing-gallery in a church

Capital, the top of a column

Capitolium, a temple of Jupiter, Juno and Minerva

Cardo, the main street of a Roman town, at right-angles to the decumanus

Caryatid, female figure used as a supporting column

Cassone, a decorated chest, usually a dower chest

Cavea, the part of a theatre or amphitheatre occupied by the rows of seats

Cella, sanctuary of a temple, usually in the centre of the building

Cenacolo, scene of the Last Supper, often in the refectory of a convent

Chiaroscuro, distribution of light and shade, apart from colour in a painting; rarely used as a synonym for grisaille

Ciborium, casket or tabernacle containing the Host

Cipollino, onion-marble; a greyish marble with streaks of white or green

Cippus, sepulchral monument in the form of an altar; a stone marking a grave or boundary

Cryptoporticus, a semi-underground covered portico used in Roman architecture for the construction of terraces or as a covered market

Decumanus, the main street of a Roman town running parallel to its longer axis

Diptych, painting or ivory tablet in two sections

Dossal, an altarpiece

Duomo, cathedral

Entablature, the continuous horizontal element above the capital (consisting of architrave, frieze and cornice) of a Classical building

Etruscan, of, relating to, or characteristic of Etruria, an ancient country in central Italy, its inhabitants, or their language

Exedra, semicircular recess in a Byzantine church

Ex-voto, tablet or small painting expressing gratitude to a saint; a votive offering

Forum, open space in a town serving as a market or meeting-place

Fresco, (in Italian, *affresco*), painting executed on wet plaster. On the wall beneath is sketched the sinopia, and the cartoon is transferred onto the fresh plaster (*intonaco*) before the fresco is begun, either by pricking the outline with small holes over which a powder is dusted, or by means of a stylus, which leaves an incised line. In recent years many frescoes have been detached from the walls on which they were executed.

Gonfalon, banner of a medieval guild or commune

Graffiti, design on a wall made with an iron tool on a prepared surface, the design showing in white. Also used loosely to describe scratched designs or words on walls

Greek cross, cross with the arms of equal length

Grisaille, painting in tones of grey

Grotesque, painted or stucco decoration in the style of the ancient Romans (found during the Renaissance in Nero's Golden House in Rome, then underground, hence the name, from 'grotto'). The delicate ornamental decoration usually includes patterns of flowers, sphinxes, birds, human figures etc, against a light ground

Herm (pl. *hermae*), quadrangular pillar decreasing in girth towards the ground, surmounted by a bust

Hexastyle, having six columns

Historiated, adorned with figurative painting or sculpture, usually comprising a narrative

Hypogeum, subterranean excavation for the internment of the dead (usually Etruscan)

Iconostasis, a screen or partition, covered with icons, that divides the public part of a church from that reserved for the clergy

Impost block, a block with splayed sides placed above a capital

Intarsia, inlay of wood, marble, or metal

Intrados, underside or soffit of an arch

Krater, antique mixing-bowl, conical in shape with rounded base

Latin cross, cross with a long vertical arm

Lavabo, hand basin usually outside a refectory or sacristy

Loggia, covered, arcaded or colonnaded gallery or balcony, usually at ground or first-floor level

Lunette, semicircular space in a vault or ceiling, often decorated with a painting or relief

Mandorla, tapered, almond-shaped aura around a holy figure (usually Christ or the Virgin)

Matroneum, gallery reserved for women in early Christian churches

Metope, panel between two triglyphs on the frieze of a Doric temple

Narthex, vestibule of a Christian basilica

Niello, black substance used in an engraved design

Nymphaeum, a sort of summer house in the gardens of baths, palaces, etc., originally a temple of the Nymphs, decorated with statues of those goddesses, and often containing a fountain

Oculus, round window or aperture

Ottonian, 10th- and 11th-century art from the Holy Roman Empire

Pala, large altarpiece

Palaeochristian, from the earliest Christian times up to the 6th century

Palazzo, any dignified and important building

Paliotto, a vestment, hanging, or covering of any material that covers the front part of a Christian altar

Pantocrator, the Almighty

Pediment, gable above the portico of a classical building

Pendentive, concave spandrel beneath a dome

Peristyle, court or garden surrounded by a columned portico

Pietà, group (usually featuring the Virgin) mourning the dead Christ

Pietre dure, hard or semi-precious stones, often used in the form of mosaics to decorate cabinets, table tops etc.

Pieve, parish church

Pinacoteca, an art gallery specialising in the exhibition of painting

Pluteus, a low wall that encloses the space between column bases in a row of columns

Podium, a continuous base or plinth supporting columns, and the lowest row of seats in the cavea of a theatre or amphitheatre

Polyptych, painting or tablet in more than three sections

Predella, small painting or panel, usually in sections, attached below a large altarpiece

Presepio, literally, crib or manger. A group of statuary of which the central subject is the infant Jesus in the manger

Pronaos, porch in front of the cella of a temple

Prostyle, edifice with free-standing columns, as in a portico

Pulvin, cushion stone between the capital and the impost block

Putto, figure of a child sculpted or painted, usually nude

Reredos, decorated screen behind an altar

Rocca, citadel above a town

Rood screen, a screen below the crucifix dividing the nave from the chancel

Scagiola, a material made from selenite, used to imitate marble or *pietre dure*

Scuola, (pl. *scuole*), Venetian lay

confraternity, dedicated to charitable works

Sinopia, large sketch for a fresco made on the rough wall in a red earth pigment called sinopia, because it originally came from Sinope on the Black Sea

Soffit, underside or intrados of an arch

Spandrel, the triangular space on either side of an arch

Squinch, small arch thrown across an angle as support block for a circular dome above a square space

Stele, upright stone bearing a monumental inscription

Stemma, coat of arms or heraldic device

Stoup, vessel for holy water, usually near the entrance door of a church

Stylobate, basement of a columned temple or other building

Telamones, see *Atlantes*

Tempietto a small temple

Tessera, a small cube of marble, glass or brick, used in mosaic work

Tetrastyle, having four columns

Thermae, originally simply baths, later elaborate buildings fitted with libraries, assembly rooms, gymnasia, circuses, etc.

Tondo, round painting or bas-relief

Trabeation, a construction system whereby verticals (eg columns) support horizontals (eg lintels) rather than arches or vaults

Transenna, open grille or screen, usually of marble, in an early Christian church separating nave and chancel

Triglyph, blocks with vertical grooves on either side of a metope on the frieze of a Doric temple

Triptych, painting in three sections

Trompe l'oeil, literally, a deception of the eye. Used to describe illusionist decoration, painted architectural perspectives, etc.

Tympanum, the face of a pediment within the frame made by the upper and lower cornices; also, the space within an arch and above a lintel or a subordinate arch

Villa, country-house with its garden

Index

Explanatory or more detailed references, or references to where an artist's work is best represented, are given in bold.

Sansovino 96, 150

Sansovino, Jacopo 17, 23, 24, 25, **27**, 28, 37, 77, 96, 107, 149, 150

Sant'Ambrogio 163

Sant'Andrea 176

Sardi, Giuseppe 30, 88

Sarego 124

Sargent, John Singer 107

Savoldo 171

Scaligeri (*see Della Scala*)

Scamozzi, Gian Domenico 123

Scamozzi, Vincenzo 62, 88, 92, 94, 95, 104, 106, 118, **120**, 123, 129, 176; (monument to) 114

Scarpa, Carlo 139, 180, 181

Scarpagnino (Antonio Abbondi) 37, 38

Schio 185

Scorel, Jan van 72

Sebastiano del Piombo 41

Segala, Francesco 81

Seitz, Lodovico 167

Semitecolo, Nicoletto 73, 86

Serena, Luigi **165–6**, 171

Shelley, Percy Bysshe 91, 95

Signorini, Telemaco 107

Sirmione 195

Soave 161, 162

Soffici, Ardengo 107

Solferino 196

Soranzen 187

Stagliano, Arturo 171

Stark, Dame Freya 178, 179

Stefano dell'Arzere 86, 88

Stefano da Ferrara 78, 85

Stefano da Zevio 134, 140, 146, 151

Stella, Paolo 77

Stra 62

Surdis, Giovanni Francesco de 81

Sustris, Lambert 80, 92

Tabacco, Bernardo 84

Tentorello, Giacomo 110

Tessari, Girolamo 87

Tezze 185

Thiene 124, 125

Tiepolo, Giambattista 34, **35**, 36, 40, 44, 51, 62, 79, 86, 95, 98, 107, 118, 124, 141, 196

Tiepolo, Gian Domenico 35, 36, **37**, 107, 118, 170

Tintoretto, Domenico 26, 27

Tintoretto, Jacopo 26, 27, 29, 30, 32, 33, 34, 37, **39**, 40, 42, 48, 72, 107, 141, 152, 187; (house of) 43

Tirali, Andrea 45

Titian 25, **32**, 33, 37, **38**, 41, 43, 72, 80, 149, 167, 170, 182; (birthplace of) 191; (monument to) 38

Tommaso da Modena 140, **165**, 167, 168, 170, 171, 172

Torbido, Francesco 135, 143, 149, 151

Torbole sul Garda 202

Torretti (Giovanni Ferrari) 178

Torri del Benaco 203

Toscolano-Maderno 200

Tosi, Arturo 187

Treviso 165

Turchi, Alessandro 110, 148

Turone di Maxio 140, 147, 149, 151

Ubertini, Francesco 156

Valdobbiadene 181

Valpolicella 161, 163

Valsanzibio 92

Vancimuglio 122

Vangi, Giuliano 86

Vecellio, Francesco 80

Vecellio, Marco 25

Vela, Vincenzo 74, 81

Venice 14ff

  Acqua alta 15, 53

  Arsenale 46

  Biennale 47

  Bridge of Sighs 24

  Burano 51

  Ca' Dario 17

  Ca' Foscari 16

  Ca' d'Oro 41

  Ca' Pesaro 40

  Ca' Rezzonico 35

  Campanile 23

  Campo Santo Stefano 30

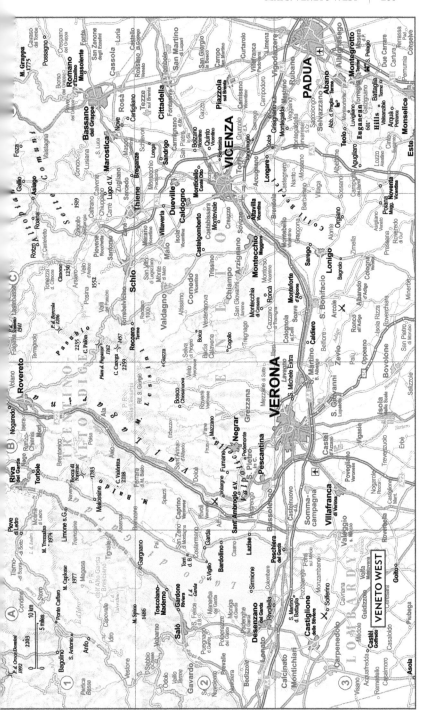

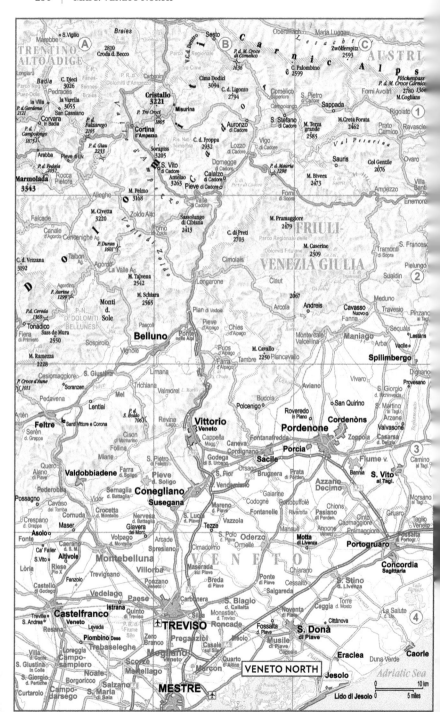

VENETO NORTH

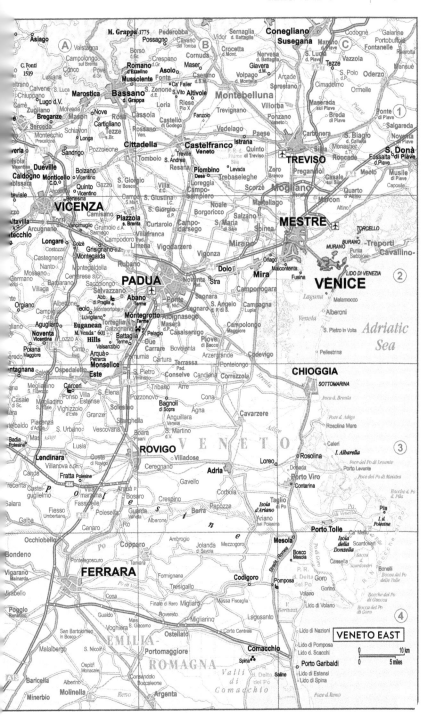

VENETO EAST

Lightning Source UK Ltd.
Milton Keynes UK
UKHW020818310519
343665UK00012B/675/P

9 781905 131785